GENDER AND PSYCHOLOGY

Edited by Karen Trew
Senior Lecturer in Psychology, Queen's University, Belfast

and

John Kremer
Reader in Psychology, Queen's University, Belfast

A member of the Hodder Headline Group
LONDON • NEW YORK • SYDNEY • AUCKLAND

Dedicated to our parents

First published in Great Britain in 1998 by
Arnold, a member of the Hodder Headline Group,
338 Euston Road, London NW1 3BH

http://www.arnoldpublishers.com

Co-published in the United States of America by
Oxford University Press Inc.,
198 Madison Avenue, New York, NY 10016

British Library Cataloguing in Publication Data
A catalogue record for this book is available from the British Library

Library of Congress Cataloging-in-Publication Data
A catalog record for this book is available from the Library of Congress

ISBN 0 340 69179 4 (Pb)
ISBN 0 340 69178 6 (Hb)

2 3 4 5 6 7 8 9 10

Production Editor: Wendy Rooke
Production Controller: Rose James
Cover Design: Mouse Mat Design

Composition by J&L Composition Ltd, Filey, North Yorkshire
Printed and bound in Great Britain by MPG Books Ltd, Bodmin, Cornwall

CONTENTS

CONTRIBUTORS

Professor Ann Colley, Senior Lecturer, School of Psychology, University of Leicester, Leicester LE1 7RH

Dr Carol Curry, Research Fellow, School of Psychology, The Queen's University of Belfast, Belfast BT7 1NN

Dr Agneta Fischer, Senior Lecturer, Department of Social Psychology, Universiteit van Amsterdam, Roetersstraat 15, 1018 WB Amsterdam, The Netherlands

Dr Brendan Gough, Lecturer, School of Health and Community Studies, Sheffield Hallam University, 36 Collegiate Crescent, Sheffield S10 2BP

Dr John Kremer, Reader, School of Psychology, The Queen's University of Belfast, Belfast BT7 1NN

Michael Lenaghan, Principal Clinical Psychologist, Child and Family Team, Bocombra Lodge, Old Lurgan Rd, Portadown, Co. Armagh, Northern Ireland

Juliet Lyon, Associate Director, Trust for the Study of Adolescence, 23 New Road, Brighton, East Sussex, BN1 1W2

Dr Majella McFadden, Lecturer, School of Health and Community Studies, Sheffield Hallam University, 36 Collegiate Crescent, Sheffield S10 2BP

Dr Carol McGuinness, Senior Lecturer, School of Psychology, The Queen's University of Belfast, Belfast BT7 1NN

Dr Geraldine Moane, Lecturer, Psychology Department, University College Dublin, Belfield, Dublin 4

Dr Orla Muldoon, Lecturer, School of Psychology, The Queen's University of Belfast, Belfast BT7 1NN

Dr Carol Percy, Lecturer, School of Psychology and Human Biology, Aston University, Aston Triangle, Birmingham B4 7ET

Dr Bridie Pilkington, Head of Clinical Psychology Services, Psychology Department, Craigavon Area Hospital, Lagan Rd, Portadown BT63 5QQ

Dr Nuala Quiery, 39 Deramore Avenue, Belfast BT7 2GH

Dr Norma Rainey, Laboratory Supervisor, School of Psychology, The Queen's University of Belfast, Belfast BT7 1NN

Dr Jacqueline Reilly, Lecturer, School of Psychology, The Queen's University of Belfast, Belfast BT7 1NN

Dr Deirdre Scully, Lecturer, School of Leisure and Tourism, University of Ulster at Jordanstown, Newtownabbey BT37 0QB

Dr Karen Trew, Senior Lecturer, School of Psychology, The Queen's University of Belfast, Belfast BT7 1NN

Dr Ian Sneddon, Senior Lecturer, School of Psychology, The Queen's University of Belfast, Belfast BT7 1NN

Dr Anneke van Wersch, Lecturer, School of Social Sciences, University of Teesside, Middlesborough, TS1 3BA

Dr Jean Whyte, Senior Lecturer, School of Clinical Speech and Language Studies, Trinity College, Dublin 1

PREFACE

INTRODUCTION

Until relatively recently, it is unlikely that the study of gender will have featured in most students' introduction to the discipline of psychology. To illustrate this point, look up the words 'gender' or 'sex' in the subject index of any introductory psychology text. Other than work relating to development or socialization, you will probably be surprised at how infrequently the terms appear. While gender may well have warranted some mention in relation to many core psychological areas, ranging across the spectrum from the biological through to the social, due recognition for gender as a distinct topic within the undergraduate curriculum has been hard fought. The reasons why this is the case are many and varied and have been well documented elsewhere (for example, see Paludi, 1992; Wilkinson, 1996).

The purpose of this book is not to dwell too long on the chequered history and politics of psychology in relation to gender (and women's) studies but to focus on the present, offering an overview of where gender currently features across a range of key areas. For convenience, these areas have been divided into three primary domains. The first considers the meta-themes or issues which recur across the discipline. Here gender plays a role which can either be explicit, for example in relation to debates around topics such as feminism, sexuality and biology, or can act in a more covert way in relation to the discipline's frameworks, perspectives and assumptions, for example in relation to discussion of roles, identity, cognition and emotion. The second section takes as its theme the role of gender across the life-span, from childhood to old age. Finally, the psychology of gender in relation to key social concerns, including health and well-being, forms the focus for section three.

Historically, psychologists now stand accused of turning a blind, or at best a jaundiced, eye to the significance of gender. One notable exception has been neuro-psychological work devoted to charting differences between the brains of men and women. This research dates back to the middle of the last century but has been singularly unsuccessful in identifying structural differences other than those known to be related to sexual behaviour, and with no evidence to suggest brain differences which relate to intelligence (see Nicholson, 1993, pp. 86–102). In contrast, those interested in individual differences, including the French psychologist Alfred Binet, discarded items from IQ tests when gender differences were found in order to ensure that the test did not differentiate between boys and girls (Terman and Merrill, 1937, p. 22).

While this book is concerned with both genders, there is no question that one gender in particular has suffered during the evolution of psychology, namely women. With higher education traditionally regarded as a male preserve on both sides of the Atlantic until the 1950s, it is small wonder that from the time of Wilhelm Wundt, working in Leipzig in the 1870s, up until the 1960s, psychology has been described as a discipline run by men for men. While the contribution made by women psychologists over the years should never be ignored, women have remained in the minority in terms of numbers and power, and as a consequence many psychological theories have developed with an inherent androcentric bias; they were developed by men and they were tested on men (Bohan (ed.), 1992).

This led to a situation where the psychology which we inherited in the 1970s had become deeply infected by a host of biases which served to maintain male dominance and to keep women in their place. Again, as a quick illustration, name the ten individuals from the history of psychology who immediately spring to mind. How many are men and how many are women? Likewise, in terms of the perpetuation of this status quo, consider your first reaction when you see a reference, such as Smith, 1997. Without any further information, what gender do you assume the author to be?

To see how this bias continues to influence the discipline, take a typical profile of a present-day psychology department, perhaps considering one with which you are especially familiar. While women will normally heavily outnumber men in undergraduate student classes, at postgraduate level it is likely that the ratio of men to women will be closer to 50:50. Among academic staff, men are likely to outnumber women, with senior academic grades likely to show an even greater preponderance of men. What is more, where women do appear in academic posts they are likely to be concentrated in areas such as developmental and social psychology.

Structural and attitudinal changes to these patterns will not occur overnight but there have been slow but inexorable shifts in the gender of psychology occuring for some considerable time. Most significantly, in the late 1960s and 1970s, what has become known as second-wave feminism launched a challenge to the existing male dominance, a challenge which has renewed itself and continues to exert a powerful and positive influence on the development of the discipline. In comparison with the USA, the structures which have underpinned and cemented this movement in Western Europe have been somewhat slower to develop but they have made their mark nevertheless. For example, while the American Psychological Association (APA) had formed a Psychology of Women Division (No. 35) by 1973, it was not until December 1987 that, at the second attempt, the British Psychological Society (BPS) finally ratified the formation of a Psychology of Women Section (Wilkinson, 1990). Over the last decade, the influence of women, and particularly feminist psychologists, on the discipline has been constant and has often served as a valuable counterbalance to more traditional approaches, for example in relation to methodologies (Nielsen, 1990). At the same time, attempts to bring women further into the mainstream of psychology continue to meet with resistance, creating a tension which is often healthy but which at times has become decidedly acrimonious (Wilkinson, 1996).

GENDER AND PSYCHOLOGY – WHAT'S IN A NAME?

Feminist psychologists have fought long and hard to place women on the political map of contemporary psychology, and should be given due credit for the advances which they have made. Among those who believe that many battles remain to be fought in that particular war it could be argued that by using the title gender and psychology, instead of perhaps women and psychology, the wrong signals are being sent at the wrong time, by deprioritizing and perhaps depoliticizing women's position in psychology.

Having pondered over this issue, we took a considered decision to use the title gender and psychology. First and foremost, our choice was driven by what we regarded as student demand and student opinion. Since 1983, we have both organized and taught a final year Women and Psychology course at Queen's University. While the course has remained extremely popular over the years, it was becoming increasingly difficult to disregard murmurings of discontent among both women and men. Indeed these murmurs had grown to a shout, arguing that a unisex title had become inappropriate for various reasons. First it politicized the course in the eyes of many students (and particularly men) and hence reduced access to a wider constituency. Second, the title was seen as a misnomer because a great deal of the material was not solely about women but about the relationship between men and women. For example, even when discussing women's issues such as the menstrual cycle and maternity, the literature often has as much to say about men's attitudes and responses to these issues as women's themselves. Third, the course was in danger of ignoring the growing literature which was charting men's studies and masculinity. From the Iron John movement of the early 1990s (Bly, 1990) to the present day, the spotlight has turned to issues such as men's response to the women's movement, and this literature has many interesting things to say about gender relationships in the 1990s and beyond. Fourth, use of the term gender was felt to sit more comfortably within third-wave feminism, where the battle lines which marked the political territories of the early 1970s had become blurred in the postmodern world of the 1990s. In this climate, the need to make political statements through the use of particular course titles was seen to warrant reassessment.

TEACHING GENDER AND PSYCHOLOGY

Higher education has undergone revolutionary change over the last twenty years, some change for the better, some for the worse. As journals such as *Psychology Teaching Review* testify, if nothing else this time of change has made teachers of psychology ask questions about the nature of teaching and learning in higher education, and to query the efficacy of traditional methods (Sneddon and Kremer (eds), 1994). Simultaneously, employers have made their voice heard in calling for change in order to improve the product of higher education, namely the graduate. For example, employers consistently argue that they need graduates who not only 'know' but more importantly, have the skills and the competences so as to be able to apply that knowledge (Sneddon et al., 1995). One way to achieve this is through a greater emphasis on small-group work and active learning strategies. This sentiment finds strong support from educationalists, who for long have promoted the case for active learning at the expense of chalk and talk (Brown, 1997).

Taken together, all these forces have produced considerable pressure for change. At the same time, acting against these forces have been increasing numbers of students, rising student/staff ratios and the practical difficulties of implementing active learning strategies and innovative teaching methods in an environment where one of the most significant criteria of success is still judged to be cost effectiveness. A challenge is therefore presented – to promote active learning (and preferably in small-group settings) and to empower the student within the learning process, but at the same time to put in place a scheme which is sustainable within a climate of economic stringency.

Available evidence supports the value of techniques where the student is encouraged to play a more active role in both the learning experience and subsequent assessment (Falchikov, 1995), and one strong contender for consideration, and a technique which has been used over a number of years at The Queen's University of Belfast (Kremer, 1997) is student-led discussion groups. To facilitate those contemplating the organization of a new gender and psychology course, or the modification of an existing course, the practicalities of running student-led discussion groups are outlined below.

Teaching gender and psychology: the Queen's experience

The final-year optional module on gender and psychology runs each year and is normally attended by approximately 70 students. The course is based around a series of ten or eleven discrete topics or themes and runs in two blocks of two hours per week throughout one term. A lecture together with an associated discussion is offered for each topic. The lecture first presents a general overview of the topic, covering major theories and contemporary research but deliberately leaving loose ends which are addressed during the discussion groups. These are timetabled in the alternate two hours the following week.

At the introductory lecture, students are allocated to a discussion group, comprising between nine and 12 students. At the end of this and each subsequent lecture, a list of five selected readings is handed out to all class members. From the list, each group member is expected to read a minimum of one item. To ensure that there has been a breadth of reading in the group, each member is assigned a number from one to five and they are asked to read the article, chapter, report, etc. which corresponds with this number on the reading list.

The discussion groups take place in a large flat teaching room containing free-standing chairs. When students arrive, they arrange a circle of chairs for their group and are asked to ensure that the physical set-up of the group feels 'right' – for example pulling the chairs closer if necessary and closing gaps.

At the start of the discussion, working around the group each person briefly informs the others what they have read and offers an informal evaluation of its worth. These evaluations are very short; students are not allowed simply to read a summary but instead must assess the worth of the article, chapter, etc. and indicate any issues or questions worthy of debate. They are also advised that if they have not read for the meeting they should not attend, as it would be unfair to 'take' information from the group without giving in return.

The tutor rarely becomes involved in discussion except perhaps when asked to clarify a point and does not intervene even when it is clear the group is struggling or has headed off at a tangent. Instead, s/he 'hovers' around the groups (which can be up to six in number in the room), never sitting too close to one group but generally keeping an eye on proceedings. For example, one important ground-rule is that there can be no more than one conversation in any group at one time. After 15 minutes an attendance list is passed around each group in turn; this list records attendance, absences and excuses for absence.

After approximately 20 minutes, a number of discussion points are shown on an overhead frame but it is left to the discretion of each group whether these questions are dealt with or not. After one hour, each group is asked to summarize its discussion in terms of a few key points. At this point there is a crossover between the groups (with each group member allocated a number at their first meeting corresponding to their crossover group, to which they now move). This ensures that all students feel secure that they have had access to all the class's debates and discussion. After a further half hour the tutor leaves the room and students are free to leave whenever their discussion has run its natural course, or to continue their discussion elsewhere (which is often the case).

Assessment

The group assessment procedure endeavours to take account of various forms of contribution. First, a register of attendance is kept and attendance itself forms a small component of final assessment. Second, during the final group meeting, each member is asked to complete a group evaluation form on which s/he rates members of the group (including her/himself) in terms of five dimensions (scored on a seven-point Likert scale):

- Preparation: S/he had done the required reading for the group discussion.
- Sharing: S/he was willing to share information with the group.
- Support: S/he was sensitive and supportive of others in the group.
- Facilitating: S/he was prepared to help discussion keep moving.
- Membership: S/he was an effective group member.

(0 = Never; 1 = Very infrequently; 2 = Infrequently; 3 = Quite frequently; 4 = Frequently; 5 = Very frequently; 6 = Invariably)

In accord with Bales's taxonomy of group contributions (Bales, 1950), it was felt that these dimensions allowed for assessment of both task and socio-emotional contributions to the group. Together with attendance, this score is used to derive a group contribution score for each student. The other course-work components include an interview report (based on a semi-structured interview) and an integrative essay. These marks are combined with those obtained from a two-hour written examination (based on ten short, compulsory answers [one per topic]) to derive the overall mark for each module.

Not surprisingly, correlations between the mark for group contribution and other forms of assessment on the course are not always high (nor are they between the other forms of assessment) but these weak correlations are not viewed with concern. Put simply, those who made the most telling contribution to group discussion are not always those who are able to write a cogent integrative essay, who in turn are not always those who are able to write a series of short answers under examination conditions. However, it is felt that each form of assessment is valid in its own right.

Formal student evaluations consistently indicate that this teaching method is valued, and anecdotal information from individual students confirms this impression. Group discussions are inevitably lively, they appear to involve the majority of students in each group and keep the attention of almost all group members. The tailoring of such schemes to the idiosyncracies of different institutions may be necessary but our experience would suggest that the investment is worthwhile. Certainly, the underlying philosophy behind the teaching approach, involving empowerment and ownership of the learning process, is one which we believe sits very comfortably with the aims of a course in gender and psychology.

References

Bales, R.F. (1950). *Interaction process analysis: a method for the study of small groups.* Reading, MA: Addison-Wesley.

Bly, R. (1990). *Iron John: a book about men.* Shaftesbury, Dorset: Element.

Bohan, J.S. (1992). *Seldom seen, rarely heard: women's place in psychology.* Boulder, CO: Westview Press.

Brown, G. (1997). Teaching psychology: a vade mecum. *Psychology Teaching Review* **6 (2)**, 112–26.

Falchikov, N. (1995). Peer feedback marking: developing peer assessment. *Innovations in Education and Training International* **32(2)**, 175–87.

Kremer, J. (1997). Empowerment in the learning process: the case of student discussion groups. *Psychology Teaching Review* **6(1)**, 77–84.

Nicholson, J. (1993). *Men and women: how different are they?* Oxford: Oxford University Press.

Nielsen, J. Mc. (1990). *Feminist research methods.* Boulder, CO: Westview Press.

Paludi, M.A. (1992). *The psychology of women.* Dubuque, IA: Brown & Benchmark.

Sneddon, I. and Kremer, J. (1994) (eds). *An enterprising curriculum: teaching innovations in higher education.* Belfast: HMSO.

Sneddon, I., Kremer, J. and Lindsay, B. (1995). *Evaluating enterprise at Queen's.* Belfast: APAS.

Terman, L.M. and Merrill, M.A. (1937). *Measuring intelligence: a guide to the administration of the new revised Stanford-Binet tests of intelligence.* London: Harrap & Co.

Wilkinson, S. (1990). Why psychology (badly) needs feminism. In Aaron, J. and Walby, S. (eds), *Out of the margins: women's studies in the nineties.* (pp. 191–203). London: Falmer Press.

Wilkinson, S. (1996). Feminist social psychologies: a decade of development. In Wilkinson, S. (ed.), *Feminist social psychologies: international perspectives.* (pp. 1–18). Buckingham: Open University Press.

Introductory reading

Beal, C. (1994). *Boys and girls: the development of gender roles.* New York: McGraw-Hill.

Beall, A.E. and Sternberg, R.J. (eds) (1993). *The psychology of gender.* New York: Guilford Press.

Bohan, J.S. (ed.) (1992). *Seldom seen, rarely heard: women's place in psychology.* Boulder, CO: Westview Press.

Brannon, L. (1996). *Gender: psychological perspectives.* Needham Hts, MA: Allyn & Bacon.

Burman, E., Alfred, P., Bewley, C., Goldberg, B., Heenan, C., Marks, D., Marshall, J., Taylor, K., Ullah, R. and Warner, S. (1995). *Challenging women: psychology's exclusions, feminist possibilities.* London: Open University Press.

Burn, S.M. (1996). *The social psychology of gender.* New York: McGraw-Hill.

Crawford, M. and Gentry, M. (1989). *Gender and thought: psychological perspectives.* London: Springer-Verlag.

Freeman, J. (1992). *Women: a feminist perspective.* Mountain View, CA: Mayfield.

Frieze, I.H., Parsons, J.E., Johnson, P.B., Ruble, D.N. and Zellman, G.L. (1978). *Women and sex roles: a social psychological perspective.* New York: Norton & Co.

Hargreaves, D.J. and Colley, A. (eds) (1986). *The psychology of sex roles.* London: Harper & Row.

Hyde, J.S. (1996). *Half the human experience: the psychology of women.* Lexington, MA: D.C. Heath.

Jacklin, C.N. (1992). *The psychology of gender.* Vols. 1–4. Aldershot, Hants: Edward Elgar.

Lips, H.M. (1993) *Sex and gender.* Mountain View, CA: Mayfield.

Matlin, M.W. (1996). *The psychology of women.* Fort Worth, TX: Harcourt Books.

Nicholson, J. (1993). *Men and women: how different are they?* Oxford: Oxford University Press.

Paludi, M.A. (1992). *The psychology of women.* Dubuque, IA: Brown & Benchmark.

Renzetti, C. and Curran, D. (1995). *Women, men and society.* Boston: Allyn & Bacon.

Rollins, J.H. (1996).*Women's minds, women's bodies: the psychology of women in a biosocial context.* Upper Saddle River, NJ: Prentice Hall.

Siann, G. (1994). *Gender, sex and sexuality.* London: Taylor & Francis.

Stockard, J. and Johnson, M.M. (1992). *Sex, gender and society.* New York: Prentice Hall.

Tavris, C. (1992). *The mismeasure of women.* New York: Simon & Schuster.

Tavris, C. and Wade, C. (1984). *The longest war: sex differences in perspective.* New York: Harcourt, Brace & Jovanovich.

Unger, R. and Crawford, M. (1992). *Women and gender: a feminist psychology.* New York: McGraw-Hill.

Wilkinson, S. (ed.) (1986). *Feminist social psychology: developing theory and practice.* Milton Keynes: Open University Press.

Wilkinson, S. (ed.) (1996). *Feminist social psychologies: international perspectives.* Buckingham: Open University Press.

Part 1

Themes and Perspectives

1

IDENTITY AND THE SELF

Karen Trew

INTRODUCTION

Within social and personality psychology, gender identity and the gendered self are increasingly looked upon as integral components in any description of the relationship between gender and social behaviour. At the same time, interesting questions are now being asked about the precise meaning of the terms gender and identity, terms which are in common usage as well as being the focus of academic research. By way of example, Hawkesworth (1997) has recently identified at least 25 different uses of the term gender. At various times it has been described as an attribute of individuals, as a feature of interpersonal relationships, as a type of social organization, and even in terms of the symbolism or ideology of a society. It has also been represented as an effect of language, a structural feature of power and as a matter of behavioural conformity.

The many alternative meanings attributed to the term gender which have emerged over the last decade serve to indicate the complexity of gender, as well as the current level of interest shown in gender as an analytic concept by researchers from many different backgrounds. In the light of her analysis, Hawkesworth (1997) has developed a lexicon which summarizes a number of important terminological and conceptual distinctions, where gender is thought of either in terms of:

- *Sex*, construed in biological terms
- *Sexuality*, understood to encompass sexual practices and erotic behaviour
- *Sexual identity*, referring to designations such as heterosexual, homosexual/gay/lesbian, bisexual, transsexual or asexual
- *Gender identity*, as a psychological sense of oneself as a man or a woman
- *Gender-role*, as a set of prescriptive culture-specific expectations about what is appropriate for men and women

- *Gender-role identity*, defined as the extent to which a person approves of and participates in feelings and behaviours considered as appropriate to his or her culturally constituted gender.

Hawkesworth considers that this taxonomy provides an analytic vocabulary for exploring some of the paradoxes and apparent contradictions associated with the analysis of gender. For example, given these distinctions it is possible to ask questions about how it is that individuals who have an equally clear and unqualified sense of themselves as being a man or a woman, can have very different conceptions of the nature of femininity or masculinity, or differ in their sexuality. This vocabulary also provides a framework for exploring a specific facet of gender in depth, such as gender identity, while acknowledging that this is only one level of a complex, multifaceted gender system.

Historically, it was assumed that a person's biological sex could account for all aspects of 'normal' masculinity or femininity. At that time, the term gender identity was confined to the medical literature where the expression was used to refer to an individual's sense of being masculine or feminine, in the context of inconsistent biological markers (Frable, 1997). Nowadays, although psychological and biological sex are assumed to be distinct, the term gender identity has lost its medical connotations and instead is widely used to refer to the individual's fundamental sense of maleness or femaleness which, with few exceptions, complements awareness and acceptance of biological sex (Spence, 1985). This chapter provides a brief historical overview of psychologists' attempts to understand the meaning of gender for the individual as a background to some contemporary approaches to gender identity and the gendered self.

THE STUDY OF SEX, GENDER AND THE INDIVIDUAL: HISTORICAL TRENDS

Following Ashmore (1990), it is useful to consider the study of sex, gender and the individual in relation to four relatively distinct historical periods. Together these provide a summary picture of how psychological interpretations of the constructs masculinity and femininity have developed throughout this century.

1894–1936: sex differences in intelligence

Early psychologists' interest in intelligence testing, and the development of measures of mental and personality traits, set the agenda for subsequent approaches to sex differences insofar as differences between men and women were seen almost exclusively as part of the study of individual differences. This paradigm, in which gender was viewed as a 'subject variable', led psychologists to consider that it was appropriate to try to measure masculinity–femininity in the same way as any other individual difference.

1936–1974: masculinity–femininity as a global personality trait

During this period it came to be generally assumed that the family provided the basic social milieu within which boys and girls were socialized into their natural roles, namely masculine, task-oriented, bread-winning men, and feminine, socio-emotional, nurturant, caring women. These cultural beliefs were clearly reflected in the first test of mental masculinity–femininity (Terman and Miles, 1936), a test which helped to give academic respectability and credence to the view that masculinity–femininity was a single psychological dimension which in turn reflected on a deep-seated and enduring aspect of human personality.

1974–1982: androgyny as a sex-role ideal

In 1974, Bem introduced the concept of androgyny, which is now widely accepted by psychologists to signify, 'the blending or balancing of psychological traits that are stereotyped masculine or feminine' (Unger and Crawford, 1996, p. 51). The publication of the Bem Sex Role Inventory (BSRI) (Bem, 1974) and the Personal Attribute Questionnaire (PAQ) (Spence et al., 1974) allowed psychologists to empirically demonstrate that masculinity and femininity, as defined by these tests, were independent rather than orthagonally related constructs.

Although the BSRI and PAQ are still widely administered, these tests and the related concept of androgyny have been shown to be less revolutionary and less robust than they originally appeared. Spence (1985) later acknowledged that the scales were based on a very limited definition of femininity–masculinity and she argued that despite the rhetoric surrounding their work, neither Sandra Bem's BSRI test nor her own PAQ test had advanced the study of gender far beyond the dispositional continuum as exemplified by the Terman–Miles test in the 1930s. Masculinity and femininity were still defined in terms of stable individual dispositions which enabled the individual to be categorized and sex-typed.

1982–1990: sex as a social category

Moving through to the present day, three articles published in the 1980s can be seen as providing the bedrock on which current accounts of gender have been constructed. First, in order to convey her view that masculinity and femininity were 'cultural lenses' rather than dimensions of personality, Bem (1981) shifted her focus from the concept of androgyny to the concept of gender-schematic information processing. This move encompassed a view which now looked upon gender not as a conglomeration of personal characteristics but as a culturally embedded schema, defined as an affective/cognitive structure which is created to lend meaning and coherence to individual experience. Hence gender was to be seen as a cognitive representation of experience which guided behaviour. Following her interest in the androgynous individual, Bem (1983) focused her attention on comparisons between sex-typed and non-sex-typed individuals, and the development of strategies which would help parents raise children who were described as gender aschematic.

Second, the period was defined by a seminal paper by Sherif (1982) in which she argued that the psychological analysis of gender must begin with a recognition that gender is best described as a social category system operating principally at a societal level. Nowadays, there is almost universal acceptance that gender does represent a primary and significant social category (Deaux and Major, 1987) and hence gender identity has emerged as a construct of considerable interest (Frable, 1997). The paradigm shift which occurred once gender had been reformulated in this way provided a major impetus for research which looked upon gender as a process rather than a dispositional characteristic. From this perspective, gender could be thought of as dynamic and as situationally determined, rather than as a stable personality disposition.

Finally, Gilligan's (1982) work dealing with the moral development of girls reintroduced the idea that there are major differences between men and women but added the essential caveat that these differences should not be couched in androcentric terms implying female deficits, as had been so often the case previously. According to Gilligan, a woman's way of knowing could be compared positively to that of a man. For example, while girls grow up thinking of themselves as connected to others, boys grow up thinking of themselves as separate from others.

In sum, psychological understanding of the meaning of femininity and masculinity to the individual progressed from an early view of gender as a unidimensional, biologically determined, bipolar construct, to the related concepts of gender being either socially constructed, a stable personality disposition or an information processing structure. Following the paradigm shift in the 1980s, although gender continues to be viewed from some perspectives as a subject variable, most theoretical accounts of gender now concentrate almost exclusively on gender as a social category, thus implicating differences between men and women in terms of their relative power and prestige in society. Such societal-based realities are assumed to have an impact on how an individual thinks, acts and feels.

1990s: gender and the self-concept

During the 1990s, a range of theories have been added to those which have explored the meaning of gender at the interpersonal level. At one extreme, constructionist theories argue that gender is not a stable internal characteristic of the individual but exists in particular transactions that are understood to be appropriate to one sex (see Chapter 2). At the other extreme, there are theories which locate gender in primarily biologically or genetically determined sex differences (see Chapter 7). These diverse approaches to gender are complemented by social psychological theories which view self or identity as the key concept for locating sex and gender at the individual level, while taking account of both its biological and social dimensions. Four of these approaches serve to demonstrate the range of meanings which have become attached to the term gender identity in recent years:

- *Multifactorial approaches,* in which gender identity is seen as a self-label within a multifaceted construct which includes personality traits and attitudes as well as self-perceptions (for example, Spence, 1993)
- *Schematic approaches,* in which gender is viewed as a schema for self-categorization (for example, Lavallee and Pelletier, 1992)
- *Social identity approaches,* in which gender identity is viewed in terms of membership in a social group and as a collective identity (for example, Yee and Brown, 1994)
- *Self construal approaches,* in which the self-concepts of men and women are seen to differ in structure and function as well as content (for example, Cross and Madson 1997).

MULTIFACTORIAL GENDER IDENTITY THEORIES

Following a review of the literature, Janet Spence (1985) argued that no single personality dimension or trait-like quality, such as femininity–masculinity, sex-role orientation or gender schematization, can account for gender differences but simultaneously most people are clear as to their maleness or femaleness. Her own research indicated that although masculinity and femininity were personally important to her informants, these normally articulate, middle-aged and middle-class men and women had difficulty in specifying what constituted masculinity and femininity in themselves and in others.

This paradox led Spence to suggest that gender identity should be thought of as 'a primitive unarticulated concept of self initially laid down at an essentially preverbal stage of development and maintained at an unverbalized level' (Spence, 1985, pp. 79–80). She considered a child learns his or her fundamental gender identity at an early age and this leads the individual to take on interests and traits which define and maintain gender identity throughout the life-span. From this perspective, knowledge of a person's gender identity, defined as his or her private sense of being a male or female, does not provide information on acceptance of gender roles or attitudes. Instead, each person develops a personal sense of masculinity and femininity which is usually specified within culturally defined boundaries (Spence, 1993; Koestner and Aube, 1995).

Spence's approach to gender identity does account for the lack of interrelationship found between the various facets of gender, but it provides only a very loose definition of gender identity, a definition which is not embedded in a wider interpretation of the self-system.

THE SCHEMATIC APPROACH

The importance of gender for the self-concept is acknowledged by most theorists of the self. Nevertheless there has been suprisingly little research which has examined the role of gender schema in ongoing behaviour. Instead, research which derives from the perspective of gender as a self-schema (Bem, 1981) has been concerned primarily with the cognitive correlates and social determinants which distinguish between gender-typed or gender schematic and non-gender-typed or gender aschematic people.

Bem (1993) extended and elaborated her original gender schema theory to analyse how androcentric and gender-polarizing social practices transfer unspoken assumptions about sex and gender, the 'lenses of gender', from the culture to the individual. However, although Bem has shifted the focus of her analysis from the individual to society she still maintains that gender is a pervasive feature of the self-definition of the gender schematic person, but is largely irrelevant to the person who is gender aschematic. The associated assumption, that having a prominent gender self-schema has a marked and systematic effect on how the person processes incoming information about him/herself, has been demonstrated empirically in a range of studies in which the gender schematic person has been found to be more efficient than the gender aschematic in processing gender-relevant information (see Cross and Markus, 1993, for a review).

Although specific aspects of Bem's gender schema theory have been criticized (Spence, 1985), the notion of gender as a schema is still widely employed as a heuristic for understanding the importance of gender in how the individual processes and organizes information (Bem, 1993).

THE SOCIAL IDENTITY APPROACH

Gender is a social category as well as a personal attribute, and gender identity involves not merely labelling the self as male or female but the process of identification of self with others who share the classification. The social identity approach is a general theoretical perspective which has been employed as a theoretical tool by a number of psychologists who are interested in the relationship between gender identification and social behaviour.

Initially, social identity theory was developed by Henri Tajfel as a theory of intergroup conflict and change, while self-categorization theory later evolved from social identity theory as a more general theory of group processes. The term social identity approach is normally used to refer to both theories, as both share the fundamental hypothesis, namely that 'individuals define themselves in terms of their social group memberships and that group-defined self perception produces psychologically distinctive effects in social behaviour' (Hogg and Abrams, 1988, p. xi). According to a social identity approach, gender is one of the many societal categories or groups which stand in power and status relations to one another and which are used by individuals to define themselves. In this context, identifying oneself as male or female on the one hand accentuates the similarities between the self and others of the same gender, and, on the other hand, exaggerates the differences between the self and those not of the same gender, the 'opposite sex'. Gender identity, as one of the possible social identities available to the individual, involves viewing oneself as a member of a group, as compared with viewing oneself as an individual. As you may expect, social identity theorists have been especially interested in those situations where individuals see themselves in terms of their group membership, that is when their social identity is salient or prominent.

The salience of an identity is thought to be a function both of its importance to the individual and of the nature of the immediate situation. At the same time, there are situations which force most people to consider their gender identity as salient, however weak their identification with other men and women. For example, students in a gender and psychology class, who possibly feel they have to defend the behaviour and attitudes of their own gender during group discussions, can offer a clear demonstration of how powerful some situations can be in determining the salience of gender identity!

Skevington and Baker (1989a) considered that social identity theory had potential for understanding both the nature and the content of women's group identification, and hence brought together a range of studies, based on both qualitative and quantitative research methods, to probe the meaning of womanhood for women. Almost unanimously, the authors of these studies found that social identity theory was unable to offer a paradigm which could account for the complexities of women's lives. Their major criticisms were related to the exclusion of social context in social identity theory, the simplification of womanhood implicit in this approach, and the trivialization of the relationship between men and women. Most of the researchers agreed that women could not be viewed as a unified coherent social category with a shared meaning for all women. However, while these criticisms may be justified, it was perhaps naive to assume that a pervasive societal category such as gender could be wholly explained in terms of the intergroup relations between men and women.

In more general terms, many of the criticisms levelled against social identity theory, in relation to its applicability to the study of gender, appear to derive from its origins as a theory of intergroup conflict rather than as a theory dedicated to understanding the self. These criticisms aside, the theory remains a useful heuristic for examining intergroup relations between men and women, and the impact of self-stereotyping on the behaviour and activities of men and women in contexts where gender identity is salient (Deaux, 1997; Swan and Wyer, 1997).

SELF-CONSTRUAL AND GENDER

Until recently, theories of gender and the self-concept have viewed gender in terms of the content of the self-concept and in terms of how people identified themselves. However, there has been a growing view that the social environment can have an impact on the nature of the self-system as well as its content. In other words, gender is assumed to have an impact on how one thinks or understands the nature of the self.

The traditional theories of identity and self were based on the Western view of the person as individualistic and autonomous. More recently, cross-cultural research has demonstrated that other societies construct a self that is thought to be more interdependent and relational (Markus and Kitayama, 1991). Cross and Madson (1997a; 1997b) have enlisted the literature on cross-cultural differences in self-construals as a heuristic to integrate a variety of gender differences recorded in the psychological literature. According to these authors (Cross and Madson, 1997b), many documented gender differences in behaviour are attributable to men's tendency to define themselves as independent or separate from others, and women's tendency to define themselves, at least partially, in terms of close others. The authors describe these differences in terms of stable gender differences associated with the process of construing the self, using the term to refer both to the content and the structure of self-representations, and proposing that these self-construals provide the fundamental basis for regulating and influencing behaviour.

Cross and Madson (1997b) maintain that even in traditionally individualistic Western countries, most women develop an interdependent self-construal in which the self is flexible and roles and relationships are emphasized. The main goals of individuals (primarily women) with an interdependent self-construal are seen to be the development of self-defining relationships and the maintenance of connectedness. In contrast, they suggest that although the life experiences of men in Western societies afford them the potential to be as sociable as women, the tendency for most men is to develop an independent self-construal, thereby involving representations of their relationships as separate from the self. Hence the principal goal for individuals with an independent self-construal (primarily men) is to maintain a sense of autonomy, and set against this goal, interpersonal relationships are seen as important contexts for demonstrating uniqueness and for enhancing individualistic targets.

Already, there is considerable evidence to support Cross and Madson's premise that, during socialization, men and women make the divide between self and non-self in very different ways (see Chapters 8, 9 and 10), and wide agreement that socialization leads women to define the self through relations with others whereas men develop a more 'separate identity'. The growing literature can be illustrated by the findings of one study where students were asked to take a series of photographs so as to communicate to others who they were (Clancy and Dollinger, 1993). Subsequent analyses revealed that female students were more likely than males to photograph themselves with friends and family whereas male students more often portrayed themselves either alone, engaging in physical activity or posing with objects such as their cars.

Cross and Madson (1997a), in reviewing the psychological literature, have demonstrated that many gender differences in cognition, motivation, emotion and social interaction can be accounted for by differences in the self-construals of men and women. Gender differences in cognitive processes, such as attention, memory and perspective-taking, as well as behaviours such as self-disclosure, non-verbal sensitivity and aggression (which are related to the development and maintenance of close relationships), are all shown to be consistent with the differences between individuals with interdependent self-construals and those with independent self-construals as predicted by these models of the self.

The emergent picture suggests that Cross and Madson have been largely successful in integrating diverse findings of gender differences and similarities by the use of a simple and coherent construct which links existing evidence on gender differences with social cognitive research on the self. In addition, their perspective on self-construals and gender differences in social behaviour is compatible with Eagly's social role theory (Eagly, 1987). Cross and Madson emphasize the intra-individual structures and processes that direct behaviour, whereas the social role approach (see Chapter 2) focuses on behaviour and personal attributes. Divergent self-construals can therefore help to explain how gendered social roles and societal expectations are internalized and influence subsequent social behaviour.

The idea of divergent gender-related differences in self-construals has potential to provide a new basis for exploring gender differences, although, as Martin and Ruble (1997) suggest, there are many aspects of the proposal which still require closer empirical scrutiny. For example, gender is stereotypically associated with a wide range of attributes such as dominant versus submissive, active versus passive, and Martin and Ruble rightly ask why the interdependent versus independent self-construals are considered to be more basic and central than these other gender-related self-construals. Is it assumed that this dimension subsumes the other gender-related attributes? Surprisingly, since the pioneering studies of Gilligan (1982) on moral behaviour, there has been little research which has demonstrated sex differences in self-construals, and little evidence to support the proposed direct link between self-construals, behaviour and cognition. This aside, it would seem that as psychologists gain more understanding of the complexity of the self-system they are raising many new and interesting questions about the psychology of men and women.

CONCLUSIONS

The study of gender identity and the gendered self is relatively recent and has followed from the general acceptance of the notion of gender as a social category rather than a personality trait. While this represents a significant advance, at the same time Frable's (1997) recent review of gender, racial, ethnic, sexual and class identities has highlighted the narrowness of the focus of research on identity to date, and the paucity of evidence which explores the inter-relationships between different identities. Furthermore, Hurtado (1997) has also noted that while the research literature on sex differences is based on literally hundreds of studies, most have only examined either one or a small number of dimensions. As she notes, 'In order to truly understand the significance of gender for human behaviour we would have to study a substantial number of variables simultaneously' (Hurtado, 1997, p. 315). In trying to account for gender differences, psychologists in the 1980s moved beyond a consideration of the individual in order to encompass the gender system and the relative power and status of men and women across society. As we approach the end of the 1990s it may be appropriate to extend the analysis of gender yet further, to take account of how gender is manifested in different social groups, and the problems that we will continue to encounter so long as we assume that gender can ever be represented by a simple dichotomy. Gender identity is a complex, dynamic and multifaceted social phenomenon, and due acknowledgement of this complexity must now be afforded if genuine understanding is to be progressed.

REFERENCES

Ashmore, R.D. (1990). Sex, gender and the individual. In Pervin, L.A., *The handbook of personality: theory and research.* (pp. 486–526). New York: The Guilford Press.

Bem, S.L. (1974). The measurement of psychological androgyny. *Journal of Consulting and Clinical Psychology* **42**, 165–72.

Bem, S.L. (1981). Gender schema theory: a cognitive account of sex-typing. *Psychological Review* **88**, 354–64.

Bem, S.L. (1983). Gender schema theory and its implication for child development: raising gender aschematic children in a gender schematic society. *Signs: Journal of Women in Culture and Society* **8**, 598–616.

Bem, S.L. (1993). *The lenses of gender.* New Haven: Yale University Press.

Clancy, S.M. and Dollinger, S.J. (1993). Photographic depictions of the self: gender and age differences in social connectedness. *Sex Roles* **29(7/8)**, 477–495.

Cross, S.E. and Markus, H.R. (1993). Gender in thought: a cognitive approach. In Beall, A.E. and Sternberg, R.J. (eds), *The psychology of gender.* (pp. 55–98). New York: The Guilford Press.

Cross, S.E. and Madson, L. (1997a). Models of the self: self-construals and gender. *Psychological Bulletin* **122(1)**, 5–37.

Cross, S.E. and Madson, L. (1997b). Elaboration of models of the self: reply to Baumeister and Sommer (1997) and Martin and Ruble (1997). *Psychological Bulletin* **122(1)**, 51–55.

Deaux, K. (1997). Social identification. In Higgins, T. and Kruglanski, A., *Social psychology: handbook of basic mechanisms and processes.* (pp. 777–98). New York: Guilford Press.

Deaux, K. and Major, B. (1987). Putting gender into context: an interactive model of gender related behaviour. *Psychological Review* **94**, 369–89.

Eagly, A. (1987). *Sex differences in social behaviour: a social role interpretation.* Hillsdale, NJ: Lawrence Erlbaum.

Frable, D.E.S. (1997). Gender, racial, ethnic, sexual and class identities. *Annual Review of Psychology* **48**, 139–62.

Gilligan, C. (1982). *In a different voice: psychological theory and women's development.* Cambridge, MA: Harvard University Press.

Hawkesworth, M. (1997). Confounding gender. *Signs: Journal of Women in Culture and Society* **22(3)**, 649–84.

Hogg, M.A. and Abrams, D. (1988). *Social identification: a social psychology of intergroup relations and group processes.* London: Routledge.

Hurtado, A. (1997). Understanding multiple group identities: inserting women into cultural transformations. *Journal of Social Issues* **53(2)**, 299–328.

Koestner, R. and Aube, J. (1995). A multifactorial approach to the study of gender characteristics. *Journal of Personality* **63(3)**, 681–701.

Lavallee, M. and Pelletier, R. (1992). Ecological value of Bem's gender schema explored through females' traditional and nontraditional occupational contexts. *Psychological Reports* **70**, 79–82.

Markus, H.R. and Kitayama, S. (1991). Culture and the self: implications for cognition, emotion and motivation. *Psychological Review* **98**, 224–53.

Martin, C.L. and Ruble, D.N. (1997). A developmental perspective on self-construals and sex differences: comment on Cross and Madson (1997). *Psychological Bulletin* **122(1)**, 45–50.

Sherif, C. (1982). Needed concepts in the study of gender identity. *Psychology of Women Quarterly* **6**, 375–98.

Skevington, S. and Baker, D. (1989a). Introduction. In Skevington, S. and Baker, D. (eds), *The social identity of women.* (pp. 1–14). London: Sage.

Skevington, S. and Baker, D. (1989b). Conclusion. In Skevington, S. and Baker, D. (eds), *The social identity of women.* (pp. 194–203). London: Sage.

Spence, J.T. (1985). Gender identity and its implications for the concept of masculinity and femininity. In Sondregger, T.B. (ed.), *Nebraska Symposium on Motivation* **32**, 59–96. Lincoln: University of Nebraska Press.

Spence, J.T. (1993). Gender-related traits and gender ideology: evidence for a multifactorial theory. *Journal of Personality and Social Psychology* **64(4)**, 624–35.

Spence, J.T., Helmreich, R.L. and Stapp, J. (1974). The Personal Attributes Questionnaire: a measure of sex role stereotype and masculinity–femininity. *JSAS: Catalog of Selected Documents in Psychology* **4(43)**, *(Ms No 617).*

Swan, S. and Wyer, R.S. (1997). Gender stereotypes and social identity: how being in the minority affects judgments of self and others. *Personality and Social Psychology Bulletin* **23**, 1265–76.

Terman, L.M. and Miles, C.C. (1936). *Sex and personality.* New York: McGraw-Hill.

Unger, R. and Crawford, M. (1996). *Women and gender: a feminist psychology.* 2nd edn. New York: McGraw-Hill.

Yee, M. and Brown, R. (1994). The development of gender differentiation in young children. *British Journal of Social Psychology* **33**, 183–96.

FURTHER READING

Ashmore, R.D. (1990). Sex, gender and the individual. In Pervin, L.A., *The handbook of personality: theory and research.* (pp. 486–526). New York: The Guilford Press.

Cross, S.E and Markus, H.R. (1993) Gender in thought: A cognitive approach. In Beall, A.E. and Sternberg, R.J. (eds), *The psychology of gender.* (pp. 55–98). New York: The Guilford Press.

Cross, S.E. and Madson, L. (1997). Models of the self: self-construals and gender. *Psychological Bulletin* **122(1)**, 5–37.

Frable, D.E.S. (1997). Gender, racial, ethnic, sexual and class identities. *Annual Review of Psychology* **48**, 139–62.

Skevington, S. and Baker, D. (eds) (1989). *The social identity of women.* London: Sage.

DISCUSSION QUESTIONS

1. What are you? Write down 20 statements in reply to that question. How many are social identities? How many are personal traits? How important is gender in your self-concept? How was your self-description influenced by your immediate social situation?
2. Are you a man or a woman? How would you define the psychological characteristics which identify you as masculine or feminine?
3. How important is it to you to identify yourself with other men and women?
4. Do you think that gender is equally important as a social category to men and women?
5. Should women try to become more independent and should men attempt to become more interdependent? What will be the consequences should they succeed?

2

ROLES AND DISCOURSE

Brendan Gough

Introduction

The term role is now used routinely as an everyday part of conversation, and in turn the concept of sex roles is widely used to characterize activities seen to be predominantly or exclusively male or female. While the concept of roles was first formally introduced into the social scientific literature some sixty years ago, the metaphor about people wearing various masks on the stage of life has been around for centuries and certainly well before Shakespeare declared, 'All the world's a stage, and all the men and women merely players' (*As You Like It*, 1599).

A role can readily be defined as a set of expectations and associated behaviours which are peculiar to a specific social setting, in the same way as a theatrical role comprises a script, a stage and various props. A priest, for example, is normally expected to be helpful, courteous, pious and reserved whereas one anticipates that an accountant will be pedantic, dour, conscientious and thorough.

The Canadian sociologist Erving Goffman is closely identified with discussion of roles and what is known as the dramaturgical approach to understanding social interaction. For example, his book *Asylums* (1961) offers a vivid account of the implicit norms and interdependent roles which govern social relations between staff and inpatients in a psychiatric hospital. According to Goffman, the enactment of many roles is realized without much conscious deliberation, at least until a disruption in mundane routines occurs, for example when a patient refuses medication and therefore challenges the quiet obedience that is expected of his or her role. It is this mindless or unconscious facet of roles which seems especially true of sex roles, roles which seem to be ingrained (or internalized) from a very early age and which continue to have such a profound effect on behaviour and cognition throughout life.

Initially, it is important to recognize that there is no one theory of sex roles. Instead, such roles have been viewed from a variety of psychological and sociological perspectives. Through each of these perspectives, one common assumption remains, namely that men and women are expected to behave in differing ways consistent with (but not necessarily caused by) their distinctive biologies. The content of these stereotypes of femininity and masculinity is well known – men are supposedly more rational, competitive and independent and hence are encouraged to pursue activities in the public realm (work, sports, etc.). According to Pleck and Sawyer (1974), this male sex role can be succinctly captured by two features: 'get ahead' and 'stay cool'. In contrast, women, regarded as the fairer or weaker sex (soft, emotional, nurturant, etc.), are confined to the domestic domain and are required to play the primary role of carer and supporter to their husband and children. While there may be agreement as to the characteristics associated with such gender roles, there is less agreement concerning how men and women are socialized into these roles. In recent times several perspectives have appeared in the literature and these are outlined below.

THEORIES OF ROLE ACQUISITION

Early contributions

Most commentators agree that Talcott Parsons, a sociologist writing in the 1940s and 1950s, was responsible for originally developing the specific concept of the sex role. Based on his studies with small groups, he came up with the terms 'instrumental' and 'expressive' to classify the two primary orientations thought necessary for social cohesion. The former category neatly maps on to masculine capacities such as reason and physical labour, whereas the latter connotes feminine domains including emotionality and nurturance. The two forms of orientation were deemed complementary, working together in order to ensure the smooth functioning of society (hence functionalism, the name given to Parsons's broader sociological theory).

Parsons also drew on psychoanalysis to help explain how people became socialized into sex roles, notably the Oedipus and Electra complexes, wherein young boys and girls come to identify with the same-sex parent and hence internalize sex-appropriate attributes. This focus on early family dynamics qualifies Parsons's account as genuinely social, although his reliance on what were seen as unobservable and untestable Freudian constructs gradually attracted much criticism from sociological and psychological quarters which were increasingly concerned to flag their scientific status. This drive towards quantification in the pursuit of scientific respectability culminated in a widespread rejection of psychoanalysis and, with it, Parsons's functionalism.

Social learning theory

Following in the wake of this debate, in the 1960s and 1970s social learning theory (Mischel, 1966; Bandura, 1977) emerged as the dominant approach to understanding sex-role socialization. According to social learning theory, individuals are encouraged to behave in sex-appropriate ways through identifying with significant others of the same sex (parent, athlete, cartoon character, etc.), and by virtue of the social rewards and punishments which are issued by appropriate socializing agents. A wealth of evidence documents how a range of agents, popularly known as role models (including parents, teachers, peers and media figures) reinforce traditional sex roles. For example, Fagot (1974) found that parents typically promote assertiveness in boys by responding to their demands while ignoring, and therefore discouraging, equivalent behaviour from girls. Similarly, many studies indicate that in the classroom boys attract more praise for the intellectual quality of their work, whereas girls receive more attention for the neatness of their work. Conversely, children are frequently reprimanded – and indeed caution their peers – for engaging in activities thought to be inappropriate or deviant for their gender (boys playing with dolls, girls climbing trees, etc.) (see Garvey, 1977).

Recently, this modelling explanation has become popular with mass media and the general public alike, as exemplified by the current debate in the UK around the influence of the Spice Girls, a female pop group considered by many to be setting 'a bad example' to young girls (they often wear revealing clothes, promote 'girl power' and behave assertively). The theme of inappropriate role models has also been offered to account for increasing juvenile violence, most notoriously in the UK with the James Bulger case, where a specific video-movie was cited as a key influence leading to the murder of a toddler by two eleven-year-old boys.

Cognitive theories

Despite the commonsense appeal of social learning theory, the burgeoning cognitive revolution within academic (social) psychology had effectively spawned the current dominant perspective on gender socialization by the 1980s. Emerging from the work of Piaget, Kohlberg and others, this perspective favoured an analysis of internal phenomena (thought processes, mental representations, etc.) as opposed to external stimuli (rewards, punishments, role models, etc.) in order to account for the internalization and endurance of sex-role stereotypes. Consequently, the concept of role in social psychology was displaced in favour of social categories (and categorization).

Simplistic or prejudiced thinking is said to follow from the basic, natural and adaptive process of categorization, whereby order is imposed on the complexity of our social and physical world in order to enable everyday functioning and interaction. The category of sex, perhaps the most visible or salient of all social discriminators, proves useful in making sense of the social world. Together, the supposition of a natural tendency towards categorization and the real biological distinction(s) between the sexes combine to yield a rather inevitable division of the social world around sex. Thus, certain behaviours, phenomena and characteristics are readily perceived as male/masculine (fixing cars, watching sport, displaying anger, etc.) while others are ascribed to the female/feminine domain (cooking dinner, supermarket shopping, showing vulnerability, etc.).

The focus of attention has tended to be not the social origins and content of stereotypes (perhaps falsely regarded more as the province of sociology or politics), but instead the extent to which people rely on these stereotypes as part of social perception and identity formation. Bem's (1981; 1985) Gender Schema Theory, for example, assumes that people will vary according to the importance they ascribe to the category of gender, with strongly sex-typed people (highly masculine or feminine) prone to classifying information about themselves and the world in terms of gender, and vice versa for those not strongly sex-typed. A gender schematic person may, for example, be inclined to categorize fitness activities into feminine aerobics and masculine weightlifting; likewise the term masculine may be used to denote certain supermarket products, such as red meat and beer, whereas baby food and shampoo could be labelled feminine. Experimental support for this hypothesis has been generated, although there are some criticisms of Bem's analysis (see Spence and Helmreich, 1978).

THE ROLE OF ANDROGYNY

Although embedded in a cognitive framework, much of Sandra Bem's work can actually be read as a critique of conventional writings on sex roles. Her work was influenced by the first (or perhaps second, see Chapter 3) wave of feminism in the early 1970s which asserted that traditional sex roles restricted personal development and the realization of potential. This liberal humanistic philosophy led Bem to develop and promote the notion that any individual could possess both masculine and feminine attributes, regardless of biological sex. In turn, this led to the concept of androgyny (Bem, 1974), the category assigned to any person who scores highly on both masculinity and femininity items on the Bem Sex Role Inventory (BSRI). In this way, in Bem's work we witness a challenge to the traditional idea that only men can be masculine and only women can be feminine. According to Bem's framework, gender identity could be reformulated by individuals through the equal acquisition of masculine and feminine characteristics.

The idea that traditional sex roles could be problematic for personal development was soon taken up by male academics in the 1970s. Drawing inspiration from liberal feminists such as Bem, an argument was put forward that men as well as women suffered from conventional ideals (for example, Farrell, 1974; Harrison, 1978). Stresses and strains associated with hard work, competing for promotion, providing for dependants and generally striving for success and status were increasingly reported. The costs issuing from job immersion and physical activities were many and serious, including poor physical health, an inability to express emotion, and a reluctance to nurture. The dominant view within this burgeoning school of men's studies was that men had endured as much pain as women through adherence to traditional roles and that changing role expectations was both possible and necessary.

The emphasis on multiple roles for men and women inherent within this liberal orientation has been enthusiastically taken up by some contemporary role theorists. In particular, the work of Pleck (1987a) emphasizes the fragmentation of sex roles. It can no longer be assumed that there is one male and one female role but a range of diverse positions through which people move over time and place. For example, a married woman with children who has returned to education must perform the roles of student, wife and mother, and may well also fulfil others such as daughter, (part-time) shop assistant and football fan. A similarly fragmented picture emerges for many men, where possible roles may include single parent, rock climber, son, divorcee, unemployed and learner driver.

The requirements of such varied roles may be incompatible at given points and this has been expressed as role conflict. The clash between career woman (independent, ambitious, hard-working, etc.) and mother (nurturant, available, maternal, etc.) is the notorious case, but it is not too difficult to conceive of other (potential) tensions, such as Casanova (flirtatious, shameless, opportunist) versus married man (committed, responsible, faithful) or footballer (aggressive, sexist, uneducated) versus gay man (gentle, liberal, intelligent). Traditionally, role conflict was associated with psychological problems, such as low self-esteem, but more recent evidence suggests that the successful maintenance of many roles may actually promote well-being, so long as effective support structures are in place.

The absence of power

The under-representation of women in high-status roles has been documented by a huge body of feminist literature in the area. The (female) secretary is subordinate to the (male) boss, the supportive wife/mother looks up to the authoritative husband/father – this is seen as the reality of gender relations (Segal, 1990). Roles vary according to social value and it would seem that the claim by male liberationists that men are just as oppressed by their roles misses this important dimension of power. The positions occupied by men and women have been evaluated by feminist writers, who have invariably demonstrated inequalities in favour of men on various criteria including professional grade, salary and domestic activity (see Faludi, 1992). The research reveals a multitude of barriers, both psychological and structural, which act to preserve male dominance, typically warranted by claims that it would not be natural for women to demand equality, or that 'things have gone too far' (see Ford, 1985).

Women are thus caught in a double bind – to adhere to the norms of femininity is to remain a second-class citizen (excluded from public life, etc.) whereas to struggle for equal rights often means enduring much psychological and physical suffering. Within feminist theory, then, sex roles are situated in patriarchal societies where established social structures and relationships favour men. Instead of concentrating on encouraging individuals to become more androgynous, a strategy which ignores the deep structural constraints which inhibit free movement, the concern here is to challenge the wider (patriarchal) social, economic and historical structures which conspire to cement traditional gender relations.

Within social psychology this point has been stressed most notably by Alice Eagly (1987) through her social roles theory. This suggests that people mistakenly attribute any behavioural differences to sex, when in fact they are directly attributable to different social roles. These social roles, although gendered, have been determined by a range of social, political and economic factors. In other words, the current dominance of men in high-status positions has been (mis-)interpreted in terms of sex rather than cultural and historical factors including power, ideology and patriarchy.

This gender picture is complicated still further when other systems of difference are taken into account. It is easy to imagine various limitations on the number and type of roles which are practised, such as those imposed by social class, sexual orientation, ethnic background and occupational choice. For example, it is often difficult for gay and lesbian individuals to come out and fulfil this role in a heterosexist society. Similarly, a working-class single mother may well find it difficult to hold down a full-time job or register for a course because of childcare responsibilities and/or lack of transport. These examples highlight one of the most potent criticisms of existing role theories – a lack of sensitivity to, and analysis of, the relative status of, and consequences from, specific gendered roles.

More recently, some sex-role theorists have countered some of these criticisms by suggesting that, for any given role, there may well be more than one version or set of expectations, for example breadwinner father versus modern involved father (see Pleck, 1987b). It is also recognized that usually one particular version is dominant, with Pleck arguing in this case that the breadwinner role still exerts much greater societal influence. These roles are also situated within wider social and historical forces. For example, Pleck explains the emergence of the modern involved father in relation to the rise of feminism and the increasing number of women in paid employment over the past thirty years. However, Pleck's analysis is so far removed from traditional sex-role theory that it can easily be regarded as an alternative formulation – but one which is gaining ground quickly within social psychology. While Pleck continues to speak of roles, other theorists have preferred to embrace the notion of discourse.

GENDER AND DISCOURSE

Some theorists within psychology and sociology have moved away from the concept of role and towards an alternative formulation centred around discourse. There is no consensus on definition, although Parker (1992) suggests conceptualizing a discourse as a set of statements which construct an object. Statements refer to ideas or understandings, while object is a broad term meaning an entity, situation or phenomenon. For example, the (male) breadwinner can be regarded as a discourse, a traditionally powerful one, which is signalled by a range of interconnecting statements or assumptions, such as that men should go out to work while women's place is in the home, and that a man must provide for his family. As Pleck notes (above) another role (discourse) has emerged in recent times which construes fatherhood in terms of involvement, closeness and emotional support. So, at any given historical moment there will be more than one understanding (or discourse) of fatherhood (or any other object for that matter) which a particular culture makes available. Further, following the work of Foucault, discourses exist in relationships of power so that usually one discourse will be socially dominant. In the case of fatherhood, one could argue that the traditional breadwinner discourse remains ascendant in spite of the evolution of alternative discourses.

The discourse perspective does not stop at identifying and describing the range of roles/discourses present in society. Rather, there is an effort to study how discourses are re-presented (or re-produced) in everyday talk and, significantly, how dominant discourses are resisted or reworked (there is no assumption here that socially powerful ideals are accepted and practised uncritically). For example, a study on unemployed men by Willott and Griffin (1997) found that, rather than reinvent themselves as domestic workers or involved caregivers, unemployed men often choose to adhere to the traditional discourse of the male breadwinner by resorting to 'fiddling', thereby finding money to support the family (and, of course, *public* consumption):

Frank *I've done some casual, and it don't satisfy yer. But I'll tell you something it does do for yer, it gets you off your arse and cos you enjoy going to work it puts you . . .*
Madge *And puts food on the table.*
Nick *It pays the bills don't it?*
Ray *Yeah.*
Frank *You're not walking around the house and you're not getting around your missus and the child, you're going out and doing something. Whether you have to get up at five or six o'clock in the morning, you enjoy doing it.*

(Willott and Griffin, 1997)

Even with men who are positioned as relatively powerless (in terms of income and status) the pull of traditional discourses is so strong that it structures their talk – and practice. In this way these oppressed men retain access to power and continue to affirm relations of inequality between themselves and their partners (positioned domestically within this discourse).

As well as addressing how gender is constructed within multiple discourses, this discourse approach is also sensitive to contradictions within a given text (such as an interview transcript, a newspaper report, a magazine article, or even a television programme). In other words, a speaker (or writer) may well employ two or more discourses during the course of conversation with diametrically opposed meanings and implications. In the field of gender, my own research on masculinity (Gough, 1997) has generated many instances where competing discourses are deployed, often in the same extract. In the following example Kevin (a university student) is ranting about feminism:

Brendan	*What do you not like about feminist women?*
Kevin	*Ah, so many things I disagree with, like quite a lot of it fair enough but at the same time they take it too far, I mean women obviously should be allowed to have jobs and stuff but there's just some jobs they gotta accept they can't do, like you get bloody women pilots and stuff, they just can't make the fitness don't you think? . . . there are situations women shouldn't be in, I mean they're good in business and stuff like that, no problem there but its just sometimes they take it too far, all this equal rights stuff . . .*

(Gough, 1998)

This is not a straightforward profession of sexism but rather one which is intermingled or softened with the projection of libertarian credentials. The speaker moves from pronouncements that could easily be read as sexist (bloody women pilots . . . just can't make the fitness . . .) and those which suggest an element of tolerance (quite a lot of it fair enough . . .). The two discourses, one reactionary, one liberal, are objectively in conflict, although scrutiny of the text would invite the view that the liberal discourse works in the service of the sexist discourse by functioning to mitigate, and therefore enable, its expression in a cultural climate which eschews overtly prejudiced talk.

Conceptualizing gender in terms of discourse moves beyond role theory (where individuals are at the mercy of normative expectations) to consider how social ideals are negotiated during social interaction. The common theme is the social construction of gender, that is, a concern with how men and women are variously represented at various sites (for example, in the media, education, the family) and how these images/ideas are reproduced by people in their everyday understandings. This turn to discourse thus situates particular identities in social, cultural and historical contexts and often signals an analysis of power, in recognition that roles and representations exist in relations of difference/dominance.

This type of discourse analysis thus moves far away from the biological connotations which for long surrounded the concept of *sex*-role. As such, the idea that men and women unproblematically accept or follow prescribed roles is challenged and replaced by the notion that negotiating gender in the 1990s is a complicated, dynamic business informed by particular perspectives and social meanings, as well as the positions of class, race, sexuality and so on.

The problem of experience

At the same time, the foregoing discussion should not be taken to imply that a discourse perspective is without blemish – a number of criticisms have been generated (indeed, Burman and Parker [1993] list 32 problems!). There is insufficient space to explore these in any detail but we may briefly consider one of the most serious charges, that discourse analysis singularly fails to capture the personal and emotional dimensions of talk – that is, the problem of subjective experience.

To focus exclusively on language, power and construction does little to convey the desires and anxieties invested in particular speaking positions within discourses. To adopt the position of househusband within a discourse of the new man is perhaps to be marginalized in a society still obsessed with the ideal of a nuclear family, but how does this *feel* for a man in the 1990s? Similarly, how does it feel for a woman to be positioned as a single mother in the 1990s, or an unemployed man, a career woman, a supermarket worker or a mature student? Although these various positions can be analysed in terms of their relative status and historical production, a discourse analysis cannot convincingly capture the experience of inhabiting a given position. To be fair, the whole notion of experience is called into question by social constructionism (something which is mediated or framed by language and convention) but this does not satisfy many critics. As a result, some contemporary social scientists have returned to Freud in order to complement discourse analysis.

Social psychologists such as Hollway (1983; 1989) and Frosh (1993) have proposed (after Freud and Lacan) unconscious desire as the key to understanding subjective experience. Of course, much (unacceptable) desire is routinely repressed in social interaction, so it becomes important to consider what is repressed and how it is defended in talk. Thus, discourse analysts are encouraged to use Freudian concepts such as repression, splitting and projection in addition to the more familiar tools (multiplicity, construction, contradiction, power, etc.) in their work. In contrast to Freud, however, these psychoanalytic concepts are applied between, rather than within, individuals – a form of relational dynamics. According to Hollway (1989), one of the key tasks in social interaction is to present oneself in ways which protect and/or enhance the ego – a task which is often accompanied by anxiety and which will typically involve defensive moves.

Indeed, as applied to masculinity this analysis does seem to move close to the dissatisfaction and frustration which many men reportedly experience in relation to dominant discourses within which they have been positioned. For example, the conventional discourse which constructs men as rational and dispassionate (i.e. not feminine or irrational) ensures that feelings of vulnerability experienced by men will produce anxiety, which then pushes the emotion out of awareness – and is often projected on to women (hence the prevalence of sexism, misogyny and anti-feminism in much male discourse and practice). Indeed, this is further evidenced by reports that in certain discrete situations, such as visiting a prostitute or during fantasy, men will gladly relinquish prevailing expectations (see Friday, 1980). Accounts that are presented in talk, then, will depend on those discourses which are culturally available, the relationship with the other/s, the context of interaction and the power to present preferred alternatives (Jefferson, 1994). The turn to psychoanalysis is interesting and could be developed fruitfully to complement the broader discourse-analytic approach to gender.

Conclusions

In sum, I have suggested the merits of adopting an approach to gender based on the concept of discourse and emphasizing the social construction of gender. This perspective allows the analysis of power relations and is sensitive to subtle and local complexities and contradictions of gender. However, the discursive approach can in turn be criticized, most notably for failing to get to grips with the lived experience of gender, a dimension that could be addressed by reconsidering elements of psychoanalysis.

References

Bandura, A. (1977). *Social learning theory*. Englewood Cliffs, NJ: Prentice Hall.

Bem, S. (1974). The measurement of psychological androgyny. *The Journal of Consulting and Clinical Psychology* **42**, 155–62.

Bem, S. (1981). Gender schema theory: a cognitive account of sex-typing. *Psychological Review* **66**, 354–64.

Bem, S. (1985). Androgyny and gender schema theory: a conceptual and empirical integration. In Sonderegger, T.N. (ed.), *Nebraska symposium on motivation 1984: psychology and gender*. (pp. 179–226). Lincoln, NE: University of Nebraska Press.

Burman, E. and Parker, I. (1993). *Discourse analytic research*. London: Routledge.

Eagly, A. (1987). *Sex differences in social behaviour: a social role interpretation*. Hillsdale, NJ: Lawrence Erlbaum.

Fagot, B.I. (1974). Sex differences in toddlers' behaviour and parental reaction. *Developmental Psychology* **4**, 554–8.

Faludi, S. (1992). *Backlash: the undeclared war against women*. London: Chatto & Windus.

Farrell, W. (1974). *The liberated man*. New York: Random House.

Ford, A. (1985). *Men*. London: Weidenfeld & Nicolson.

Friday, N. (1980). *Men in love: men's sexual fantasies*. New York: Arrow Books.

Frosh, S. (1993). The seeds of male sexuality. In Ussher, J. and Baker, C. (eds), *Psychological perspectives on sexual problems*. (pp. 41–55). London: Routledge.

Garvey, C. (1977). *Play*. Cambridge, MA: Harvard University Press.

Goffman, E. (1961). *Asylums: essays on the social situation of mental patients and other inmates*. New York: Penguin.

Gough, B. (1998). Men and the discursive reproduction of sexism: repertoires of difference and equality. *Feminism & Psychology* **8(1)**, 25–50.

Harrison, J. (1978). Warning: the male sex role may be dangerous to your health. *Journal of Social Issues* **34(1)**, 65–86.

Hollway, W. (1983). Heterosexual sex, power and desire for the other. In Cartledge, S. and Ryan, J. (eds), *Sex and love: new thoughts on old contradictions*. (pp. 124–40). London: Women's Press.

Hollway, W. (1989). *Subjectivity and method in psychology*. London: Sage.

Jefferson, T. (1994). Theorising masculine subjectivity. In Newburn, T. and Stanko, E.A. (eds), *Just boys doing business?* (pp. 10–31). London: Routledge.

Mischel, W. (1966). A social learning view of sex differences. In Maccoby, E.E. (ed.), *The development of sex differences*. (pp. 56–81). Stanford, CA: Stanford University Press.

Parker, I. (1992). *Discourse dynamics: critical analysis for social and individual psychology*. London: Routledge.

Pleck, J. (1987a). The theory of male sex role identity: its rise and fall from 1936 to the present. In Brod, H. (ed.), *The making of masculinities: the new men's studies*. (pp. 21–38). Boston: Allen & Unwin.

Pleck, J. (1987b). American fathering in historical perspective. In Kimmel, M.S. (ed.), *Changing men: new directions in research on men and masculinity*. (pp. 83–97). Newbury Park, CA: Sage.

Pleck, J. and Sawyer, J. (eds) (1974). *Men and masculinity*. Englewood Cliffs, NJ: Prentice Hall.

Segal, L. (1990). *Slow motion: changing men, changing masculinities*. London: Virago.

Spence, J.T. and Helmreich, R.L. (1978). *Masculinity and femininity: their psychological dimensions, correlates and antecedents*. Austin, TX: University of Texas Press.

Willott, S. and Griffin, C. (1997) Wham bam, am I a man?: unemployed men talk about masculinities. *Feminism & Psychology* **7(1)**, 107–28.

FURTHER READING

Archer, J. and Lloyd, B. (1985). *Sex and gender*. Cambridge: Cambridge University Press.

Edley, N. and Wetherell, M. (1995). *Men in perspective: practice, power and identity*. London: Prentice Hall.

Gough, B. (1998). Men and the discursive reproduction of sexism: repertoires of difference and equality. *Feminism & Psychology* **8(1)**, 25–50.

Pleck, J. (1987a). The theory of male sex role identity: its rise and fall from 1936 to the present. In Brod, H. (ed.), *The making of masculinities: the new men's studies*. (pp. 21–38). Boston: Allen & Unwin.

Segal, L. (1990). *Slow motion: changing men, changing masculinities*. London: Virago.

Discussion questions

1. Write down the various roles you inhabit. Considering each role in turn, think about whether it is more popular with men or with women and discuss reasons for this. Do these roles sit easily together?
2. Select a text (magazine article, advertisement, interview transcript, etc.) pertinent to masculinity and identify the way[s] in which men are represented. Consider which other representations (or discourses) are excluded from the text and discuss reasons for this.
3. Discuss how the discourses reproduced by men are constrained by other identities (for example, in terms of social class, sexual orientation, race).
4. Do you agree that traditional sex roles have changed substantially during the 1990s?
5. Are men and women equally oppressed by conventional gender norms?

3

FEMINISM

Carol Percy

INTRODUCTION

What is feminism?

Feminism is a key influence on twentieth-century Western thought, a social movement and a theoretical perspective on gender and human behaviour. It takes as its focus the nature, rights and interests of women, and uses a critique of male power and authority to argue for profound changes in the way that male and female humans are produced, represented and treated. Feminist activists have driven wide-ranging changes in the political and legal systems of many countries, and continue to campaign for change in others. Feminist practitioners have set up and run support systems for women around issues of sexuality, pornography, sex work, domestic violence, rape, child abuse, and access to reproductive freedom. Feminist academics have altered the direction of theory in sociology, political and cultural studies, history, literature and the arts, and have been key contributors to the sea change in academic thought known widely as postmodernism. These achievements are all the more remarkable because they have come about against feelings of mistrust and suspicion about the term feminism and its perceived connotations among many men, and indeed many women (Percy and Kremer, 1995). To do full justice to the range of theory and practice encompassed by the single word feminism would not be feasible here. Instead, the aim of the chapter is to begin to outline what feminism is and what it has achieved, and most especially, to consider the role which feminism has played within the discipline of psychology.

Early signs

The effects of feminism on psychology were publicly acknowledged in the 1970s but its influence was undoubtedly felt for some considerable time beforehand, the length of time depending critically on how the term feminism is actually defined. For example, feminist historians such as Spender (1983) emphasize the continuity between the activities and motives of those involved in suffrage campaigns at the beginning of the twentieth century and those active in the so-called women's liberation movement from the 1960s onwards. These two periods of activity are often referred to as 'first-wave' and 'second-wave' feminism, though some speak of the tide of feminism which has run throughout this century, for example citing the ongoing activity of feminists in a whole range of areas between the 1920s and the 1970s.

Alongside this attempt to emphasize continuity and ongoing activity, there is considerable debate as to how feminism is defined and as to which activities may legitimately be labelled feminist. Leaving aside the subtleties of this debate, perhaps the most basic definition of a feminist psychology would simply be where women are present and active within the discipline.

Feminism and psychology: influence by mere presence

A common approach adopted by many 'psychology of women' texts is to examine and celebrate the contribution of women in psychology, whether such women were self-labelled feminists, and whether or not they pursued goals explicitly linked to gender. In one sense then, feminism influenced psychology first by enabling women to take and be awarded degrees in the discipline, and, to some extent, to take up positions of influence within the academe and psychological practice. Accounts of the history of psychology which attempt to 're-place' women aim to acknowledge women's contribution to the discipline, but there remains the problem as to whether having women present will inevitably lead to a feminist influence. It was not until the late 1960s and early 1970s that the rise of second-wave feminism paved the way for a debate about the role of feminism *per se*, and acceptance of feminist views within psychology. In this movement, two women psychologists are worthy of particular mention.

Sandra Bem and Carol Gilligan

Bem's (1974) work was revolutionary in that she used her powerful position as a psychological expert to persuade fellow psychologists, and later the educated public, that existing patriarchal gender roles were not simply unjust, but psychologically unhealthy. Her work with the Bem Sex Role Inventory (BSRI) was able to show that androgynous individuals (those who shared masculine and feminine traits in approximately equal proportion) experienced better mental health, and were more flexible and adaptable in their attitudes and behaviours.

As a result of media interest in Bem's work, and its timeliness in a society undergoing change as a consequence of the women's liberation movement, the term androgyny became widely known and the psychological state it supposedly described was widely advocated in popular culture. Even though later studies have contradicted Bem's claims, and she herself has reformulated her gender theory several times, Bem's work was highly influential in providing expert 'scientific' support for challenges to the existing gender status quo.

Another feminist psychologist whose work became influential in the psychology of the 1970s and early 1980s was Carol Gilligan. Gilligan's (1982) work, based on a large-scale study at Harvard University in the USA, served to challenge existing theories on moral development and in particular that of Lawrence Kohlberg. Kohlberg's (1969) theory of moral development outlined six stages of moral reasoning through which most human beings were assumed to progress, with the 'later' stages in the developmental sequence somehow deemed as superior or more advanced than those which precede them. When later research on non-white, lower-class and particularly female participants showed that these individuals failed to display the moral reasoning characteristic of Kohlberg's later stages, researchers had a choice between criticizing the participants' morality or re-examining Kohlberg's theory. Carol Gilligan chose the latter. She criticized Kohlberg's work for attempting to extrapolate from findings based on an all-male sample to the moral behaviour of women and girls. To do so, she argued, was androcentric, that is treating male morality as the norm against which women's moral reasoning can be assessed, and more often than not, found lacking.

According to Gilligan, Kohlberg's formulation of morality emphasized justice, while ignoring or underplaying the role of feeling and care in moral decision-making. Gilligan's work on women's 'different voice' was an important landmark in feminist psychology because it drew attention to the androcentricity of the traditional discipline, and because it offered a new perspective on moral behaviour. Gilligan herself, and other theorists, have taken this work further to argue that moral choices are more flexible and complex than Kohlberg's work implies, and that morality may be simultaneously guided by several sets of considerations. Gilligan's work has not gone uncriticized, both from anti-feminist critics intent on devaluing feminist psychology and by those who find some of its essentialist assumptions too simplistic to sustain. Nevertheless, her work was important in suggesting that women's psychology deserved study in its own right. Such moves towards a distinct psychology of women have been, and continue to be, a source of conflict within both feminism and psychology.

Feminism and psychology: separate or together?

Given the challenges which they made to the male-centred, male-dominated and highly professionalized discipline of psychology, it is perhaps not surprising that feminists soon found themselves in conflict with 'the system'. Feminists and their projects have encountered opposition within psychology in similar ways to their counterparts in other disciplines, and indeed wider society. As we shall see later, feminist psychology has been seen as a threat to the mainstream, as seeking to introduce emotion and politics into a discipline which claims to be rational, objective and scientific. In turn feminist psychology has been labelled as exclusionary, in attempting to pursue the needs and rights of women at the expense of those of men. These debates have centred not only on the way in which theory is formulated and research is conducted but also on the way psychologists organize themselves into professional bodies to regulate and police the boundaries of the discipline and its professional practice.

In the USA, the Association for Women in Psychology was founded in 1969 and played a pivotal role in the establishment of a special division of the American Psychological Association in 1973, Division 35, Psychology of Women (Paludi, 1996). As a consequence, feminist psychology became a formally legitimated component of the discipline, supported through journals, conferences and networks of academics working on issues of gender. In the UK, formal recognition for feminist psychologists took longer to achieve. The establishment of a Psychology of Women Section of the British Psychological Society in 1987 was permitted only after a lengthy struggle in which objections were raised that a section would be unnecessarily separatist and political (Wilkinson, 1990).

As a result of these struggles, feminist psychology in the UK in the late 1990s has an official voice, but one which is far from unitary. Such difficulties can be recognized in the writings of two key UK researchers, Jane Ussher (1990) and Celia Kitzinger (1991). While both identify themselves as feminists, Ussher argues strongly for activism *within* psychology and the retention of a psychological perspective on gender issues. Kitzinger, however, offers a critique so damning of psychology's humanist underpinnings and inherent heterosexism that she argues the need for active resistance *to* psychology. These tensions reflect a history of debate within feminist theory, of which some of the key arguments are outlined below.

THEORETICAL PERSPECTIVES

Any attempt to classify arguments and theories risks the dangers of oversimplification and polarization, particularly when the authors concerned are either academics or activists, or sometimes both, and the theories vary along a broad continuum from esoteric academic research through to grassroots activism. However, in order to offer the following outline of feminist theory, it is necessary to show the diversity of views which have influenced feminists in psychology.

Feminisms

Liberal feminists work on the assumption that men and women are of equal value and deserve equal rights as individuals. Their practices aim to enable the individual person to pursue their rights unhindered by gender. The early work of Sandra Bem, advocating the value of psychological androgyny, reflects this broadly liberal stance.

One of the strengths of this approach is its relative palatability to mainstream Western political thought, which has been dominated in both Europe and the USA by liberal humanism and individualism. Liberal feminism has been successful in bringing about changes in legislation relating to sex discrimination, equal pay and childcare provision in the USA and Western Europe, though there is still considerable progress to be made on these issues.

Not surprisingly, this approach has been criticized for its individualist and liberal-humanist base (Kitzinger, 1991), which asks only for correctional adjustments to the gendered status quo in order that women may participate on an equal footing to men. In doing so, it is argued that the liberal approach tends to ignore the powerful effects of 'unconscious gender', that is heterosexism, and places the responsibility for challenging oppression firmly on the shoulders of the oppressed individuals themselves.

Psychoanalytic feminists, including a wide range of Freudian and Neo-Freudian writers such as Karen Horney (1973) and Juliet Mitchell (1974), emphasize the power of the unconscious in shaping behaviour. They argue that, because of early experiences and particularly those within the so-called traditional nuclear family, girls and women internalize representations of gender where women are relatively powerless. Such unconscious representations are used to account for the development of a form of femininity which is more oriented towards others, towards caring and nurturance, rather than individualistic self-advancement. It could be argued that such qualities, if they indeed exist, disadvantage women in a world where more 'masculine' values such as ambition, independence and mastery are privileged, while other feminists have argued that the former values reflect a superiority on the part of women. The early work of Carol Gilligan reflects some psychoanalytic feminist assumptions. Psychoanalytic feminists differ in the extent to which they see women's supposed feminine qualities as predestined by biology or acquired through experience.

Essentialist feminists, on the other hand, see women as innately different from men. Using some of the same biological arguments adopted by sociobiologists, essentialist feminists, such as Mary Daly (1978), maintain the view that women are, by virtue of their biological make-up, psychologically different from men, and, some argue, naturally superior. This veneration of women's ability to bear and nurture children, and their supposed tendency to avoid conflict, war and destructive competition, has led some essentialist feminists to criticize both men and masculinity, and in some cases to advocate a rejection of both.

This approach provides an important redress to the bias in Western thought which elevates the masculine and devalues the feminine. However, its rather static and fixed approach to gender creates problems for feminists who seek change in the status quo. Essentialism alone is regarded as an insufficient theoretical base to support active gendered politics, so some feminists have taken the approach further in the form of radicalism.

Radical feminists, such as Andrea Dworkin (1974), argue for the overthrow of patriarchy through active refusal to collaborate with the structures, institutions and practices which uphold masculine power and its abuse. This can involve decisions not to engage in sexual relationships with men, to reclaim power over sexual reproduction (for example, through the use of technology such as artificial insemination), or to provide and organize in women-only spaces and organizations. As a consequence, many radical feminists have chosen to be lesbian, though some have gone further to suggest that lesbianism is women's natural state. Some other radical feminists argue for the feminization of language (for example, 'herstory' as opposed to 'history'). This focus on language anticipates a major component of constructionist feminism, a theme to which we will return later.

The radical approach highlights the oppression of lesbians by heterosexual women as well as by men, and introduces sexual orientation as an additional theoretical axis for consideration alongside gender. Radical feminism's links with the gay rights movement and women-only organizations have helped to ensure its political edge. However, the refusal of radical feminists to compromise on the issues of separatism and heterosexism has led to conflict between themselves and potential allies from elsewhere across the feminist spectrum.

Existential feminists, the first and best known of whom was Simone de Beauvoir (1974), argue that humans naturally tend to polarize the world into masculine and feminine, and then overlay these categories with value judgements which privilege the male. De Beauvoir argued that, for historical reasons, man established himself as the generic Self and placed woman as the essential Other, defined through what she lacks and the hidden, fearful qualities that she possesses. Though ideas embedded in existentialist theories can be difficult to access, because of their abstract nature and the esoteric language in which they are expressed, they have been influential across other brands of feminism, including some already discussed. For example, psychoanalytic feminists have speculated as to the ways in which woman's Otherness is incorporated into the unconscious lives of both women and men, while essentialist and radical feminists have used echoes of de Beauvoir's Self/Other scheme to make sense of misogyny, men's apparent fear and hatred of women.

Marxist feminists argue that the roots of gender oppression can be traced to capitalism as a means of production, and the power structures reproduced by class in capitalist societies. They argue that freedom from the constraints of gender-stereotyped roles and patriarchal power structures can best be achieved in a Marxist economy. This approach addresses the concerns about individualism expressed by critics of liberal feminism but can be criticized for placing gender as a second-order priority, dwarfed by the central concern, class.

Black feminists, such as African American theorist bell hooks (1989), criticize academic feminism for its white middle-class bias, and its neglect of the gendered experiences of women of colour. hooks is a black academic feminist participating in the white-dominated debates of contemporary feminist theory, but she retains contacts with her working-class black extended family and is active in the black rights movement. Given her multiple identity and membership of numerous political constituencies, hooks and her black feminist colleagues have been able to draw attention to the lack of theorizing about race inherent in white feminism.

Socialist feminists, dissatisfied with the tendency of radicals to focus on gender to the neglect of class, and Marxist feminists to do the reverse, have proposed an eclectic theory which acknowledges the multiple nature of gendered oppression. Taking on board ideas from all the other major strands of feminist thought, socialist feminism offers an account of gender which acknowledges material, social and unconscious processes and accepts that race, gender, sexuality and class combine to produce power relations which systematically disadvantage women. Socialist feminism subscribes to the notion of patriarchy as proposed by early theorists, but acknowledges it to be much more complicated than other approaches suggest. However, its admirable attempts to cope with diversity have not prevented it being superseded by a new kind of feminism with a very different agenda.

Postmodern feminism arose from several different sources and has a complicated history. It is associated with a wider movement in the social sciences which rejects certainty and structured accounts of social phenomena. Like socialist feminists, postmodern theorists were dissatisfied with the limited range of other feminist theories and their tendency to focus on single explanations of gender. However, whereas socialist feminists chose to adopt certain aspects of existing theories to construct a new eclectic approach, postmodern feminists began to question the wisdom of constructing great theories at all. Postmodern writers, such as Kenneth Gergen (1994) and Michel Foucault (1989), reject 'grand narratives', arguing that the social world is much less structured and much more fragmented than these theories suggest. They advocate a shift away from a focus on a single material 'reality' to a position where there are many alternative versions or *constructions* of reality.

The appeal of the post-structuralist approach for feminists lies in the possibility of exposing gender as being not real or fixed, but constructed and therefore amenable to change. Marginalized groups are seen as fertile sources of alternative construction, so that feminisms can be constructed from a variety of perspectives. There are potentially black, lesbian, heterosexual, white, middle- and working-class constructions of feminism; in fact, as many versions of feminism as there are combinations of experience. This approach offers one way of dealing with the diversity in feminist thought and practice, and can explain the ways in which power can be achieved through symbolic, as well as material, means.

Not all constructions are equally available and some may be systematically promoted over others. For example, constructions of sexuality which privilege heterosexuality are more widely employed in contemporary popular media than alternatives which promote lesbian, bisexual or celibate practices. Radical lesbian theory on such heterosexism demonstrates that constructions are not neutral and are often used to serve the purposes of particular individuals and groups.

Though postmodern/constructionist feminism is appealing for the reasons outlined above, it worries some feminists because of its move away from a focus on the material or real. Given the continuing existence in many parts of the world of gendered oppression such as sexual violence, enforced pregnancy, sexual slavery, unequal or non-existent pay, educational and employment discrimination, for some it would be politically damaging if feminism were to direct its attentions away from these material problems. Because of these concerns, some feminists adopt a type of constructionism which acknowledges a material basis upon which different versions of reality may be constructed.

Feminism today: a cautionary note

All of the strands of thought outlined above (and most of the practices associated with them) coexist today. There is no single orthodoxy in contemporary feminism, no end-point has been reached in the development of feminist theory. Tempting though it is to take a storybook approach, the order in which this history of feminist thought is presented should not be taken as a chronological life story of 'feminism today'. The story is continuing to be rewritten.

Feminist psychologies

The task of mapping feminist theories onto feminist psychologies is made doubly difficult because of, on the one hand, the problems in classifying feminisms outlined above, and on the other hand, the dual and potentially conflicting roles of the feminist psychologist.

As a psychologist s/he[1] is concerned with epistemological and theoretical issues, adopting a meta-theoretical stance on human behaviour and the means by which it ought to be studied. As a feminist s/he will have political motives, relating to power and gender, which may manifest themselves in the topics s/he chooses to study and the methodological approaches s/he

1 It is an assumption made by the author that a feminist psychologist may be either male or female, though this assumption would be disputed by some radical theorists.

adopts in so doing. If we examine the first of these two sets of issues, we will see how feminist psychologists differ in their meta-therorетical agendas.

Philosopher of science Sandra Harding (1986) has classified feminist approaches to the study of gender as:

- *feminist standpoint approaches* which assume that women are essentially different from men and need to be studied separately and in their own right;
- *feminist empiricist approaches* which argue that women may or may not be different, but if accurate measurements are taken then at least we will have a more accurate picture of similarities and differences;
- *feminist constructionist approaches* which argue that women's qualities are constructed and fluid, and as such, efforts to fix and measure them are misguided.

These three approaches can be detected, to a greater or lesser extent, in contemporary theory and research by feminist psychologists.

Contemporary research

Feminist standpoint approaches are reflected in a number of psychology of women courses and the textbooks used to teach these. For example, American texts such as those by Lips (1993), Hyde (1996) and Matlin (1996) do important corrective/replacing work by showing how women have contributed to the history of psychology and by highlighting the fact that the psychology of women reflects 'half the human experience'. By focusing on the study of women in their own right, such courses and texts acknowledge that women's experiences are important and have not been adequately reflected in mainstream psychology. However, by virtue of their names and labels, such courses and texts risk marginalizing the study of feminism and gender issues as something which need only be studied by or for the sake of women. For this reason, some feminists have argued that the focus should shift to the study of gender as a construct which applies to all human beings, regardless of their sex or political persuasion.

Feminist empiricist research is also given coverage in most psychology of women texts (for example, Hyde, 1996). This work often promotes classic texts, such as that by Maccoby and Jacklin (1974), as offering a more genuine picture of true gender differences. Some of this work, using techniques such as meta-analysis, pursues feminist aims by trying to demonstrate the lack of statistically or socially significant differences between women's and men's traits and abilities. The chief strength of these approaches, as far as feminist politics is concerned, lies in the rhetorical resources they have at their disposal. By using the rhetoric of evidence-based science, still widely accepted within mainstream psychology, gender difference researchers are able to challenge mainstream conceptions of women's abilities and qualities on their own scientific terms. This means that, arguably, feminist empiricist researchers are less likely than their feminist standpoint counterparts to be marginalized within the discipline of psychology. However, a criticism which has been levelled at feminist empiricist researchers is that, by adopting the methods and rhetoric of the mainstream, they miss an opportunity to offer a radical and much needed critique of the whole way in which psychology formulates theory, collects data and perpetuates the body of knowledge it has come to represent.

With this in mind, some of those involved in differences research (for example, Hare-Mustin and Marecek (eds), 1990) have moved away from the empiricist position to argue that psychology's approach to theory and research has *constructed* gender differences rather than simply measuring, documenting and accounting for them. Examples of this work show how the tendency of psychological researchers to expect and seek gender differences is compounded by publishing practices which favour studies showing significant differences, to produce a literature in which evidence of difference is highlighted and occurrences of gender similarity neglected. As a result of this critique, which sadly has not been widely heeded in mainstream psychology, many feminist psychologists (for example, Hollway, 1994) now advocate a move away from measuring the *product* of gendering to examine the *process* by which this occurs. Developmental psychologists have been pursuing such work for some time, but whereas they focus on the production of gender schemata or gender identities in individuals, and particularly in childhood, the focus of much feminist psychological theorizing has more recently been upon gendering in language throughout adult life.

The emphasis on the process of gendering has led feminist psychologists to the use of qualitative methodologies, and particularly discourse analysis. This is the study of language as an active medium in which realities are constructed, identified and negotiated, and through which social purposes are achieved. Feminists are by no means the only psychologists interested in discourse analysis but feminist psychologists (including Mary Crawford in the USA, and Margaret Wetherall in the UK) have played a key role in the development of the technique and the constructionist theory which underpins it.

A strength of the constructionist approach is that it offers a metatheoretical critique, not just of the psychology of women but of the whole basis of psychological enquiry. As part of a wider movement in the social sciences, this approach can draw support from work in political and cultural studies, sociology and literary theory, forging links across disciplinary boundaries to create a fluid and socially situated psychology. However, this very fluidity and commitment to social specificity is the basis upon which constructionist research has been criticized.

Empiricist theorists and researchers located within mainstream empiricist psychology argue that qualitative and discursive research is generally based on limited samples and as a consequence lacks generalizability. Discourse research rarely offers universal theory or general rules which apply across all situations; indeed, part of the critique offered by discourse analysts is to argue that the search for such universals is futile and counterproductive. Nevertheless, the positivist approach favoured by mainstream psychology means that constructionist work is, for the present, often treated with scepticism. Apart from the problem of convincing scientific psychologists of the merit of constructionist accounts, constructionism raises issues for feminists of a much more pressing and political nature. Feminist psychologists, fearful that discursive work could become a sterile endeavour of talk without action, argue strongly for a politicized psychology where deconstruction is always conducted with political goals in mind. It is this political agenda which drives the most interesting and relevant contemporary research (Wilkinson, 1996).

Recent trends

The feminist psychologies of the 1990s have turned to the analysis of key issues which unite and divide along sexed and gendered lines. An important strand of research in both the USA and Western Europe has been that which problematizes heterosexuality. Instead of assuming this as a normal or usual state, several authors have questioned the naturalness of heterosexuality and have theorized the ways in which it is regulated and promoted (for example, Kitzinger, 1992). Lesbian feminists have asked their heterosexual feminist psychologist colleagues to explain how their sexuality has contributed to their feminism (Wilkinson and Kitzinger (eds), 1993) and generated debates about heterosexism within the discipline.

Other issues of difference between women themselves have been a similar focus of theory and research, in feminist psychological enterprises examining race (for example, Bhavnani and Phoenix (eds), 1994), (dis)ability (for example, Morris (ed.), 1996) and mental health/illness (for example, Ussher, 1991). In response to criticisms that existing feminist theories and practices exclude certain individuals and groups, feminist psychologists are increasingly addressing the issue of 'Otherness' and questioning the right of one woman to represent another (see Wilkinson and Kitzinger (eds), 1996). Given that psychologists have traditionally assumed the right to represent the reality of their research participants, this is a critique which should have wide-ranging implications for the discipline as a whole.

Perhaps the clearest sign of this shift in focus is the growing development of a feminist psychology of *men and masculinity*. Recognizing that both feminism and psychology have failed to account for women's diversity, some theorists now argue that there can no longer be a single generic psychology of men. The interest in men's psychology, and the increasing number of courses on the psychology of gender as opposed to the psychology of women, is, at least in part, a consequence of the developing men's movement in the USA and Europe. Not all those involved in the men's movement espouse feminist politics; indeed, some authors identify aspects of the men's movement as reactionary or deliberately anti-feminist. Nevertheless, as the academic psychology of men emerges, it is feminists in the main who are equipped with the theoretical tools to fashion its future (see, for example, Edley and Wetherall, 1995).

In addition to addressing issues of difference, feminist psychologists have continued to use feminist critiques of gender, in particular those emanating from the social constructionist school, in order to engage in a critical deconstruction of the bedrock of mainstream psychology. Examples of this type of endeavour can be seen in the work of the UK clinical psychologist Jane Ussher, who has offered critiques of the biopsychology of women's bodies (Ussher, 1989), and the treatment of distressed women by clinical psychology and psychiatry (Ussher, 1991). More recently, another UK feminist, Erica Burman (1994), has offered a critical deconstruction of the assumptions underpinning developmental psychology, showing the ways in which its gendered constructions have been used for political purposes.

CONCLUSIONS

Feminist psychology is alive and relatively well, albeit constantly shifting and changing. It has an unusual relationship to the remainder of psychology in that its practitioners have a more overt, political agenda and seek to make this part of their theory, research and practices. This has brought them into conflict with the mainstream in the past and without doubt is likely to continue to do so in the future. The survival of a substantial feminist psychology depends upon the continuance of support networks and publishing outlets which legitimate its practice. Any changes in the professionalization of psychology which alter the existing structure of its national and local bodies may have implications for the survival of the feminist contribution to the discipline. This is particularly the case when, in the USA and Western Europe, several authors (for example, Faludi, 1991) have documented an anti-feminist backlash in popular culture and politics.

Concerns have been raised about the loss of focus on women through the metamorphosis of psychology of women courses into psychology of gender courses, with disagreements emerging between those who place different priorities upon the study of men and masculinity. Similarly, some feminists worry that a continuing emphasis on discourse may detract from the political realities of gendered oppression.

The issues of race, social class, (dis)ability and sexual orientation are likely to continue to divide feminists and fuel their theory and research. In the UK in particular, lesbian feminist psychologists continue to argue for greater recognition by both the British Psychological Society and their heterosexual feminist counterparts. Whether these concerns will result in a break-up of existing alliances, or a healthy friction and debate, remains to be seen. Feminism has succeeded in the past because of its willingness to change and its capacity for inclusiveness through diversity. It has formed alliances which have survived considerable conflict, and others which were dissolved when differences proved too great. In looking to its future, the psychology of gender would do well to remember the invaluable lessons of its feminist past.

References

Bem, S. (1974). The measurement of psychological androgyny. *The Journal of Consulting and Clinical Psychology* **42**, 155–62.

Bhavnani, K.K. and Phoenix, A. (eds) (1994). *Shifting identities, shifting racisms: a feminism and psychology reader.* London: Sage.

Burman, E. (1994). *Deconstructing developmental psychology.* London: Routledge.

Crawford, M. (1995). *Talking difference: on gender and language.* London: Sage.

Daly, M. (1978). *Gyn/Ecology: the metaethics of radical feminism.* London: The Women's Press.

de Beauvoir, S. (1974). *The second sex.* (Trans. and ed. H.M. Parshley). New York: Vintage Books.

Dworkin, A. (1974). *Woman-hating: a radical look at sexuality.* New York: Dutton.

Edley, N. and Wetherell, M. (1995). *Men in perspective: practice, power and identity.* London: Harvester Wheatsheaf.

Faludi, S. (1991). *Backlash: the undeclared war against women.* London: Chatto & Windus.

Foucault, M. (1989). *The archaeology of knowledge.* (English trans. by A.M. Sheridan Smith). London: Routledge.

Gergen, K.J. (1994). *Toward transformation in social knowledge.* London: Sage.

Gilligan, C. (1982). *In a different voice: psychological theory and women's development.* Cambridge, MA: Harvard University Press.

Harding, S. (1986). *The science question in feminism.* Ithaca, NY: Cornell University Press; Milton Keynes: Open University Press.

Hare-Mustin, R.T. and Marecek, J. (eds) (1990). *Making a difference: psychology and the construction of gender.* New Haven: Yale University Press.

Hollway, W. (1994) Beyond sex differences: a project for feminist psychology. *Feminism & Psychology* **4(4)**, 5538–46.

hooks, b. (1989). *Talking back: thinking feminist, thinking black.* London: Sheba Feminist.

Horney, K. (1973). *Feminine psychology.* New York: Norton.

Hyde, J.S. (1996). *Half the human experience.* Lexington, MA: D.C. Heath & Company.

Kitzinger, C. (1991). Feminism, psychology and the paradox of power. *Feminism & Psychology* **1**, 111–29.

Kitzinger, J. (1992). Sexual violence and compulsory heterosexuality. *Feminism & Psychology* **2**, 399–418.

Kohlberg, L. (1969). Stage and sequence: The cognitive developmental approach to socialisation. In Goslin, D.A. (ed.), *Handbook of socialisation theory and research.* (pp. 347–80). Chicago: Rand McNally.

Lips, H.M. (1993). *Sex and gender: an introduction.* Mountainview, CA: Mayfield Publishing Company.

Maccoby, E.E. and Jacklin, C.N. (1974). *The psychology of sex differences.* Stanford, CA: Stanford University Press.

Matlin, M.W. (1996). *The psychology of women.* Fort Worth, TX: Harcourt Brace.

Mitchell, J. (1974). *Psychoanalysis and feminism.* London: Penguin Books.

Morris, J. (ed.) (1996). *Encounters with strangers: feminism and disability.* London: The Women's Press.

Paludi, M.A. (1996). *The psychology of women.* Dubuque, IA: WCB.

Percy, C. and Kremer, J. (1995). Feminist identifications in a troubled society. *Feminism & Psychology* **5(2)**, 201–22.

Spender, D. (1983). *There's always been a women's movement this century*. London: Pandora.

Ussher, J. (1989). *The psychology of the female body.* London: Routledge.

Ussher, J.M. (1990). Choosing psychology: or not throwing the baby out with the bathwater. In Burman, E. (ed.), *Feminists and psychological practice*. (pp. 47–61). London: Sage.

Ussher, J. (1991). *Women's madness: misogyny or mental illness?* London: Harvester Wheatsheaf.

Wilkinson, S. (1990). Women organising in psychology: I. In Burman, E. (ed.), *Feminists and psychological practice*. (pp. 140–51). London: Sage.

Wilkinson, S. (1996). Prioritising the political: feminist psychology. In Ibanez, T. and Iniguez, L. (eds), *Critical social psychology*. (pp. 178–94). London: Sage.

Wilkinson, S. and Kitzinger, C. (eds) (1993). *Heterosexuality: a feminism & psychology reader*. London: Sage.

Wilkinson, S. and Kitzinger, C. (eds) (1996). *Representing the other: a feminism & psychology reader.* London: Sage.

Further reading

Hollway, W. (1991). The psychologisation of feminism or the feminisation of psychology? *Feminism & Psychology* **1**, 29–37.

Kitzinger, C. (1991). Feminism, psychology and the paradox of power. *Feminism & Psychology* **1**, 111–29.

Thompson, D. (1992). Against the dividing of women: lesbianism, feminism and heterosexuality. *Feminism & Psychology* **2**, 387–98.

Ussher, J. (1990). Choosing psychology: or not throwing the baby out with the bathwater. In Burman, E. (ed.), *Feminists and psychological practice*. (pp. 47–61). London: Sage.

Wetherall, M. and Griffin, C. (eds) (1992). Feminist psychology and the study of men and masculinity: Part I: Politics and practices. *Feminism & Psychology* **2(2)**, 133–68.

Discussion questions

1. Can a man be a feminist? If not, why not?
2. How might being heterosexual affect a woman's feminist politics?
3. Are some research methods more feminist than others? If so, why?
4. Should feminists expend their efforts studying men and masculinity? If not, why not?
5. Has feminist psychology been accepted into the mainstream? If so, how?
6. Which kinds of feminism are shown and explained in the popular media?
7. Do we still need feminism? If so, why?
8. Has feminism been beneficial or harmful? How?
9. Why might some feminists say that it is impossible to be both a feminist and a psychologist at the same time?

4

SEXUALITY

Majella McFadden and Ian Sneddon

INTRODUCTION

As we start to reflect on the end of the twentieth century and welcome the approach of a new millennium it seems that issues and questions surrounding sexuality abound. By way of example, sexuality occupied centre stage during the moral panic associated with AIDS in the 1980s, and even more recently, sexuality has been a topic hotly debated within the high institutions of state, such as the church and the army. During the 1990s, many aspects of sexuality have become explicit, with open discussions commonplace in the popular media, in magazines and even in the ever-present soap operas. Yet despite the greater coverage, and the younger age at which exposure to issues associated with sexuality begins, many seem still unsure about their own and others' sexuality, and about the factors which influence the development and sustenance of sexual identities. Among academics too, within psychology and related disciplines, what sexuality means and how we can approach its study remain fiercely contested issues. This chapter aims to guide the reader through a consideration of these debates and their implications for those trying to understand sexuality within the discipline of psychology.

ESSENTIALIST MODELS OF SEXUALITY

The sociobiological perspective

Since sex is often referred to as one of our more animal instincts, perhaps we should 'naturally' turn to biology for an explanation of our sexuality. This approach is associated with a long tradition which views aspects of human behaviour from within a wider biological context. Supporters of these biological theories would claim that they offer insight into something fundamental, not just about human behaviour but about human nature. Unfortunately, the reality has been that such theories have enjoyed a chequered history, including their use as scientific justifications for policies of sexual or ethnic repression and social division (Rose et al., 1984).

Although political misuse of ideas does not necessarily make the ideas in themselves wrong, many academics remain justifiably cautious of attempts to apply theories from the field of biology to the study of human behaviour. These cautions aside, over the past few decades animal behaviour researchers have not been slow to make several forays into the area of human social behaviour (for example, Wilson, 1978; Dawkins, 1989; Diamond, 1997). Theorists working on animal behaviour look for common patterns across different species, trying to explain how an animal's biology, together with the environment in which it lives, may come to shape and constrain behaviour, ultimately resulting in the evolution of the behaviours we see today. In relation to sexuality, many aspects of sexual relationships, such as courtship, mating systems and the division of child rearing by males and females, have now been examined in detail across a wide number of species. The resulting theoretical framework for non-human species is now widely accepted and largely uncontroversial (Gould and Gould, 1989).

Based on the fundamental idea that individuals are driven to maximize the number of offspring which they successfully produce, sociobiologists would argue that, due to basic differences between males and females, the two sexes go about this task in different ways. Females, who produce resource-rich eggs, can achieve this most effectively first by being selective about the males with whom they mate, and second, by then ensuring the successful rearing of any offspring produced. Males, on the other hand, produce metabolically inexpensive sperm and hence they can more successfully maximize their breeding success by competing with other males for access to females and by attempting to mate with as many females as possible. In some cases, environmental conditions require that the two mates co-operate in rearing their offspring and a monogamous system evolves. In other cases conditions may favour polygyny (a male with multiple female mates) or, more rarely, polyandry (a female with multiple male mates) (Emlen and Oring, 1977).

The conditions pushing animals towards a monogamous system are usually those such as scarce or difficult-to-obtain food, a harsh environment or many predators which make it difficult for one parent to rear the offspring alone. Conditions favouring polygyny often involve the ability of a male to control access to resources important to the female such as food, water or nesting sites. Polyandry is a much rarer phenomenon which seems to have evolved from a response to predator pressure on the offspring. By taking over the nurturing role, males free females to devote their energy to replacing those young who have been taken by predators. It is argued that females then exploit the situation by producing offspring with several males.

Clearly, elaborate explanatory frameworks have been developed over recent years to cover many aspects of animal sexual behaviour, and it will come as no surprise to learn that theorists have been tempted to cast their nets wider in order to try to explain human sexuality. This extrapolation has met with far from universal approval both within and without the academic community and the underlying assumptions behind the approach have been the subject of close scrutiny. Primarily, the approach is predicated on the belief that the sole function of sex (and, by inference, our sexuality and sexual preferences) is the production of offspring and that males and females have different forces driving them towards this end. It is but a short step from making this assumption to viewing non-reproductive sex as aberrant, and to prescribing different roles to males and females.

Furthermore, in early sociobiological speculations on human social behaviour (for example, Alexander, 1974), the assumption was often made that the drives or predelictions towards certain behaviours were not only influenced by our genes but encoded in those genes. Recently a more subtle attempt to bring the biological tradition to bear on human social behaviour has been made by evolutionary social psychologists (Buss, 1990). Although this approach may have the potential to offer fresh insights into a range of human social behaviours, in the area of human sexuality the core arguments still rest upon the calculus of reproduction. Individuals are seen as maximizing reproductive success and sex is fundamentally about procreation. There is little acknowledgement of concepts such as love or bonding, or other social roles played by sex. Hence, while the sociobiological approach may have made strides towards understanding sexual behaviour and gender differences across the animal kingdom, it appears inadequate as an explanation of the range and diversity of human sexuality.

The Freudian legacy

Within the discipline of psychology, discussion of the origins of our sexuality has often been set against the ubiquitous nature–nurture debate, with the nature side of the argument dominating proceedings prior to the 1960s. A key figure in this tradition was Sigmund Freud (1856–1939) and his theory of psychosexual development (see also Chapter 11). Grounded in the ideas of psychic (unconscious), biological and social development, Freud envisaged our sexuality as stemming from infancy before developing through a series of age- and sex-related phases. Adult sexuality was finally achieved in the genital phase, with women's and men's sexuality deriving from the differential resolution of what Freud refers to as the Oedipus (boys) and Electra (girls) complexes in early childhood. These are seen as occuring during the phallic stage of development when the child becomes aware of others (and most especially the father) impinging on her/his exclusive relationship with the mother (seen as the primary object of an infant's love).

For the young boy, awareness of the father's relationship with the mother ignites a fierce hatred for the father. In fact the son wishes to kill the father in order to retrieve his exclusive possession of the mother. At the same time, the boy is all too aware of the power of the father and fears that he will be punished by his father, by removing that part of his anatomy from which the boy derives his primary pleasure at this stage of development, his penis. Castration anxiety motivates the boy to repress his desire for the mother and to come to identify with the father. The identification process requires the boy to respect not only the wishes of the father but, on a societal level, that which the father represents, namely law and morality. Hence the young boy acquires a distinct sexuality and, with the development of his superego, what Freud regarded as full entry into mature, human culture.

According to Freud, this rocky road to men's sexuality was simply not open to women. Indeed, the development of women's sexuality caused Freud somewhat of a headache, as an extract from his 1933 lecture on femininity illustrates: 'Throughout history people have knocked their heads against the riddle of the nature of femininity ... Nor will you have escaped worrying over this problem – those of you who are men; to those of you who are women this will not apply – you are yourselves the problem' (Freud, 1933, p. 224). For women, the resolution of the Electra complex can best be described as complexity heaped on complexity. In common with young boys, the young girl becomes aware of the presence of a third figure entering into the mother–daughter relationship (the father), and of the relationship that exists between the mother and the father. Again, like her male counterpart, the young girl is enraged by the mother's desire for the father and wishes to kill the father. At the same time, the young girl becomes aware of anatomical differences between her primary source of pleasure (her clitoris) and that of boys. Believing that her penis has already been cut off by her mother, the young girl develops a hatred for her mother and all that she represents (that is, her femininity). In despair she turns to her father in a bid to win back that which she (and all women) desire, a penis. Thus the girl's love object changes from being the mother to being the father. However, soon the young girl realizes that she will never possess a penis and, accepting her loss, reluctantly she is compelled to identify with her mother. Completion of this phase for the young girl occurs when her envy for the penis is replaced by her desire for a (male) baby: 'if woman can positively wish for a baby as a substitute source of power and identity, so much the better for the quality of her femininity' (Freud, 1933, p. 231). The hurdles of childhood development and the young girl's inability to completely resolve the conflict culminate in a rather complicated picture of women's development in the writings of Freud. In his mind, the lack of castration anxiety experienced by young girls deprives them of the psychic momentum necessary for the development of a strong superego. In turn, the wound of inferiority created by the young's girl's realization that she does not possess a phallus continues to weep throughout adult development, resulting in womenkind being characterized by jealousy, insecurity and masochism. It is little wonder that classical Freudians see the acquisition of femininity as providing a fertile breeding ground for a variety of neuroses (Figes, 1970), and it is also little wonder that many women working within the psychoanalytic tradition have long been prepared to take issue with Freud's thesis regarding female sexual development (Horney, 1924).

Freud's contribution to the study of sexuality remains a contested issue. For many, he has provided a powerful insight into gender inequality which continues to outshine traditional socialization theory by its inclusion of the psychological acquisition of femininity and masculinity. For others, Freud's inclusion of infantile sexuality and the bisexual nature of early sexual desires has provided tools for understanding the multiple gendered identities that exist today (see Mitchell, 1974). In contrast to such approval, both Freud's research philosophy and his conceptions of sexuality have been criticized on a number of fronts, and these are outlined below.

Politically biased: Freud has been accused by many writers of providing accounts of sexuality which, rather than being objective scientific theories (as he claimed), have merely served to protect and enhance male hegemony. Similar criticisms have been levelled at accounts of lesbianism produced in the late nineteenth and early twentieth centuries. For instance, Penelope (1992) and Faderman (1991) believe that sexual theorizing was profoundly influenced by changing social and sexual relations during this period. To illustrate, they highlight how attitudes to romantic friendships among women changed during this period. Intimate female friendships had been seen as providing an important social service (teaching women the art of loving for when they later became wives) but came to be redefined as representing a menace to the moral stability of society.

Penis envy or power envy: Although broadly in agreement with Freud's theory of psychosexual development, Karen Horney (1924) dismissed the notion that young girls experience penis envy during the phallic stage. Instead she introduced the concept of womb envy, that boys may come to envy those parts of a woman's anatomy which they palpably lack. She suggested that young girls desire not the anatomical penis but the social penis – the power and identity that the phallus seems to ensure her male counterpart, a theme taken up by later writers such as Juliet Mitchell (1974).

Femininity as riddle: For Cixous (1975), Freud's insistence that femininity should be regarded as a riddle (the 'feminine mystique') has meant that female sexual identity and practices are not explored, nor are the social implications of sexuality recognized. The suggestion that a male agenda underpinned Freud's work continues to be forcefully expressed in the writings of contemporary researchers of female sexuality. To quote Frosh (1987),

> it is as if the recognition of the precariousness of masculinity is still too daunting for full articulation in Freud's theory: femininity is continually derogated and the power of social construction repeatedly circumscribed by a biologism that seeks to sustain an image of male superiority, of masculine activity and power
>
> (p. 201)

Active male, passive female: Work from other disciplines has been cited by some psychologists in order to question Freud's dichotomous representations of femininity (passive, caring and nurturing) and masculinity (active, aggressive and philandering), and the biological universals of gender which underpin his whole approach. Historically, the work of anthropologist Margaret Mead (1935), which described behavioural diversity coexisting among women and men in Polynesian tribes, provided a basis for challenging biological representations of sexuality (albeit that controversy still surrounds Mead's research). For example, Mead found that among the Arapesh, both females and males were co-operative and non-aggressive, among the Mundugumour both females and males were hostile and detached, whereas among the Tchambuli it was females who were active, aggressive and detached while males were passive and nurturing. More recently, La Fromboise et al. (1990) have offered insights into the warrior women in native American cultures which further weaken biologically based representations of the universality of gendered behaviour. Once more, this work demonstrates that simple and sovereign, deterministic approaches seem unable to capture the breadth of human experience.

HOMOSEXUALITY: SICKNESS AND BEYOND

In his writings on sexuality, Freud (1905) described homosexuality as a condition originating in childhood as a result of abnormal developmental experiences. For boys, an overly possessive and seductive mother who rejects her son's attempts at independence was thought to facilitate the development of male homosexuality. For girls, their failure to relinquish their active sexuality and accept the more passive sexual practices that characterized femininity predisposed them to lesbianism.

During this period, the focus was not confined simply to understanding 'homosexuality' but also to rectifying the imbalanced psychic/sexual stages and thus curing a perceived illness (Kitzinger, 1987). For example, representations of lesbian women as being in some way biologically abnormal predominate in Havelock Ellis's (1936) *Studies in the psychology of sex*. 'Female inverts' (as Ellis [1936] labelled lesbian women), although perhaps maintaining the clothes and appearance of a woman, were betrayed by their innately masculine behaviours and practices:

> There are all sorts of instinctive gestures and habits which may suggest to female acquaintances the remark that such a person 'ought to have been a man'. The brusque energetic movements, the attitude of the arms, the direct speech, the inflexions of the voice, the masculine straightforwardness and the sense of honour, and especially the attitude towards men, free from any suggestion of shyness or audacity, will often suggest the underlying psychic abnormality to a keen observer.
>
> (p. 250)

Furthermore, intrinsic to such perceptions were queries relating to the moral and mental stability of such individuals, in particular to their impact on society. For instance, Ellis not only linked lesbianism to particular types of social instability (including the demise of heterosexual marriage) but expressed concerns relating to lesbians' impact on the overall moral fabric of society. According to Ellis, normal women were in danger of being seduced into becoming pseudo-homosexuals by real lesbians who set out to lure them into their immoral lifestyle (see Jeffreys, 1985).

Challenges to essentialist notions of sexuality during the 1960s and 1970s brought about changes not only in how femininity and masculinity were viewed but also in accounts and interpretations of homosexuality. Within psychology, representations of homosexuality as sickness, as deviant in relation to the norm of heterosexuality, and as dangerous, were replaced by liberal humanistic understandings of homosexuality (Kitzinger, 1987). Within these new paradigms, differences between homosexual and heterosexual individuals were dismissed and lesbian women and gay men were presented as normal individuals who had made a personal life choice which was 'as natural, normal and healthy as heterosexuality' (Kitzinger, 1987, p. 45). In addition, notions that lesbian women and gay men were a danger to the moral and social stability of society were strongly denied. For gay men in particular, during the 1980s this proposition had to swim against a growing tide of homophobia (that is, fear, intolerance or hatred of homosexuality), fuelled by descriptions of AIDS as a 'gay plague' or judgment on homosexual men. How AIDS continues to impact on attitudes towards homosexuality in the late 1990s remains to be seen but certainly available evidence from the 1980s and early 1990s would suggest that homophobia is still far from uncommon (Sneddon and Kremer, 1991).

Against this backcloth of public opinion, liberal accounts of homosexuality have been welcomed by many individuals either living in homosexual relationships or contemplating 'coming out', as well as writers and practitioners critical of the pathological model of homosexuality. At the same time, this paradigm has also been criticized on a number of fronts. For example, rather than liberating lesbians, Kitzinger (1987) believes that liberal accounts may reduce the adoption of a lesbian identity to no more than a personal choice. In doing so, such women are denied the opportunity to define or express themselves collectively in socio-political terms (for example, as actively resisting patriarchy through the politicization of lesbianism through radical feminism). Kitzinger and Wilkinson (1997) level the same charge against advocates of 'queer theory', who argue that deliberate use of the term 'queer', so long a term of abuse used against homosexuals, can be looked upon as a positive, confrontational, proud and deliberate expression of nonconformist sexualities. Further, it is suggested that defining lesbianism in terms of fulfilment of the self, or as a natural part of self-development, instead of as a source of empowerment, may actually obscure the political dimensions of lesbian identities and thus may contribute to maintaining the (heterosexual) status quo.

Clearly the discourse surrounding homosexuality is extremely active, and the issues and challenges which this discourse throws up are likely to continue to drive debate for a considerable time to come. Despite the alarming intricacies and political intrigues often associated with these discussions, one positive outcome has been an ongoing and vibrant consideration of the nature of sexuality, and a successful challenge to the notion of 'compulsory heterosexuality' (Rich, 1980) which had dominated the discipline for so long.

Compulsory heterosexuality

Many authors suggest that the most prevalent construction of sexuality is that which presents it as synonymous with heterosexual ideology and practices. Undoubtedly, one of the most outspoken critics of this definition in relation to female sexuality has been Adrienne Rich. In her ground-breaking paper 'Compulsory heterosexuality and lesbian existence', written almost twenty years ago, Rich (1980) questioned the 'naturalness' of heterosexuality (that is, the representation of femininity and masculinity as innate, penetrative sex as 'normal' and marriage as the only legitimate sexual arrangement). She achieved this via two interrelated arguments: (i) the manufactured and coercive nature of heterosexuality; and (ii) lesbian continuum and lesbian existence.

With respect to the first, the so-called naturalness of heterosexuality, Rich argued that heterosexuality as a practice is not only socially manufactured but coercively imposed on many women through various means including romantic ideologies, the use of physical force or the censorship of alternative sexual arrangements.

> Whatever its origins, when we look hard and clearly at the extent and elaboration of measures designed to keep women within a male sexual purlieu, it becomes an inescapable question whether the issue feminists have to address is not simple 'gender inequality' nor the domination of cultures by males nor mere 'taboos against homosexuality' but the enforcement of heterosexuality for women as a means of assuring male right of physical, economic and emotional access.
>
> (Rich, 1980, pp. 434–5)

Contrary to accepted wisdom, and following from Freud's description of the development of the Electra complex, she argued that girls must learn how to become heterosexual, because their first emotional attachment is homosexual. Furthermore, as the above quotation shows, Rich viewed the political consequences of heterosexuality as central to Western definitions of female sexual identity and expression. The definition of female sexuality using heterosexual criteria, and the specification of these as social norms, coerce women into accepting subordinate sexual roles and so deny them the opportunity for developing a critique of existing sexual relations.

Rich argued that defining heterosexuality as 'the norm' across a variety of practices and contexts (for example, scientific and cultural theorizing, political and social milieux, as well as everyday language and thinking) effectively ensures the eradication of knowledge relating to alternative sexual arrangements. In addition, defining female sexuality in terms of heterosexual criteria establishes false and divisive boundaries between women, ignoring both the sense of community and practical support many women have experienced.

In order to redress this perceived imbalance, she has radically reconstructed the concept of lesbian by introducing the term 'lesbian continuum' to include not only those who desire sexual contact with other women but any women who have enjoyed a variety of 'woman identified experiences', including 'the sharing of a rich inner life, the bonding against male tyranny, the giving and receiving of practical and political support' (Rich, 1980, p. 635).

Rich's discussion of the socially manufactured and coercive nature of heterosexuality has informed much of the subsequent theorizing on sexuality. For example, Bleier (1984) describes the ideology of heterosexuality and the practices it legitimates as one of the most powerful social forces shaping the lives and consciousness of women and men (although through different practices and with different consequences for each gender). She describes how, in school, in the home, and through the media, women 'learn that the normal way to be is to be identified with a man, to have a primary emotional commitment to a man' (p. 184). In turn, obligatory heterosexuality teaches men about their unlimited access (even when this entails using force) not only to women's bodies but to their emotional, social and economic resources. These themes are also prevalent in the work of Holland et al. (1990) and Gavey (1993). Gavey (1993) goes on to suggest that broad definitions which describe heterosexuality as 'normal' may serve to bind and constrain female sexuality, not only by prescribing particular sexual practices and arrangements but also by depicting women who resist these, or who indulge in 'other sexual practices' (including lesbianism), as abnormal.

Other work has been more critical of what is perceived as Rich's mistaken assumption that all heterosexual relationships are coercive or compulsory. For example, Ferguson (1982) has argued that Rich 'ignores the existence of some heterosexual couples in which women who are feminist maintain an equal relationship with men. Such women would deny that that their involvement is coercive, or even that they are forced to put second their own needs, their self-respect, or their relationships with women' (p. 159). Ferguson also maintains that by assuming passivity among women, many important instances of women's agency are overlooked, a concern voiced by more recent commentators such as Richardson (1990), Gergen (1993) and Gill and Walker (1993). In addition, Ferguson is critical of Rich's focus on heterosexuality as the central mechanism of women's oppression. Instead, she suggests the need for a more complex analysis of women's oppression, one which includes the impact of other social systems such as capitalism and racism. Again, such issues have been taken on board in more recent considerations of heterosexuality (see Wilkinson and Kitzinger (eds), 1993).

SEXUALITY: LINGUISTIC AND SOCIAL PRACTICES

The discourse which surrounds sexuality has attracted considerable attention over recent years, and in particular that relating to female sexuality. From the 1970s onwards, approaches to gender and sexuality such as those discussed so far have been increasingly challenged from a diverse number of sources and at a number of levels, including the epistemological, methodological and political. Gradually the concepts of masculinity and femininity have been reconstructed as critical thinkers have re-evaluated concepts at the heart of mainstream social psychology. Three key issues to emerge from this debate which have particular relevance to a discussion of sexuality are presented below.

Subjectivity

The concept of an inner core self and the private space which this inhabits has been deconstructed and replaced with notions of fluid and multifaceted identities which are negotiated and given shape within public, social space (see Chapter 2). Thus, dualistic representations of the individual and the social have been replaced by the individual as the social. In order to avoid the trap of social determinism, which many social theories of sexuality had fallen into, within this critical paradigm individuals are not perceived as passive recipients of social practices but as actively working towards various social positions and representations. For example, many 'thirty-something' women are resisting representations of woman as wife and mother and presenting themselves as positively single (Smith, 1988). In the literature on sexuality this acceptance of multiplicity is reflected in the ongoing difficulties associated with defining terms such as homosexual and heterosexual, or indeed even gender itself.

Language and social practice

Language is viewed as the raw material underlying identities and practices (Burman and Parker, 1993), with sexuality a common theme for those interested in linguistic construction. For example, Foucault (1976) wrote extensively about sexuality, dispelling the notion that it is situated inside the person and instead presenting it as the product of a number of discourses including the religious, the medical and the scientific. In this way, sexuality is posited as the fulcrum around which social relationships, positions and practices are organized. Since Foucault, understandings of sexuality as the product of culturally placed discourses have been prevalent within the work of both British and American critical social psychologists (for example, Fine, 1988; Holland et. al, 1990; McFadden, 1994; Wetherall, 1997).

By way of example, Holland et al. (1990) maintained that the portrayal of women as potential victims of an uncontrollable male sex drive is one of the dominant discourses pervading the information which women receive regarding sexuality. In addition, Fine (1988) points out that such victimization does not concentrate solely on the sexual dangers that men present to women and their reputations but extends to include the need for women to protect themselves from pregnancy and disease. She also notes that another common representation of female sexuality is that of women as some type of moral vanguard. As well as having the responsibility for protecting themselves against pregnancy and disease, presentations of men as driven by uncontrollable sexual urges place the responsibility for 'sensible' sexual behaviour with women. Within this discourse, female subjectivity is given recognition in the language of self-control and sexual restraint. Against this backdrop of danger, Thomson and Scott (1991) note that within the information available for women in relation to their sexuality, strong associations between sexuality and reproduction are evident. In this context, sex for women is presented primarily in terms of how it affects their roles as wives and mothers.

According to Vance (1984), various discourses on female sexuality, whether they present it as dangerous, as a means of victimization, or as a case of individual morality, share one common theme which starkly distinguishes female from male sexuality – that is, little recognition is given to women's desire to be sexually active. Even in the 1990s, many women continue to be taught about their bodies only in relation to menarche and pregnancy; sexual pleasure remains uncharted territory (Thomson and Scott, 1991). While these formal discourses are undoubtedly significant, this does not mean that women passively accept them. Again, Fine (1988) acknowledges that formal literature (including school-based education, parental advice, health education and religious doctrines) often fails to address the issue of female sexual desire and pleasure, in response women turn to other sources (for example, peers, partners, magazines, television and political groups) to construct their notions of sexual pleasure and desire.

Political discourse

By suggesting that concepts such as sexuality are the product of social, cultural and political discourses, critical social psychology is able to examine and contribute to so-called real life struggles. Understandings of sexuality as constructed rather than innate (Gergen and Davis (eds), 1997) call into question the very processes involved in defining it as we know it. The function of sexuality is thus exposed and issues of power, ideology and equality move to centre stage. In addition, the integration of a constructionist perspective poses questions about the current shape of psychology as an academic discipline and the nature of the knowledge which it produces.

Conclusions

This chapter has attempted to offer an overview of the debates around sexuality within psychology, moving from essentialist perspectives which view sexuality as predominantly biological/anatomical, through the work of Freud and his similar concern with anatomy as destiny and towards contemporary approaches. These, through a constructionist perspective, have begun to explore the various shades of sexuality and sexual identities which make up human experience. At the very least contemporary work is prepared to acknowledge that our sexuality develops and is sustained in response to a great many personal and social forces, and that the pathways which we follow towards our current sexuality are many and varied. No longer is heterosexuality viewed as compulsory or 'right', but in turn it should not be portrayed as politically incorrect or 'wrong' to be comfortable with that sexual identity. Postmodernism dictates that the social sciences should respect difference and diversity and nowhere should this message be more powerful than in relation to that most personal aspect of our identity, our sexuality.

References

Alexander, R.D. (1974). The evolution of social behaviour. *Annual Review of Ecology and Systematics* **5**, 325–83.

Bleier, R. (1984). *Science and gender: a critique of biology and its theories on women.* London: Pergamon Press.

Burman, E. and Parker, I. (1993). *Discourse analytic research.* London: Routledge.

Buss, D.M. (1990). Evolutionary social psychology: prospects and pitfalls. *Motivation and Emotion* **14**, 265–86.

Cixous, H. (1975). Cited in Minsky, R. (1996), *Psychoanalysis and gender.* London: Routledge.

Dawkins, R. (1989). *The selfish gene.* New edn. Oxford: Oxford University Press.

Diamond, J. (1997). *Why is sex fun? The evolution of human sexuality.* London: Weidenfeld and Nicolson.

Ellis, H. (1936). *Studies in the psychology of sex.* New York: Random House.

Emlen, S.T. and Oring, L.W. (1977). Ecology, sexual selection and the evolution of mating systems. *Science* **197**, 215–23.

Faderman, L. (1991). *Odd girls and twilight lovers.* London: Penguin.

Ferguson, A. (1982). Patriarchy, sexual identity and the sexual revolution. In Keohane, N., Rosaldo, Z. and Gelpi, B. (eds), *Feminist theory: a critique of ideology.* (pp. 147–61). Chicago: Chicago University Press.

Figes, E. (1970). *Patriarchal attitudes.* New York: Stein & Day.

Fine, M. (1988). Sexuality, schooling and adolescent females: the missing discourse of desire. *Harvard Educational Review* **58**, 29–53.

Foucault, M. (1976). *The history of sexuality.* Vol. 1. London: Allen.

Freud, S. (1905). Three essays on the theory of sexuality. Repr. in vol. 7 of *The standard edition of the complete psychological works of Sigmund Freud,* trans. and ed. J. Strachey. London: Hogarth Press, 1961.

Freud, S. (1933). *New introductory lectures on psychoanalysis.* London: Hogarth Press.

Frosh, S. (1987). *Psychology and psychoanalysis.* London: Sage.

Gavey, N. (1993). Technologies and effects of heterosexual coercion. In Wilkinson, S. and Kitzinger, C. (eds), *Heterosexuality: a Feminism & Psychology reader.* (pp. 93–120). London: Sage.

Gergen, M. (1993). Unbundling our binaries – genders, sexualities, desires. In Wilkinson, S. and Kitzinger, C. (eds), *Heterosexuality: a Feminism & Psychology reader.* (pp. 62–5). London: Sage.

Gergen, M. and Davis, S. (eds) (1997). *Towards a new psychology of gender.* New York: Routledge.

Gill, R. and Walker, R. (1993). Heterosexuality, feminism, contradiction: On being young, white heterosexual feminists in the 1990s. In Wilkinson, S. and Kitzinger, C. (eds), *Heterosexuality: a Feminism & Psychology reader.* (pp. 68–73). London: Sage.

Gould, J.L. and Gould, C.G. (1989). *Sexual selection.* New York: Scientific American Library.

Holland, J., Ramazanoglu, C., Scott, S., Sharpe, S. and Thomson, R. (1990). *Pressure, resistance and empowerment: young women and the negotiation of safer sex.* London: Tufnell Press.

Horney, K. (1924). On the genesis of the castration complex in woman. *International Journal of Psychoanalysis* **5**, 50–60.

Jeffreys, S. (1985). *The spinster and her enemies: feminism and sexuality 1800–1930.* London: Pandora Press.

Kitzinger, C. (1987). *The social construction of lesbianism.* London: Sage.

Kitzinger, C. and Wilkinson, S. (1997). Virgins and queers: rehabilitating heterosexuality. In Gergen, M. and Davis, S. (eds), *Towards a new psychology of gender: a reader.* (pp. 403–20). London: Routledge.

La Fromboise, T., Helye, A. and Ozer, E. (1990). Changing and diverse roles of women in American Indian cultures. *Sex Roles* **22**, 455–86.

McFadden, M. (1994). *Female sexuality in the second decade of AIDS.* Unpublished PhD thesis, The Queen's University of Belfast.

Mead, M. (1935). *Sex and temperament in three primitive societies.* New York: William Morrow.

Mitchell, J. (1974). *Psychoanalysis and feminism.* Harmondsworth: Penguin.

Penelope, J. (1992). *Call me lesbian: lesbian lives, lesbian theory.* Freedom, CA: The Crossing Press.

Rich, A. (1980). Compulsory heterosexuality and lesbian existence. *Signs: a journal of women in culture and society* **5(4)**, 631–57.

Richardson, D. (1990). *Women and the AIDS crisis.* London: Pandora Press.

Rose, S., Lewontin, R.C. and Kamin, L.J. (1984). *Not in our genes: biology, ideology and human nature.* Harmondsworth: Penguin.

Smith, D. (1988). Femininity as discourse. In Roman, L.G., Christian-Smith, L.K. and Ellsworth, E. (eds), *Becoming feminine: The politics of popular culture.* (pp. 37–59). Lewes: Falmer Press.

Sneddon, I. and Kremer, J. (1991). AIDS and the moral climate. In Stringer, P. and Robinson, G. (eds), *Social attitudes in Northern Ireland.* (pp. 120–41). Belfast: Blackstaff Press.

Thomson, R. and Scott, S. (1991). *Researching sexuality in light of AIDS: historical and methodological issues.* London: Tufnell Press.

Vance, C. (1984). *Pleasure and danger: exploring female sexuality.* London: Routledge.

Wetherall, M. (1997). Linguistic repertoires and literary criticism: new directions for a social psychology of gender. In Gergen, M. and Davis, S. (eds), *Towards a new psychology of gender: a reader.* (pp. 149–71). London: Routledge.
Wilkinson, S. and Kitzinger, C. (eds) (1993). *Heterosexuality: a Feminism & Psychology reader.* London: Sage.
Wilson, E.O. (1978). *On human nature.* Cambridge, MA: Harvard University Press.

Further reading

Emlen, S.T. and Oring, L.W. (1977). Ecology, sexual selection and the evolution of mating systems. *Science* **197**, 215–23.
Gergen, M. and Davis, S. (eds) (1997). *Towards a new psychology of gender.* New York: Routledge.
Holland J., Ramazanoglu, C., Scott, S., Sharpe, S. and Thomson, R. (1991). *Pressure, resistance and empowerment: young women and the negotiation of safer sex.* London: Tufnell Press.
Kitzinger, C. (1987). *The social construction of lesbianism.* London: Sage.
Wilkinson, S. and Kitzinger, C. (eds) (1993). *Heterosexuality: a Feminism & Psychology reader.* London: Sage.

Discussion questions

1. Think back to your attitudes towards homosexuality before reading this chapter. Has your reading influenced your attitudes and if so, why?
2. If you are homosexual, or have talked to someone who has declared their homosexuality, how would you describe his/her/your experience of living in a 'heterosexual world'?
3. Do you feel that Freud has much to contribute to our understanding of psychosexual development?
4. Why does Freud's work continue to generate so much interest and especially outside the discipline of psychology?
5. Gay men or gays? Lesbian women or lesbians? Discuss the implications of using these different form of words when defining sexual identity. Which form of words are you most comfortable with and why?

5

BIOLOGY

Orla Muldoon and Jacqueline Reilly

INTRODUCTION

Biological or essentialist explanations of gender differences are often viewed as irrefutable or as 'hard' scientific fact, and are given greater weight than findings or explanations emanating from the 'softer' social sciences. However, social factors, and in particular construals of gender, have often influenced scientific enquiry and as a result the objectivity of 'hard science' in this area can be questioned, so much so that the biological definition of sex itself becomes untenable (see also Chapter 17).

Although biological definitions of gender are unconvincing, reproductive structures and functions do impinge on our experience of gender. Generally such effects have been highlighted in relation to women but rarely in relation to men. Perhaps the most notable research in this area is that which relates to the influence of reproductive hormones and menstruation on women's performance and behaviour. Analysis of the literature in this area emphasizes the importance of considering not only biological but also cultural, social and psychological factors when attempting to understand the relationship between biology and gender.

BIOLOGICAL FOUNDATIONS OF GENDER

Many of the arguments underpinning cognitive, behavioural and role differences between males and females have their foundations in the anatomical and physiological differences between the sexes. In biological terms, sex is most often defined on the basis of reproductive function (Ross and Wilson, 1983). Biological sex in humans is determined genetically; eggs fertilized by a sperm cell bearing an X chromosome develop into girls, while those fertilized by a Y-bearing sperm cell develop into boys. Humans carry a total genetic code consisting of 23 pairs of matched chromosomes, one half of the set being inherited from each parent. Fusion of a sperm and an ovum results in the development of an embryo containing 23 such pairs of chromosomes, the final pair usually being one of two possible combinations, either XX or XY. Individuals with the XX pair reproduce egg cells with X chromosomes, and are known as female, whereas individuals with an XY pair will reproduce sperm cells containing either an X or a Y chromosome, and are known as male.

Although the role played by the twenty-third pair of chromosomes in sexual development is poorly understood (Fausto-Sterling, 1985), its importance in pre-natal development is widely accepted. The twenty-third pair of chromosomes begins to affect the development of the embryo at about six weeks of gestational age; until this time XX and XY embryos are anatomically identical. At this time, genetic coding on the Y chromosome in males causes the gonads to develop into testes, and in females, where there is a second X chromosome, the gonads develop into ovaries. After the testes have developed at around six weeks of gestational age, they begin to produce testosterone and Müllerian Inhibiting Substance (MIS) which stimulates the Wolfian ducts to develop into the male reproductive tract. In contrast, the development of ovaries in female embryos may occur as late as 12 weeks of gestational age (Kessler and McKenna, 1985).

For many years, it was the absence of the androgens secreted by foetal testes which was thought to result in the development of the Müllerian ducts, which subsequently developed into the female reproductive tract. More recently, however, a female-determining gene has been located on the X chromosome (Unger and Crawford, 1996) and it has been suggested that female embryos begin synthesizing large quantities of oestrogens at about six to eight weeks of gestational age (Fausto-Sterling, 1985). These oestrogens are thought to play a key role in the development of the female reproductive system. Nonetheless, the genetic and biochemical basis for female differentiation during pre-natal life is still less well understood than that for males (Fausto-Sterling, 1992), with far greater research efforts being directed towards the latter (Fausto-Sterling, 1989). No doubt this research bias is related to the long-standing impact of cultural ideas on what is defined as the 'scientific' process (Hubbard and Wald, 1993). Researchers seem to be willing to accept at face value the notion of passive female development, consonant with the historic and androcentric idea that being female results from the lack of something male, in this case androgens during pre-natal life.

At birth, the gender of a child is normally ascribed on the basis of the child's external genitalia and this attribute is generally viewed as immutable (Kessler and McKenna, 1985). Thus, from birth onwards the exact roles of nature and nurture in the development of gender-related processes become difficult to disentangle. In distinguishing between individuals' genotypes and phenotypes, modern genetics endorses the impracticality of attempting to dissect the effects of the inherited from that of the environment. Genotype refers to the specific composition of genetic material possessed (regardless of whether it is expressed), whereas phenotype, on the other hand, refers to the observable characteristics of the individual (Hubbard and Wald, 1993). Accepting the biological definition of male as being capable of producing sperm and/or having an XY pair of chromosomes, alongside the equivalent female definition, is problematic. This is primarily because infertile individuals who are incapable of producing reproductive cells or with chromosomal abnormalities (such that they do not have the usual XX or XY constellation of the twenty-third pair of chromosomes) fall outside the biological definition for either gender. At the same time these individuals do exhibit a 'gender phenotype'. In essence therefore, biological definitions of sex are not as irrefutable as they would first appear.

Assumptions Underlying Definitions of Sex and Gender

Although it is normally biology that determines gender ascription at birth, cultural factors also play a role. Both cultural and biological prescriptions of sex generally have two core assumptions (Kessler and McKenna, 1985). First, maleness and femaleness are viewed as dichotomous, mutually exclusive categories, and second, sex is seen as unchanging. These assumptions can, however, be challenged.

A chromosomal anomaly that affects sexual development provides evidence to refute the first assumption. Turner's Syndrome is a rare chromosomal abnormality where the second sex chromosome, which could have been either an X or a Y, is absent. These individuals are classified genetically as 45, XO (Moore and Persaud, 1993). At birth, individuals with Turner's Syndrome are identified as female on the basis of their external genitalia which are ostensibly female. However, these individuals do not mature as females at adolescence; they are unusually short, rarely exceeding four and a half feet, their reproductive system does not develop or function and they are therefore sterile. Essentially, Turner's Syndrome represents how development proceeds in the absence of all sex hormones, excepting maternal hormones to which the foetus has been exposed pre-natally. Biologically, therefore, individuals with Turner's Syndrome represent a third sex, being neither female nor male but neuter individuals (Unger and Crawford, 1996). However, our restrictive, dichotomous cultural definition of gender results in such individuals being ascribed as female, though biologically they are no more female than male. Once more, the traditional thesis of 'woman as deficient man' appears to have underpinned this particular labelling process.

Deficiencies and abnormalities of hormone production provide evidence which undermines the second assumption, that gender is a fixed attribute. One such deficiency, known as Five Alpha-Reductase Deficiency, is an inherited disorder which results in an inability to convert testosterone to dihydrotestosterone, an androgen that plays a key role in the development of the penis and the scrotum (Fausto-Sterling, 1992). Individuals with this disorder have a normal male internal reproductive system but an underdeveloped penis and scrotum. Although the external genitalia of these individuals may be ambiguous in appearance they were usually assumed to be female in the absence of modern scientific methods.

A group of individuals affected by this disorder and reared as females has been studied extensively in the Dominican Republic (Imperato-McGinley et al., 1979). At puberty, because of the presence of normal testes, large amounts of testosterone are produced, resulting in the development of secondary male sex characteristics such as deepening of the voice and hair growth on the chest and face. In addition, the enlargement of the penis and testicles occurs and erections and ejaculations begin. All 38 individuals in this study assumed a male gender identity subsequent to puberty, despite the fact that, in the earliest cases in particular (19 of the 38), they had lived their childhood unambiguously as females.

The evidence obtained from individuals who are affected by chromosomal and hormonal anomalies is important for a number of reasons. In the first instance this evidence challenges cultural assumptions. Unusual cases such as those described above demonstrate that ascribed sex is not always contingent on a person's biology. Further, the work highlights that many of our beliefs about sex and gender are in fact socially constructed. In effect, it can be said that sex is not always biologically determined, rather culture and biology interact to define gender.

Gender, biology and human behaviour

Despite the shortcomings of definitions of sex that rely solely on biology, there are nevertheless identifiable effects of biology on the experience of gender. An obvious example is that of hormonal differences, which not only affect secondary sexual characteristics (such as breast development in women and beard growth in men) but also are widely assumed to contribute to personality and behavioural differences between the sexes.

Reproductive hormones are the physiological basis of the menstrual cycle in women. Each month, approximately, follicle-stimulating hormone is secreted by the pituitary gland, which then stimulates a pre-selected ovarian follicle to develop into its mature form, an ovum, and which also stimulates the ovaries to produce oestrogen. Oestrogen causes the proliferation of the uterine lining and triggers the release of a second hormone which causes the release of the ovum (ovulation). Following ovulation, the follicle that released the egg becomes a temporary gland, known as the corpus luteum, which then secretes progesterone. This hormone further prepares the lining of the uterus to receive a zygote (fertilized ovum), should fertilization take place. If fertilization does not take place, a sharp decrease in oestrogen and progesterone production results in degeneration of the now unnecessary uterine lining, and menstruation begins.

It is important to recognize that both men and women, from puberty onwards, experience cyclical hormonal fluctuations. In fact, as hormone release is pulsatile rather than continuous, there are marked minute-to-minute variations in hormone levels in both sexes. There is evidence that men's testosterone levels are cyclical in nature, although over time the peaks and troughs are not as predictable as oestrogen shifts in women (Doering, 1974). Further to this, variations in androgens in males have been related to mood and aggressive behaviours in animal and human studies (Tavris and Wade, 1984). At the same time, the paucity of the research in this area is marked when compared to the plethora of research on women's hormonal cycles, perhaps because the behaviours in question are compatible with the male sex-role stereotype. This scarcity of work has been variously attributed to the difficulty of measuring blood levels of testosterone, the absence of overt cues associated with hormonal cycles in men, and last but by no means least, the tacit cultural belief that a woman's reproductive system exerts a powerful influence on female behaviour, again raising questions about the value-free nature of scientific inquiry (Rodin, 1992; Tavris and Wade, 1984). Thus, while cyclicity is in fact the rule rather than the exception in living organisms, human female reproductive cyclicity, which is marked by menstruation, has attracted a disproportionate amount of modern research attention.

Hormones and Behaviour

That this should be the case is unsurprising, given that historically menstruation in particular has been a focus for comparisons of male and female physiology, and has been used routinely as an explanation for women's and men's relative social status and roles. For example in ancient Greece, women's biology was often deemed to be inferior to that of men because women's bodies were thought to be cold and moist, in comparison to the warm, dry male ideal. Menstruation was seen as physical proof of this inferior system, being a necessary function in females in order to excrete their superfluous moisture. In the nineteenth century, women were thought to possess finite amounts of energy which should not be depleted by academic study or physical exercise lest their reproductive function become impaired (see Chapter 17). In the twentieth century, as medical understanding of the physiological processes underlying the menstrual cycle was expanded, sex-related hormones came under intense scrutiny as they were incorporated into a similar essentialist and reductionist explanation of the social and behavioural differences between the sexes.

Hormones are chemicals produced by glands within the endocrine system which circulate by means of the vascular system to reach various target organs where they have an effect. While there are many such hormones, those most frequently regarded as relevant to discussions of gender are the sex-related hormones, of which there are two major classes, the androgens and the oestrogens. The androgens (such as testosterone) are generally found at higher levels in males than in females, while the oestrogens (such as oestradiol) are generally found at higher levels in females. However, it is important to understand that androgens are not 'male hormones' nor oestrogens 'female hormones'. Both classes are found in both sexes, in fact oestrogen was first identified in the urine of male horses and the androgen, testosterone, is thought to be related to libido in both men and women (McNeill, 1994).

While there are other hormonal differences between males and females, with regard to the relationship between hormones and gender only the sex-linked hormones are generally assumed to play a significant role. This is unsurprising; the treatment of transsexuals often includes administration of hormones of the desired sex in order to produce appropriate secondary sexual characteristics, and this is also widely assumed to have a direct effect on gender identity and behaviour.

Stereotypically, androgens are associated both with aggression and male sexuality, resulting in the hypothesis that they may be implicated in the propensity to rape, although feminist analyses have long emphasized the power motive over the sexual motive in cases of rape (see Chapter 18). In reality, much of the evidence relating testosterone to aggression is derived from animal studies, and there are well-documented problems associated with extrapolating from animal studies to human behaviour. In particular, while a given behaviour may have a biological cause in animals, in humans the cause is likely to be socially mediated (see Chapter 4). Alternatively, if the research involves primates, it may be the case that what is thought to be a biologically based behaviour in both species is in fact a result of social factors, as primates generally form hierarchical, male-dominated groups.

Oestrogens are associated with the menstrual cycle and female fertility and sexuality, and women's hormones are widely believed to have pervasive and significant effects throughout the life-span. Menarche (when menstruation begins), the menstrual cycle and menopause are all assumed to have an important effect on women's psychology and behaviour, and this long-standing assumption has contributed to the perpetuation of stereotypical notions of women as unstable, irrational and unreliable in comparison to men (Choi, 1994).

In order to consider the relationship between hormones and behaviour in women, a useful example is that of premenstrual syndrome (PMS). First documented by Frank in 1931, PMS was described as a mood disturbance occuring in the days prior to menstruation, often accompanied by physical symptoms such as oedema, causing swelling of the abdomen and/or breasts. As research progressed, the list of symptoms attributed to PMS in the scientific and medical literature grew, and the assumption that these were the result of the lowered hormone levels prior to menstruation became well established, notably so after Katharina Dalton reported successfully treating the condition with progesterone, although later studies did not support her findings (Laws, 1985). PMS also became the focus for a great deal of media attention, with numerous articles in women's magazines. The condition was also accepted as a defence for murder in several widely publicized court cases in the 1970s, thus receiving extensive coverage in national newspapers and on television (Walker, 1995).

However, the evidence pointing to a hormonal aetiology for the syndrome was questioned as feminist researchers began to examine the issue. First, it was pointed out that most of the evidence was correlational in nature. From a scientific perspective, this is unsatisfactory because it does not establish the direction of causal relationships between variables. If women display symptoms such as negative mood premenstrually, at a time when levels of oestrogen, for example, are low, it does not follow that the low level of oestrogen has necessarily caused the symptoms.

Second, it was realized that women's reporting of symptoms could be manipulated, for example if a researcher told women that they were in the premenstrual phase, they tended to report PMS symptoms even if this was not in fact the case. Moreover, if women were told that PMS was the focus of an experiment, they were liable to report more symptoms than if the experiment was conducted 'blind'. Thus, a feminist analysis of PMS was developed which attributed the causes of PMS to psychological, social and cultural factors rather than to hormonal ones. PMS (when designated a psychiatric disorder) was described as a dangerous political construct which could be used by men within the context of patriarchal society to the detriment of women as a class (Caplan et al., 1992), perpetuating the notion that women were unsuited to positions of responsibility by virtue of their biology.

This feminist analysis drew on a wide range of psychological, anthropological and historical evidence. Historically, menstruation had been viewed as a source of female instability, and PMS was viewed as a modern variation on this theme (Rodin, 1992). Cross-cultural evidence indicated that PMS was a phenomenon found only in Western, developed societies, suggesting that it could not have a simple physiological explanation (Johnson, 1987). Psychological perspectives, including social cognition theory and attribution theory, were used to explain why women perceived themselves to have more negative moods premenstrually than at other phases of the menstrual cycle, in the absence of objective evidence of any such changes (Koeske and Koeske, 1975; Ruble and Brooks-Gunn, 1979). However, this analysis has been contested both by medical researchers, who continue to work to a medical model of the disorder, and by women who report that they experience PMS. Clearly, the assumption that women are prey to the ravages of their raging hormones is one which should not be uncritically accepted in relation to PMS, and a biopsychosocial approach to the subject has been advocated (Ussher, 1992; Walker, 1997).

Moreover, as Asso (1992) so pertinently points out, if the whole of the menstrual cycle is taken into account, rather than focusing narrowly on the premenstrual phase, it is evident that women's internal hormonal environment is in fact conducive to positive mood for the majority of the cycle. Even in the premenstrual phase, some studies have found positive changes, for example with some women reporting increased energy or creativity, although evidence on this is mixed. Moreover, while many women report that they do experience PMS, most women are not severely affected, and the idea that women have any significant cognitive impairment premenstrually has proved to have little foundation (Sommer, 1992). These observations in no way preclude the acknowledgement that a small proportion of women may suffer, in the true sense of the word, from severe and debilitating symptoms premenstrually. They do, however, call into question the continuing uncritical acceptance of the socially constructed notion that the hormonal fluctuations of the normal menstrual cycle render most women dysfunctional once a month throughout their reproductive years, barring pregnancy.

At the same time, female hormones are also assumed to have behavioural effects during and after pregnancy, and in contrast to PMS, these assumed effects are consonant with stereotypical notions of femininity. In particular, pregnant women and new mothers are commonly viewed as particularly nurturant and serene, in an almost idyllic representation of the benefits to women of the motherhood mandate (see Chapter 11). Woollett (1996) describes how this, coupled with conceptions of infertility as a medical problem, translates into an assumption that any well-adjusted woman who finds herself to be infertile will pursue infertility treatment to its fullest extent. This cultural tendency to idealize pregnancy ignores the reality for many women, who may experience nausea, exhaustion and anxiety at least some of the time. While it is true that oestrogens remain at a high and stable level throughout most normal pregnancies, this is by no means universally accompanied by similar effects on mood.

In addition, in the 1970s the idea that mothers must 'bond' with their children during a critical period after birth (when hormone levels drop radically) became popular. This idea was based on studies of imprinting in animals, where such a critical period has been shown to be crucial to the survival of the offspring. The evidence for this in humans is scanty, however, and this trend can be viewed as a direct descendant of earlier conceptions of women as less evolved and closer to nature than men. It can also be viewed as a development of Bowlby's concept of maternal deprivation (see Chapter 11). The idea that women are 'instinctive' in that they are hormonally predisposed to 'fall in love' with their babies after chilbirth has been superseded by the realization that women differ in the rate at which they become attached to their babies. However, the widespread view that mothers *ought* to feel an instantaneous and enduring affection for their offspring has been related to the possible later development of post-natal depression in those who do not experience such an immediate attachment.

Another aspect of women's lives where hormonal influences are assumed to have an impact is menopause, notoriously labelled a state of 'living decay' by Wilson (1966). At the end of the reproductive years, the menstrual cycle is discontinued and women cease to produce the large amounts of oestrogen which have until that time protected them against coronary disease and other ailments (see Chapter 14). The advent of hormone replacement therapy (HRT) was welcomed by many women who were delighted to learn that it also slowed down the visible effects of ageing, and enhanced sexuality (assumed to decline after menopause). Gannon (1994) notes, however, that the image of the postmenopausal woman as asexual is not supported by the evidence, and seems to derive in part from the tacit assumption that women are at the mercy of their hormones. She also notes that the effects of ageing on men are seldom described in negative terms, despite the fact, for example, that testosterone levels in men also gradually decline after around 50 years of age, with concomitant effects on sexuality.

The assumed and taken for granted nature of the relationship between women's hormones and their behaviour has been exemplified here by issues such as PMS, pregnancy and menopause, but similar observations could be made with respect to both lay beliefs about and much scientific research into other female experiences in which hormonal changes are implicated (for example menarche). Moreover, the relationship between the assumption that hormones influence women's lives to a greater extent than men's and the amount and nature of scientific enquiry about each sex illustrates again the susceptibility of science to social influences. This is true whether considering PMS in women or the relationship between testosterone and aggression in men. While the sex-related hormones, and indeed the differences between male and female anatomy, may well have behavioural and other effects, any such effects are inevitably mediated by social and cultural variables. Moreover, if scientists uncritically assume a direct causal relationship between sex-related hormones and, for example, a sex-role specific behaviour such as aggression or emotionality, they may well find evidence supporting such a relationship. Unless they consider possible mediating influences, however, they are likely to miss the point, that biology is but one part of the experience of gender.

CONCLUSIONS

The relationship between biology and gender is a complex one; there is no simple or single cause that can ever explain complex patterns of gendered behaviours. It is also worth noting that there is a great degree of variability in the behaviours of both genders. Many women are emotionally stable throughout the menstrual cycle; many men are less aggressive than some women. Nevertheless, the social construction of the categories 'woman' and 'man' has historically been justified by reference to biological differences, and the modern tendency to provide essentialist and reductionist explanations which include the effects of genes and hormones can be viewed as a contemporary manifestation of this long-standing tradition. It is concluded that biology rarely has a monopoly on cogent explanations of gender differences, and that, historically, the attention and significance attached to biological explanations of gender differences has been disproportionate to their true effect.

REFERENCES

Asso, D. (1992). A reappraisal of the normal menstrual cycle. *Journal of Reproductive and Infant Psychology* **10(2)**, 103–10.

Caplan, P.J., McCurdy-Myers, J. and Gans, M. (1992). Should 'Premenstrual Syndrome' be called a psychiatric abnormality? *Feminism & Psychology* **2(1)**, 27–44.

Choi, P.Y.L. (1994). Women's raging hormones. In Choi, P.Y.L. and Nicolson, P. (eds), *Female sexuality: psychology, biology and social context*. (pp. 128–47). Hemel Hempstead: Harvester Wheatsheaf.

Doering, C.H. (1974). Plasma testosterone levels and psychological measures in men over a two-year period. In Friedman, R.C., Richart, R.M. and Varde Wiele, R.L. (eds), *Sex differences in behaviour*. New York: Wiley.

Fausto-Sterling, A. (1985). *Myths of gender: biological theories of women and men*. New York: Harper-Collins.

Fausto-Sterling, A. (1989). Life in the XY corral. *Women's Studies International Forum* **12**, 319–31.

Fausto-Sterling, A. (1992). *Myths of gender: biological theories of women and men*. Rev. edn. New York: Basic Books.

Frank, R.T. (1931). The hormonal causes of premenstrual tension. *Archives of Neurology and Psychiatry* **26**, 1053–7.

Gannon, L. (1994). Sexuality and menopause. In Choi, P.Y.L. and Nicolson, P. (eds), *Female sexuality: psychology, biology and social context*. (pp. 100–24). Hemel Hempstead: Harvester Wheatsheaf.

Hubbard, R. and Wald, E. (1993). *Exploding the gene myth*. Boston: Beacon Press.

Imperato-McGinley, J., Peterson, R.E., Gautier, T. and Sturla, E. (1979). Androgens and the evolution of male-gender identity among male pseudohermaphrodites with 5 alpha reductase deficiency. *New England Journal of Medicine* **300**, 1233–7.

Johnson, T.A. (1987). Premenstrual syndrome as a western culture-specific disorder. *Culture, Medicine and Psychiatry* **11**, 337–56.

Kessler, S.J. and McKenna, W. (1985). *Gender: an ethnomethodological approach*. Chicago: The University of Chicago Press.

Koeske, R.K. and Koeske, G.F. (1975). An attributional approach to moods and the menstrual cycle. *Journal of Personality and Social Psychology* **31(3)**, 473–8.

Laws, S. (1985). Who needs PMT? A feminist approach to the politics of premenstrual tension. In Laws, S., Hey, V. and Eagan, A. (eds), *'Seeing red': the politics of premenstrual tension*. (pp. 17–64). London: Hutchinson.

McNeill, E. (1994). Blood, sex and hormones: a theoretical review of women's sexuality over the menstrual cycle. In Choi, P.Y.L. and Nicolson, P. (eds), *Female sexuality: psychology, biology and social context*. (pp. 56–82). Hemel Hempstead: Harvester Wheatsheaf.

Moore, K.L. and Persaud, T.V.N. (1993). *Before we are born*. London: Saunders.

Rodin, M. (1992). The social construction of pre-menstrual syndrome. *Social Science and Medicine* **35(1)**, 49–56.

Ross, J.S. and Wilson, K.J.W. (1983). *Foundations of anatomy and physiology*. Edinburgh: Churchill Livingstone.

Ruble, D.N. and Brooks-Gunn, J. (1979). Menstrual symptoms: a social cognition analysis. *Journal of Behavioural Medicine* **2(2)**, 171–94.

Sommer, B. (1992). Cognitive performance and the menstrual cycle. In Richardson, J.T.E. (ed.), *Cognition and the menstrual cycle*. (pp. 39–66). New York: Springer-Verlag.

Tavris, C. and Wade, C. (1984). *The longest war: sex differences in perspective.* San Diego: Harcourt, Brace, Jovanovich.

Unger, R.K. and Crawford, M. (1996). *Women and gender: a feminist approach.* New York: McGraw Hill.

Ussher, J.M. (1992). The demise of dissent and the rise of cognition in menstrual-cycle research. In Richardson, J.T.E. (ed.), *Cognition and the menstrual cycle.* (pp. 132–73). New York: Springer-Verlag.

Walker, A. (1995). *Premenstrual syndrome: mind, body or media construction?* Paper presented at the annual conference of the British Psychological Society, Warwick, 1–4 April.

Walker, A. (1997). *The menstrual cycle.* London: Routledge.

Wilson, R. (1966). *Feminine forever.* New York: M. Evans.

Woollett, A. (1996). Infertility: from 'inside/out' to 'outside/in'. In Wilkinson, S. and Kitzinger, C. (eds), *Representing the other: a Feminism & Psychology reader.* (pp. 68–71). London: Sage.

Further reading

Eagly, A.H. (1995). The science and politics of comparing women and men. *American Psychologist* **50(3)**, 145–58.

Fausto-Sterling, A. (1985). *Myths of gender: biological theories of women and men.* New York: Harper-Collins.

Unger, R. and Crawford, M. (1996). *Women and gender: a feminist approach.* New York: McGraw Hill. (particularly chapters 6 and 3).

Ussher, J.M. (1992). Research and theory related to female reproduction: implications for clinical psychology. *British Journal of Clinical Psychology* **31**, 129–51.

Walker, A. (1992). Premenstrual symptoms and ovarian hormones: a review. *Journal of Reproductive and Infant Psychology* **10(2)**, 67–82.

Discussion questions

1. Are we able to define sex, when is it necessary to define sex and why is it necessary to define sex?
2. In relation to understanding sex differences, can scientific endeavour ever be regarded as value free? Why not?
3. Are women at the mercy of their raging hormones? What about men?
4. Does PMS exist and if it does, why should feminists regard it as a dangerous political construct?
5. Think of slang words used to describe men and women. What do they tell us of how the sexes are differentiated?

6

COGNITION

Carol McGuinness

INTRODUCTION

When comparing the cognitive abilities and intellectual achievements of men and women, with a view to identifying similarities and differences, a host of scientific as well as political questions are raised. As you may expect, writers disagree on the answers to a great many of these questions, and indeed whether the questions should ever be asked in the first place. For example, do gender differences in cognition exist at all or do they exist only in very specific areas, like spatial ability, or at specific ages, or in highly selected samples? Furthermore, if they do exist, are they so small as to be of no practical significance, or if they existed in past generations, are they now disappearing as educational opportunities increase and gender stereotypes are challenged? Has the political climate become such that it is now impossible to consider gender differences in a dispassionate way, or does the issue of gender and cognition expose a view of science that can no longer be sustained?

First and foremost, students who are studying the psychology of gender need to know what these questions are, how they are framed, what research methodologies are used to gather relevant evidence, and how the arguments are formulated which lead to one conclusion or another. Bearing this in mind, the chapter aims to:

- Enable students to read the literature on gender and cognition with a critical eye on both the methodologies used to collect data and the conclusions reached.
- Identify the main cognitive domains where gender-related comparisons have been made (that is, verbal, spatial and mathematical abilities).
- Show how new developments in reviewing methods have had a profound impact on the conclusions reached about gender and cognition, and on the issues raised.

- Place comparisons between males and females in the context not only of scientific debate but also of political climate.

In order to achieve these aims in the available space, the chapter will focus on the emerging story of the *extent* of gender-related differences in cognition, rather than on the theoretical *origins* of presumed differences.

THE CONTROVERSIES

Research on the cognitive abilities of men and women has a long history. Therefore a new reader could well assume that clear-cut answers to questions about the extent and origins of similarities and differences would now be agreed. That is not so. In a recent comprehensive review of gender differences in cognitive abilities, Halpern (1992) still described it as a 'hot topic in contemporary research' (p. 1).

One reason is that 'theories' about how men and women think and reason pervade everyday conversation and the popular media, as well as scientific discourse. These everyday theories tend to endorse the viewpoint that men and women think differently, that they have preferred modes of reasoning, and that they have different cognitive areas in which they excel. For example, the popular view is that men are logical while women are more intuitive in their reasoning style; men are better at mathematical thinking and spatial reasoning, like reading maps, while women excel when language and communication skills are required; men's cognitive style enables them to embrace the new technologies while women are computer-phobic. Earlier psychological research tended to confirm these viewpoints, thus giving additional 'truth' status to the more everyday views (for reviews, see Maccoby, 1966; Maccoby and Jacklin, 1974). However, as this chapter will show, the picture in the late 1990s is a good deal more complex than it seemed 25–30 years ago.

Another reason for controversy relates to the linkages between the psychology of gender, the politics of the women's movement, and feminist critiques of power structures. For example, conclusions reached about gender and cognition have implications for understanding employment patterns and questions of equal opportunity, with research findings having the potential to explain and subsequently justify the differential proportions of men and women who occupy certain jobs. For example, it has been argued that the reason why a greater proportion of men become engineers, computer scientists and architects is because men are better at logical, mathematical or spatial reasoning and are thus more suited to these occupations than women. Rarely, of course, are the findings used to question why women do not dominate occupations which rely on linguistic skills, such as the media, law or public relations.

Yet another reason why research on gender and cognition is controversial is because it raises a central question about the origins of human behaviour

– that is, the extent to which behaviour (including differences in the nature of cognitive processing) is biologically determined or socially constructed. If so-called gender differences in cognition can be traced to biological factors, such as genetics, brain structures/functions or hormonal influences, then they can be viewed as 'natural' and unlikely to change. On the other hand, if gender differences are socially constructed, and are the result of socialization practices and gender stereotypes, then reconstructing these practices and stereotypes could radically alter patterns of cognitive achievements.

Because of the long history of research on gender and cognition, a substantial database has now accumulated and within this, several phases in the research effort can be identified (Hyde, 1990). Early research, at the turn of the nineteenth century, studied neuroanatomical differences and particularly the differences between the sizes of male and female brains (Romanes, 1887; see Shields [1975] for a critique of this early period of research). Even today, considerable effort continues to be devoted to examining differences in male and female brain structures and functions (for example, Kimura, 1987; see Halpern [1992, Chapter 5] for a review of this research). However, over the years the greatest volume of research has considered mental testing, using standardized psychometric tests of cognitive ability (similar to those used to measure intelligence). The focus of this type of research is normally on *variability* and on *individual and group differences.*

The sheer volume of such research has placed it in a dominant position. More importantly, new methods for reviewing research literatures, called meta-analysis, have permitted writers to produce quantitative syntheses of literally hundreds of individual studies, thus yielding new answers to old questions, as well as generating some entirely novel questions. This *quantitative* tradition, which forms the basis of much of this chapter, has been enthusiastically embraced by several feminist writers. Indeed, Hyde (1994) has argued that meta-analysis 'is capable of making feminist transformations in psychology' (p. 451).

In contrast, other feminist writers have launched a powerful critique on the quantitative tradition from both a constructivist and a postmodern viewpoint. They claim that a psychology of gender from an individual differences perspective 'constructs', and necessarily exaggerates, the differences between men and women (for example, Hare-Mustin and Marecek, 1988). These tendencies to exaggerate differences, or *alpha biases* as they are called, have been much more evident in psychological theorizing than *beta biases*, or the tendency to ignore or minimize differences. Indeed some writers have gone so far as to argue that gender differences should not be studied at all (Baumeister, 1988). Throughout the late 1980s and 1990s these debates among feminist writers were conducted particularly within the pages of the *American Psychologist*, the monthly journal of the American Psychological Association (Baumeister, 1988; Eagly, 1990, 1995; Hare-Mustin and Marecek, 1988; Hyde and Plant, 1995; Marecek, 1995). More recently, a similar set of arguments have been put forward in a special issue of the UK-based journal *Feminism and Psychology*, edited by Celia Kitzinger (1994), and as yet no satisfactory conclusion to the debate appears to be in sight; the jury is still out.

As you may by now appreciate, students who come to the research literature on gender and cognition soon realize that not only do they have to grasp the more usual conceptual and methodological issues, as found within any research literature, but they must also be sensitive to the political and ideological climate within which research studies are conducted and interpreted. Only if both tasks are negotiated successfully can a satisfactory personal epistemological standpoint be attained.

One further word of caution at this point. The chapter reports primarily on the quantitative syntheses or meta-analyses of research studies conducted over the past decade or so. Because of the nature of the answers revealed by these meta-analyses, and the additional questions posed, no attempt will be made here to review either biological or sociocultural theories about the origins of cognitive differences. A full review of these theories can be found in Halpern (1992) and a very useful guide for thinking critically about research on sex and gender is offered by Caplan and Caplan (1994). Additionally, an invaluable source of original papers is a four-volume collection edited by Jacklin (1992), which contains reprints of both classical and recent papers on the psychology of gender. (The papers in Volume II are particularly relevant for studying gender and cognition.)

METHODS AND MEASUREMENTS

The mental testing tradition has made its mark on gender-related research most obviously in the cognitive domains, with frequent comparisons being drawn between males and females. The main measuring instrument for mental testing is the IQ test, with early tests of intellectual abilities based on the notion that intelligence is a single ability, thus yielding a single score or IQ. More recently emphasis has shifted to differences on the subtests which relate to the processing of different types of symbols, including words, numbers and diagrams.

This idea of primary mental abilities, as opposed to a single ability, was first developed by Thurstone in the 1930s (Thurstone, 1938), with a more contemporary version described in Gardner's theory of multiple intelligences or frames of mind (Gardner, 1983). From 60 different types of ability tests, Thurstone reported that three sets of clusters or factors were identifiable, namely verbal, number (quantitative) and perception (visual-spatial). Sixty years later, the idea of multiple abilities continues to provide the foundation for gender-related research into verbal, spatial and mathematical reasoning.

That these major subdivisions are central to cognitive processing is given added weight by contemporary theories of brain functioning and lateralization. Lateralization research indicates that the left brain hemisphere is dedicated primarily to linguistic processing while the right hemisphere is devoted to visuo-spatial manipulation. Unfortunately, no specific brain lateralization hypothesis relates to the capacity for mathematical reasoning.

No single study can hope to provide a definitive answer to the question of gender similarities and differences in cognition. Instead, there is a need to survey and review existing studies in order to gain a sense of prevailing trends. Although there were several earlier surveys of the research literature, Maccoby and Jacklin's review published in 1974 represents the modern benchmark against which subsequent reviews are compared, both in terms of the conclusions reached and the method of reviewing. Maccoby and Jacklin surveyed over 1000 studies published prior to 1974 and concluded that, in three cognitive areas (and one personality area), gender differences were fairly well established. Girls had greater verbal ability than boys, boys had greater visual-spatial abilities, and boys were better at mathematical reasoning. While several cautionary notes were struck about the size of the differences, and about developmental trends, overall their review crystallized what Hyde has called the 'holy trinity of gender differences in abilities' (Hyde, 1990, p. 60).

Alongside these conclusions, Maccoby and Jacklin's review marked the beginnings of a more quantitative approach to reviewing literature in this area. Traditional reviews of literature had relied on the method of narrative review. That is, the reviewer located as many studies as possible, organized these within a systematic framework, and then offered a conclusion in a narrative form. As an alternative, Maccoby and Jacklin adopted the systematic use of the method of vote counting; that is, they listed all the studies which found a difference in favour of one sex or the other and all the studies that found no difference. The percentage of studies in each category was then examined, thus offering some kind of numerical weight to the evidence.

Although innovatory at the time, this vote counting method has limitations. Most importantly, it is difficult to decide how large a percentage in favour or against a difference indicates a true difference. Hence the technique has been superseded by a quantitative or statistical method for conducting a literature review known as meta-analysis (Hedges and Olkin, 1985).

Meta-analysis is a way of summarizing the results of a large volume of studies which have examined a question in roughly the same way. It permits an estimate to be made of both the extent and the direction of gender differences and it has served to raise discussions about gender similarities and differences to a new level of sophistication. When conducting a meta-analysis, the first step is to assemble as large a set as possible of studies which examine the same topic (computerized databases, such as *PSYCHLIT*, *ERIC* and *BIDS* have made this step very much easier in recent years). Next, the effect size statistic, *d*, is estimated for each individual study. Effect size is calculated as the difference between mean scores for males and females in a study, divided by the standard deviation for the two groups. Essentially, the *d* statistic tells how far apart means for males and females are in standard deviation units, with the larger the value the bigger the effect size. The *d* statistic is very similar to a standardized score; it can be positive or negative with a mean of 0 and is likely to vary no more than three standard deviation units at the most. In gender research, ordinarily convention dictates that a positive *d* denotes a difference favouring males, while a negative *d* signifies a difference favouring females.

Once computed, the *d* values are then averaged over all the studies, yielding a quantitative basis from which to draw conclusions about the extent and direction of gender differences (weighted averages are normally used which take into account the number of subjects in each of the original studies). The final step in the meta-analysis is to carry out a homogeneity test which examines the extent to which the values of *d* in the sample are uniform. This test allows decisions to be made about the logic of averaging *all* the *d* measures into a single overall effect size. For example, if half the studies yielded large effect sizes in favour of males and half showed large effect sizes in favour of females, it would not be reasonable to combine all the effect sizes and conclude that there were no gender differences (one set of large effects cancelling out the other set). Rather, further classification and regrouping of the variables would be indicated. The homogeneity test has proved very useful for testing specific hypotheses about gender effects (for example, age trends and year of publication of the study), as well as for examining subcomponents of the main types of cognitive abilities, such as spatial perception; spatial visualization and mental rotation within spatial ability or vocabulary; reading comprehension; and verbal analogies within verbal ability.

After completing the meta-analysis, interpretation of the effect size is of primary importance. When is an effect size big or small? Reported effect sizes within the gender and cognition literature rarely exceed plus or minus 1.0 standard deviation unit, and the majority are much smaller. According to Cohen's (1969) statistical guidelines, $d = 0.20$ is a small effect size, $d = 0.50$ is moderate and $d = 0.80$ and above represent a large effect. Writers continue to argue whether the use of statistical benchmarks is an appropriate way to judge the importance of size effects, pointing out that small to moderate size effects are the norm rather than the exception in other areas of psychological research and yet are still deemed to be of practical significance (Eagly, 1995, and a reply by Hyde and Plant, 1995).

In order to gain a better grasp of what is at stake in these discussions Figure 6.1 shows three hypothetical distributions of male and female performance on a cognitive test. Figure 6.1a shows the distributions for a small size effect favouring females ($d = -0.20$) while Figures 6.1b and 6.1c show the patterns for moderate ($d = -0.50$) and large effects ($d = -0.80$) respectively.

Two points should be noted about the distributions. First, although the means may differ, there is substantial overlap between the male and female distributions even in the case of so-called large size effects. Whichever gender performs better on a task overall, considerable numbers of the higher-performing group will continue to score below the average of the lower-performing group. Second, the figures assume that variability or the shape of the curve is similar for both genders and yet this is not always the case. This vexed question of variability will be returned to in the final section of the chapter.

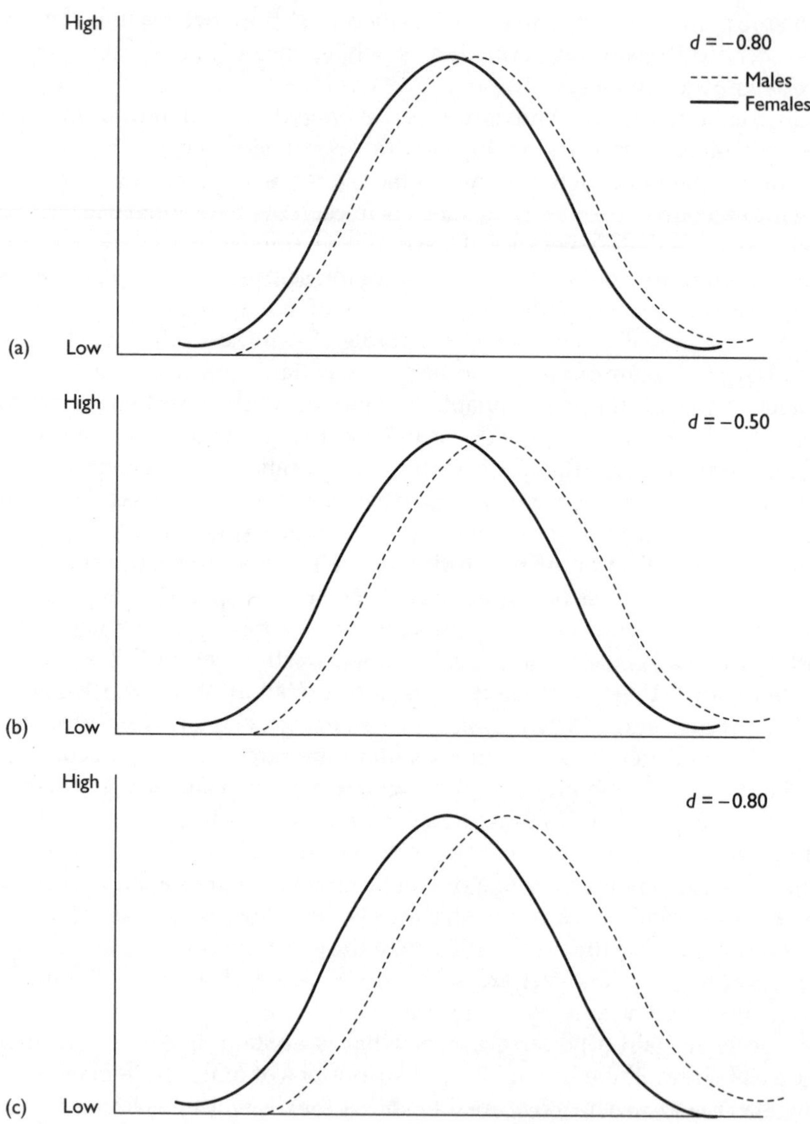

FIGURE 6.1 Male and female distributions showing different size effects

COGNITIVE DIFFERENCES: 'FIRST YOU SEE THEM, THEN YOU DON'T, AND THEN …'

We are now in a position to consider the results from the main meta-analytic reviews which have been conducted during the past 10–15 years in the three cognitive areas where gender has been debated: verbal, visuo-spatial and mathematical/quantitative abilities. Several themes emerge in all three cognitive domains and these are worth previewing before the details of each are discussed in turn. First, many writers have been critical of using blanket terms such as verbal ability, spatial ability or mathematical ability because it is felt they mask an array of performances on tasks which may well require very different cognitive processes. For example, tasks used to measure verbal ability can range from vocabulary tests (where a person is asked to supply a definition for a word) to essay writing (where the requirement is to express complex ideas in coherent and fluent written prose). Spatial tests can vary from finding simple forms embedded in more complex figures, to mentally manipulating objects which require shifts in orientation and perspective in both two and three dimensions. Similarly with mathematical ability, tests range from simple computations like addition and subtraction to problem-solving and calculus. One of the outcomes of meta-analytic reviews has been to further partition each of the three main cognitive domains to reveal that even subcomponents of the same ability can be more or less sensitive to gender influences.

A second theme to emerge relates to age effects. Several hypotheses about gender differences and age trends have been reported, for example that girls show advanced language skills, and especially in the early years, that male superiority in spatial ability does not emerge until early adolescence, and that gender differentials in mathematical achievement become more evident throughout adolescence and early adult years. Meta-analyses have permitted these hypotheses to be more thoroughly tested than was previously possible.

A third theme concerns change over time. Several of the reviews have used Maccoby and Jacklin's (1974) publication as the state of the art on gender and cognition up to the early 1970s and have reported on gender effects for studies pre-1973 and post-1973. By identifying chronological time as an important variable, the reviews help to recognize changing patterns of gender effects (or at least, the reporting of these effects), thus enabling hypotheses about changing cultural beliefs and gender stereotypes to be tested.

Spatial differences

Linn and Petersen (1985) reported the first meta-analytic review of gender and spatial ability, a review which included 172 studies published since Maccoby and Jacklin's (1974) work and before June 1982. Three major types of spatial reasoning were identified and measured by different types of tests. First, spatial perception tests, such as the rod and frame test, require people to 'determine spatial relationships with respect to the orientation of their own bodies, in spite of distracting information' (p. 1482). Second, mental rotation tests require 'the ability to rotate a two or three dimensional figure rapidly and accurately' (p. 1483); while third, spatial visualization tasks 'involve multistep manipulations of spatially presented information' (p. 1484) and are distinguished 'by the possibility of multiple solution strategies'.

The gender effect sizes reported for the different types of test were: spatial perception, $d = 0.44$; mental rotation, $d = 0.73$; spatial visualization, $d = 0.13$. All values were positive, indicating the males performed better on the tests than females. Using Cohen's (1969) guidelines to interpret the size of the effects, it is clear that the spatial visualization effect is small, the spatial perception effect is close to moderate and the mental rotation effect is relatively large. The overall mental rotation effect was dominated by the size of the effect for 3-D rotation ($d = 0.94$) rather than 2-D rotation ($d = 0.26$).

Only spatial perception tests showed any sign of a developmental trend insofar as over-18-year-olds showed a larger size effect ($d = 0.64$) than those aged 13–18 years ($d = 0.37$) and under 13 ($d = 0.37$). Year of publication was not analysed in this review but Feingold (1988), in a separate analysis using US norms from four standardizations of major psychometric tests over a 30-year period, found that the traditionally observed gap between girls and boys on mechanical and spatial reasoning (subtests of the Differential Aptitude Test) had halved over the period.

A more recent meta-analysis of spatial abilities by Voyer et al. (1995), which included studies from both Maccoby and Jacklin's (1974) and Linn and Petersen's (1985) reviews, together with all studies up to 1993 (286 effect sizes overall), provided a more fine-grained analysis of gender effects on specific types of tests. Nevertheless, it substantially replicated Linn and Petersen's findings. Size effects were $d = 0.56$ for mental rotation; $d = 0.44$ for spatial perception; and $d = 0.19$ for spatial visualization. Age effects were test specific and were largely due to over-18-year-olds showing larger effect sizes in favour of males. Of the 12 different types of spatial test surveyed in this review, the size of the effect appeared to decrease with time on four tests, no significant change was observed on seven tests, and the gender-related size effect increased on only one test, mental rotation.

The general conclusion from these reviews is that it can no longer be claimed, without qualification, that males are superior to females in terms of spatial ability. Overall, differences tend to be small, with the exception of mental rotation and in particular 3-D rotation. What has been called the most persistent finding in gender-related research continues to persist even in the face of disappearing differences on other spatial tests.

Developmental trends are mixed; under-13-year-olds show the smallest differences, 13–18-year-olds show mixed effects, and over-18-year-olds show the largest effects. Of course, these data cannot be used to infer that gender differences increase with age; the sampling is cross-sectional and may simply reveal a generational effect showing that changing socialization practices and reduced gender stereotyping are having an impact on the cognitive achievements of younger people.

Although the general view is that gender-related cognitive differences in spatial ability are disappearing, the practical significance of size effects, even if small in statistical terms, is still hotly contested (Halpern, 1992, p. 87; Eagly, 1995, p. 255).

Verbal differences

In 1988, Hyde and Linn reported a meta-analysis on gender differences in verbal ability. Although confining the review to US and Canadian studies, they surveyed 165 studies representing 1,418,899 participants. Tests were included which covered a wide range of verbal and linguistic processing, namely retrieval of the definition of a word (vocabulary); retrieval of the name of a picture (vocabulary); analysis of the relationship between words (analogies); selection of relevant information from text (reading comprehension); and verbal production (essay writing and measures of spoken language), with many tests requiring a combination of the above processes.

From this analysis, the overall *d* metric was negative and small ($d = -0.11$), showing a female advantage. Seven of the eight tests also revealed negative values, the one exception being analogies where the direction favoured males ($d = 0.16$). Again, following Cohen's advice on interpreting size of effects, only three tests yielded size effects above 0.20 and these were speech production ($d = -0.33$), anagrams ($d = -0.22$) and general/mixed tests ($d = -0.20$).

Differences at all age groups tested were small and below 0.20 with the exception of over-26-year-olds ($d = -0.20$) and there was no developmental trend. Studies were grouped into two categories; pre-1973 studies yielded $d = -0.23$, and post-1973 yielded $d = -0.10$, indicating that the advantage for women on measures of verbal ability was disappearing with time. This finding was confirmed by Feingold's (1988) work on US standardization norms which also reported disappearing verbal ability differences over 20- and 30-year periods.

The general conclusion from this review is that gender differences between males and females in verbal abilities are small relative to spatial ability and are disappearing. Nevertheless, Halpern (1992), in her commentary on these trends, believes that female superiority is underestimated in these analyses because of the absence of low-performing groups in the samples. She points out that males tend to be over-represented in groups of stutterers, dyslexics and those with reading difficulties. She argues that 'if more of the studies included in the meta-analysis had contained samples from the low end of the distribution, the overall effect size favouring females would have been much larger' (p. 85).

Mathematical differences

Hyde et al. (1990) reported a comprehensive meta-analytic review on gender differences in mathematical performance. The reader will note that in this domain, the more neutral word 'performance' is used rather than 'abilities'. This is because mathematical achievement represents an even more heterogeneous domain than do either the verbal or visuo-spatial domains.

Additionally, mathematical achievement is believed to draw on abilities in other areas, particularly spatial reasoning (for example, Fennema and Sherman, 1977). Hence, writers are reluctant to attribute the term 'ability' to the overall domain. The term 'quantitative' is more readily used but it necessarily refers to a more limited range of mathematical achievements.

The Hyde et al. review surveyed studies from 1967–87, including the Maccoby and Jacklin (1974) bibliography and large sets of US normative data but excluding studies which report classroom grades rather than psychometric tests of mathematical achievement. Overall the review covers 254 effect sizes and 3,175,188 participants. The mathematical tests were divided into four categories according to 'cognitive level' as the authors defined it.

> *Computation* refers to a test that requires the use of only algorithmic procedures to find a single numerical answer. *Conceptual* refers to a test that involves analysis or comprehension of mathematical ideas. *Problem solving* refers to a test that involves extending knowledge or applying it to new situations. *Mixed tests* include a combination of items from these categories.
>
> (Hyde et al., 1990, p. 141)

All of the obtained d values were small according to Cohen's benchmarks (that is, below 0.20). Two indicated female superiority, computations ($d = -0.14$) and concepts ($d = -0.03$), while the other two showed male superiority, namely problem solving ($d = 0.08$) and mixed ($d = 0.19$). Analysis by age was classified into four groups which showed a shift from marginally favouring females at the younger ages (5–10-year-olds, $d = -0.06$; 11–14-year-olds, $d = -0.07$) to moderate/large effects favouring males in the later years (15–18-year-olds, $d = 0.29$; 19–25-year-olds, $d = 0.41$; over-26-year-olds, $d = 0.59$). However, a more interesting pattern showed the changing age effects for tests at different cognitive levels. For the two younger age groups, females showed superior performance for computation ($d = -0.20$ and -0.22 respectively); while for two older age groups the males showed an advantage for problem solving ($d = 0.29$ for 15–18-year-olds; and $d = 0.32$ for 19–25-year-olds). All differences for the concepts category were close to zero.

One of the most pervasive hypotheses in the literature on mathematics achievement is that the higher the levels of achievements that are compared, the greater the disparity between male and female performance (Benbow, 1988). Consequently, gender effect sizes were calculated as a function of selectivity of the sample. The magnitude of the d values showed unambiguously that male advantage in mathematical achievement increased as samples were more selected. The d value was close to zero for the overall sample but as samples became more selected the effect sizes shifted in favour of male superiority (moderately selective, $d = 0.33$; highly selective, $d = 0.54$; precocious, $d = 0.41$).

Analysis based on year of publication showed that effect sizes are becoming smaller. For pre-1973 the d value was 0.31 but for post-1973, $d = 0.11$.

However, Feingold's (1988) study on US norms concluded that, 'The important exception to the rule of vanishing gender differences is that the well-documented gender gap at the highest levels of performance on high school mathematics has remained constant from 1960 to 1983' (p. 101).

Compared to the consistency shown in verbal and spatial performance in favour of one sex over the other, the picture to emerge with regard to mathematical performance is very mixed. Young girls seem marginally better at computational tasks than young boys but these differences are not sustained as they grow older. In contrast, boys seem to surpass girls at mathematical problem-solving as they grow older. The most striking finding is superior performance of males in highly selected samples.

At the same time, the findings in these meta-analytic studies should be interpreted cautiously, as the gender differences reported on mathematical tests of achievement are not always reflected in school grades or public examinations in mathematics. (See Chapter 10 for further discussion of gender differences in mathematical performance.)

Conclusions

From this review of meta-analytic studies comparing gender differences in cognition, several conclusions can be reached.

First, the picture is more complex than it appeared 20 years ago, yet at the same time it maintains coherence. Within the three cognitive domains which were examined, the smallest differences are found in verbal abilities and are in favour in women; the largest differences are in spatial processing and are in favour of men. Mathematical performance falls in between in terms of the size of the difference and presents a mixed pattern; on some tasks and at some ages females perform better than males while on other tasks and at other ages the reverse is true.

Second, over a 20–30 year period the trend shows that differences are becoming smaller and, in some cases, have disappeared completely, but there are exceptions. Notably, males continue to be superior on tasks requiring spatial manipulation in three dimensions and, in highly selected school samples, they continue to excel in mathematical achievement. The possible causes for disappearing gender differences reported in the research literature are not straightforward. They may be taken at face value and reflect 'true' changes in cognitive performance due to changing gender stereotypes and socialization practices, but other influences may also be at work. For example, changing publication policies on the part of journal editors may mean that studies which report no gender differences are more likely to be published than they were 20 years ago. Also, some writers have commented that the samples used in more recent studies are drawn from general populations where previously more highly selected samples were studied. The extent of these influences and their impact on changing patterns of gender differences cannot be fully assessed.

Third, gender differences are generally small, with effect sizes rarely exceeding one unit of standard deviation. At the same time, Eagly (1995) has argued that if gender size effects are compared with other size effects reported in the literature then they are not unusual. Indeed, she claims that the small-to-moderate range appears to be more typical in psychological research than large effects. This point has been contested by Hyde and Plant (1995) who claim that, from their analysis, 25 per cent of gender effect sizes are below 0.10, compared to 6 per cent in other types of psychological research. Perhaps another way of deciding the extent of effect sizes is to examine their practical significance in the real world. Here again Eagly (1995) is critical of the effect size *d*-statistic, claiming that it frequently misleads psychologists into discounting findings which may have important practical significance. In contrast, if gender differences were expressed as a percentage of each group which performs above the average of the whole group (men and women combined), a different message may be conveyed. For example, Eagly (1987) showed that in a study on gender and aggressive behaviour, the effect size was $d = 0.29$ (moderate), yet when the same result was communicated in terms of the percentage of each group performing above the average, 43 per cent of women and 57 per cent of men scored above average in aggressive behaviour.

Fourth, in the heated debates about the size/importance of effect sizes, it should not be forgotten that effect size refers only to differences in average performances and tends to ignore questions concerning variability. If women and men differ in variability on a cognitive test, the more variable sex will be over-represented at both high and low levels of performance, even when average performances are the same. Feingold (1992) expressed surprise at the neglect of gender comparisons in variability in cognitive performance, given its historical significance in explaining gender differences. For example, male variability was frequently used to account for the over-representation of men in remedial samples and among the gifted and the eminent. Using meta-analytic techniques, he reported that higher male variability was confined to visuo-spatial and mathematical abilities for US samples, while no gender difference in variability was found for verbal ability. Differences in variability of samples are important especially when comparing gender in highly selected groups. Feingold's work permits a 'new look at an old controversy' and adds another layer of interpretation to meta-analytic studies.

Fifth, many writers have commented on the bias in the gender and cognition literature towards samples from Western industrialized nations and especially the USA. This is particularly true for the meta-analyses reported in this chapter. The importance of establishing a cross-cultural literature on gender comparisons should not be underestimated for the light it would shed on the influences of culture, language, ethnicity, gender beliefs and roles on the construction of gendered cognitive competence. As Halpern (1992) notes, 'we do not know much about sex differences in cognitive abilities in societies with social structures very different than our own' (p. 234).

The available literature would suggest both similarities and differences across cultures, as well as differences across ethnic groups within the same culture (for example, Born et al., 1987). Additionally, Feingold (1992) reported that the US findings of consistently greater male variability in mathematical and spatial abilities were not invariant across other cultures and nations. More generally, the topic of cross-cultural gender comparisons is under-researched.

In conclusion, notwithstanding the criticisms levelled at the quantitative tradition in gender research, there is little doubt that meta-analyses have transformed the area of cognitive comparisons. They have provided a coherent framework within which to pose questions about gender differences and have permitted the testing of hypotheses related to subcomponents of cognitive abilities and to age and generational effects, as well as probing the relationship between statistical effects based on group performance and an individual's life chances. These are old questions which have been given new vigour and vitality from feminist scholarship which is rooted on this occasion within a quantitative tradition.

At the beginning of the chapter I stated that one of its primary purposes was to enable students to read the contemporary literature with a critical eye and with a view to developing a personal epistemological standpoint on the question of gender and cognition. Keep in mind a comment from a leading constructivist, when discussing current developments in the psychology of women, and of gender: 'Feminist psychology today is certainly not monolithic. A number of areas of controversy have developed among those whom one would clearly identify as feminist psychologists' (Unger, 1997, p. 27). From this chapter, I hope that you will begin to understand why.

REFERENCES

Baumeister, R.F. (1988). Should we stop studying sex differences altogether? *American Psychologist* **42**, 1092–5.

Benbow, C.P. (1988). Sex differences in mathematical reasoning ability in intellectually talented preadolescents: their nature, effects and possible causes. *Behavioral and Brain Sciences* **11**, 169–232.

Born, M., Bleichrodt, N. and van der Flier, H. (1987). Cross-cultural comparisons of sex-related differences in intelligence tests: a meta-analysis. *Journal of Cross-Cultural Psychology* **18**, 283–314.

Caplan, P.J. and Caplan, J.B. (1994). *Thinking critically about research on sex and gender.* New York: Harper Collins.

Cohen, D. (1969). *Statistical power analysis for the behavioral sciences.* New York: Academic Press.

Eagly, A.H. (1987). *Sex differences in social behaviour: a social-role interpretation.* Hillsdale, NJ: Erlbaum.

Eagly, A.H. (1990). On the advantages of reporting sex comparisons. *American Psychologist* **45**, 560–2.

Eagly, A.H. (1995). The science and politics of comparing women and men. *American Psychologist* **50**, 145–58.

Feingold, A. (1988). Cognitive gender differences are disappearing. *American Psychologist* **43**, 95–103.

Feingold, A. (1992). Sex differences in variability in intellectual abilities: a new look at an old controversy. *Review of Educational Research* **62**, 61–84.

Feingold, A. (1994). Gender differences in variability in intellectual abilities: A cross-cultural perspective. *Sex Roles* **30**, 81–92.

Fennema, E. and Sherman, J. (1977). Sex-related differences in mathematics achievement, spatial visualisation, and sociocultural factors. *Journal of Educational Research* **14**, 51–71.

Gardner, H. (1983). *Frames of mind*. New York: Basic.

Halpern, D.F. (1992). *Sex differences in cognitive abilities*. 2nd edn. Hillsdale, NJ: Erlbaum.

Hare-Mustin, R.T. and Marecek, J. (1988). The meaning of difference: gender theory, postmodernism, and psychology. *American Psychologist* **43**, 455–64.

Hedges, L.V. and Olkin, I. (1985). *Statistical methods for meta-analysis*. San Diego, CA: Academic Press.

Hyde, J.S. (1990). Meta-analysis and the psychology of gender differences. *Signs: Journal of Women in Culture and Society* **16**, 55–73.

Hyde, J.S. (1994). Can meta-analysis make feminist transformations in psychology? *Psychology of Women Quarterly* **18**, 451–62.

Hyde, J.S., Fennema, E. and Lamon, S.J. (1990). Gender differences in mathematics performance: a meta-analysis. *Psychological Bulletin* **107**, 139–53.

Hyde, J.S. and Linn, M.C. (1988). Gender differences in verbal ability: a meta-analysis. *Psychological Bulletin* **104**, 53–69.

Hyde, J.S. and Plant, E.A. (1995). Magnitude of psychological gender differences: another side to the story. *American Psychologist* **50**, 159–61.

Jacklin, C.N. (ed.) (1992). *The psychology of gender*. 4 vols. Aldershot, Hants: Edward Elgar.

Kimura, D. (1987). Are men's and women's brains really different? *Canadian Psychology* **28**, 133–47.

Kitzinger, C. (ed.) (1994). Should psychologists study sex differences? *Feminism & Psychology* **4** (whole issue).

Linn, M.C. and Petersen, A.C. (1985). Emergence and characterisation of sex differences in spatial ability: a meta-analysis. *Child Development* **56**, 1479–98.

Maccoby, E.E. (1966). Sex differences in intellectual functioning. In Maccoby, E.E. (ed.), *The development of sex differences*. (pp. 25–55). Stanford, CA: Stanford University Press.

Maccoby, E.E. and Jacklin, C.N. (1974). *The psychology of sex differences*. Stanford, CA: Stanford University Press.

Marecek, J. (1995). Gender, politics, and psychology's ways of knowing. *American Psychologist* **50**, 162–3.

Romanes, G.J. (1887). Mental differences between men and women. *Nineteenth Century* **21**, 654–72.

Shields, S.A. (1975). Functionalism, Darwinism, and the psychology of women: a study of social myth. *american Psychologist* **30**, 739–54.

Thurstone, L.L. (1938). *Primary mental abilities*. Chicago: University of Chicago Press.

Unger, R.K. (1997). The three-sided mirror: feminists looking at psychologists looking at women. In Fuller, R., Noonan-Walsh, P. and McGinley, P. (eds), *A century of* *psychology: progress, paradigms and prospects for the new millennium.* (pp. 16–35). London: Routledge.

Voyer, D., Voyer, S. and Bryden, M.P. (1995). Magnitude of sex difference in spatial abilities: a meta-analysis and consideration of critical variables. *Psychological Bulletin* **117**, 250–70.

FURTHER READING

***Eagly, A.H.** (1995). The science and politics of comparing women and men. *American Psychologist* **50**, 145–58.

Hyde, J.S., Fennema, E. and Lamon, S.J. (1990). Gender differences in mathematics performance. *Psychological Bulletin* **197**, 139–55.

Hyde, J.S. and Linn, M.C. (1988). Gender differences in verbal ability: a meta-analysis. *Psychological Bulletin* **194**, 53–69.

***Hyde, J.S. and Plant, E.A.** (1995). Magnitude of psychological gender differences: another side of the story. *American Psychologist* **50**, 159–61.

Linn, M.C. and Petersen, A.C. (1985). Emergence and characterisation of sex differences in spatial ability: a meta-analysis. *Child Development* **6**, 1479–98.

***Marecek, J.** (1995). Gender, politics and psychology's ways of knowing. *American Psychologist* **50**, 162–3.

Shaw-Barnes, K. and Eagly, A. (1996). Meta-analysis and feminist psychology. In Wilkinson, S. (ed.), *Feminist social psychologies: international perspectives.* (pp. 258–74). Buckingham: Open University Press.

* *Treat as one reading.*

DISCUSSION QUESTIONS

1. To what extent are you convinced by the arguments that gender differences are disappearing? Why and why not?
2. In your view, what are the limitations of the 'quantitative' approach to reaching decisions about gender differences?
3. How would you study gender and cognition qualitatively?
4. For the sake of argument, presume that some gender differences in cognition are real. What are the implications for the principle and practice of equal opportunities?
5. As a woman or a man, do you feel that you are cognitively different to the opposite sex? Have you developed an informed personal viewpoint on the question? What primarily influenced you?

7

EMOTION

Agneta Fischer

INTRODUCTION

It is generally believed that women are the emotional sex, a belief subscribed to not only in Western culture but across a range of other cultures as well. There is ample evidence that women are portrayed as being overly emotional, as less able to deal with difficult situations and as less intelligent than men (for example, Williams and Best, 1990). Emotionality is seen as the essence of womanhood. In contrast with men, women are thought to hide their emotions less often, to express tender feelings more frequently, to cry very easily, and to feel hurt more often. Overall, women's emotionality is seen to stand in sharp contrast with men's rationality.

The opposition between passions, or emotions, and reason has characterized Western philosophy from its ancient past up until the twentieth century (Lloyd, 1984; Pott, 1992). Emotions have been defined as everything that reason is not. This dichotomy does not stand alone but symbolizes the opposition between the sexes: 'The rational which belongs to mind and reason is of the masculine gender, the irrational, the province of sense, is of the feminine' (Philo, in Lloyd, 1984, p. 27). Thus, femininity is associated with the irrational, and this in turn is equated with emotionality.

This dichotomy between men's rationality and women's emotionality is not only found in the works of great philosophers, but also (though in various modifications) in the works of social scientists and psychologists throughout this century. The founder of Dutch experimental psychology, Heymans, for example, states in his book *The psychology of women* (1910) that women's emotionality inhibits their ability to think in a logical, abstract, innovative and independent way. Likewise, the American psychologist Stanley Hall describes women as being more spontaneous and more intuitive, and closer to real feelings such as fear, rage, compassion and love, than are men, who are hardly able to feel, let alone express, their emotions (Jansz and van Drunen (eds), 1996).

Women's assumed closeness to nature and their consequent emotionality can also be found in a variety of other psychological traditions. Freud not only thought women to be the more jealous sex, as illustrated by their inevitable penis envy, but also to have a greater disposition for neuroses in general. Women's perceived erratic tendencies led the behaviorist Watson to argue that women generally are bad mothers, because they cannot maintain distance between themselves and their children. More generally speaking, mothers' tendency to be emotional has been a frequent topic in American child-rearing manuals since the beginning of this century (Shields and Koster, 1989). Whereas men's objective and rather emotionless attitude towards their children was considered to be healthy for the development of the child, women's emotional relationships with their children were depicted as dangerous. Mothers were thought to have the tendency to overreact emotionally and their unrestrained emotions were felt to pose a threat to their children.

However, although some psychologists considered women's emotionality to be dangerous, emotionality was generally conceived of as a sign of mature womanhood. In the various tests of masculinity/femininity (M/F), developed since 1936, emotionality has been one of the core characteristics, employed to distinguish normal women from normal men or abnormal (masculine) women. 'Normal' women were thought to be more sensitive, emotionally expressive, and afraid of the dark, as compared to 'normal' men. These are but a few examples to illustrate how the cultural belief in women's emotionality has also pervaded the thoughts of psychologists (see also Lewin (ed.), 1984).

Before turning to the explanations that have been offered for this alleged gender difference, it is important to note a number of implicit assumptions which are shared in these views on women's emotionality (see also Shields, 1987; Fischer, 1993). First, emotionality is seen as a natural disposition rather than a reaction based on gendered socialization practices in Western society. Second, emotionality cannot exist together with intellectual capacities but rather operates to the exclusion of rational and abstract thinking. Third, emotionality is not a very desirable trait and is even considered to be problematic as it implies losing control. Being emotional is conceived of as restraining instead of inspiring. Fourth, emotionality is treated as a unidimensional state, as if there exists only one type of emotion.

THEORETICAL PERSPECTIVES

Evolutionary theories

The early twentieth-century beliefs about the different natures of men and women were based on the work of Charles Darwin. He and many of his followers asserted that females should be placed lower on the evolutionary ladder than males. Particularly because of their reproductive function, women were supposed to be closer to nature. This implied that their brains were less developed than those of men and therefore they were supposed to react more spontaneously and instinctively, and to be less suitable for intellectual work. These ideas can be found in Freudian psychoanalysis, in early twentieth-century medical and psychological theories (including those of Thorndike and Hall), but also in current sociobiological theories (for example, Kenrick and Trost, 1993), which claim that women's reproductive function is the biological basis for their emotionality.

Biological theories

More specific biological explanations focus on the differential development of male and female brains. According to some popular biological accounts (for example, Moir and Jessel, 1989), women's better verbal expression of emotions can be explained by the fact that the right hemisphere of the female brain, which controls the emotions, is better connected to the left side of the brain, which controls verbal expression, than is the case for men. However, this view has been criticized for being too simplistic. Other, more sophisticated biological explanations focus on the differences in hormonal responses between men and women. Men's higher concentrations of testosterone are supposed to elicit aggressive tendencies. At the same time, the evidence supporting this claim is rather weak as it is based exclusively on animal research (see also Van Goozen, 1994). Thus, though it is likely that testosterone plays some role in the elicitation and intensity of anger and aggression, the extent to which gender differences in aggression reflect differences in testosterone levels still remains undetermined.

Physiological differences between men and women are also employed to account for gender differences in crying. One explanation argues that:

- Higher levels of prolactin account for greater tear stimulation.
- Women have naturally higher levels of prolactin than men because of women's ability to breast feed.
- Prolactin has to be excreted because otherwise it can have negative bodily effects.
- Therefore women's greater tear production is explained by their greater need to excrete prolactin. (e.g., Kottler, 1996)

While there is evidence that women do cry more frequently when prolactin levels are higher (for example when they are pregnant), on the other hand it is also obvious that crying has important social functions, suggesting that a mere biological explanation of gender differences in crying would be too simplistic. However, most biological theories acknowledge the fact that, in themselves, biological or physiological factors cannot account for all gender differences in emotions. Instead, biological differences may offer one factor which may help to explain specific differential emotional reactions by men and women, such as aggression or crying.

Feminist psychoanalytic theories and socialization theories

From the 1970s onwards, feminist scientists challenged the negative connotations associated with women's emotionality by changing the focus to the positive effects of being emotional and the negative effects of the inability to express one's emotions. This positive twist was effected by emphasizing women's relational nature; their ability to empathize, to decode other people's feelings, and to talk about emotions with others enabled them to engage in intimate relationships with their children, with their partners and with other women (for example, Chodorow, 1978; Gilligan, 1982; Eichenbaum and Orbach, 1983).

One explanation which has been advanced to account for women's relational capacities relates to the nature of their socialization. Most feminists did not regard emotionality as a biological disposition but rather as something that had to be learned. An important feature of the traditional Western female role is women's primary responsibility in the socio-emotional domain; she attends to the personal well-being of her family, she deals with personal relationships, she has to make others feel comfortable, she consoles others. Men's traditional role, on the other hand, is to provide bread and to protect the family. In other words, girls are taught to be sweet and demure, to smile and be nice, whereas boys are supposed to be active, competitive and brave. Boys and girls have thus learned different emotional roles.

Another explanation is based on feminist reformulations of psychoanalytic theory (Chodorow, 1978). In traditional Western families, it is the mother with whom all children develop their first relationship. This is of crucial importance, because it leads to fundamentally different relations between mother and child, and father and child. Girls do not need to differentiate themselves fully from their mother, because they are like her, and they can identify themselves with her. Hence, girls develop their identity in a continuous, intimate relationship with their mother, resulting in little need for autonomy, but rather a need for emotional intimacy with others. Women's emotionality is thus regarded as being intertwined with their relational nature. Boys, on the other hand, differentiate themselves from their mothers at an early age ('I am not like her'), and their independence is the result of a process that is largely characterized by individuation and the development of firm ego-boundaries. In this process boys are supposed to suppress their affective needs far more than girls. 'Boys and men come to deny the feminine identification within themselves and those feelings they experience as feminine: feelings of dependence, relational needs, emotions generally' (Chodorow, 1989, p. 109).

Although these feminist accounts did challenge the dominant view on women's emotionality, replacing its association with negative and irrational attributes by one with positive relational effects, emotionality was still assumed to be the core essence of womanhood. Feminists at that time did not adopt a critical stance towards the concept of emotionality as such. Thus, the question still remained as to what emotionality means and what gender differences are left when emotionality is stripped of its ideological connotations.

Gender-specific social psychological theories

According to current social psychological and feminist theories (Deaux and Major, 1987; Eagly, 1987; Shields, 1991), the statement that women are more emotional than men is too simplistic and incapable of capturing all aspects of the complex emotional reality occupied by men and women. The concept of emotionality seems to refer mainly to typical female emotions, such as sadness and crying, and to exaggerated reactions. Being emotional actually means emotionally over-reacting, not adhering to the 'emotion norms' of one's culture (Shields, 1987). Indeed, when comparing research in which a global measure of 'emotionality' has been used with research in which distinct emotions are measured, it appears that gender differences are more evident in the former studies. Thus, using the global concept 'emotionality' exaggerates the differences between men and women. Therefore, in order to study gender differences in emotion, a distinction should be made not only between different types of emotions (anger, fear, sadness, joy, etc.), but also between different components of emotions (for example, experience and expression) and between different contexts in which emotions are elicited. Following current emotion theories (for example, Frijda, 1986), emotions should be thought of as processes, containing multiple components, including appraisals, action tendencies, facial expressions, bodily changes and actions. Gender differences may occur in each of these components, leading to either subtle or more overt differences in the ways in which emotions are felt, expressed or coped with by men and women.

Social psychologists who study gender differences in emotions take as their basic premise that emotions are affected by gendered belief systems (Deaux and Major, 1987) and these contain implicit knowledge and norms about how men and women should react emotionally in a particular context. This does not imply that the individual is always aware of these norms. The strength of these gendered belief systems is that they represent an intrinsic and 'natural' part of the way in which men and women, mothers and children, fathers and children, boys and girls interact with each other, silently reproducing differences. Because women are expected to behave emotionally in a different way to men, this may affect the likelihood of admitting particular emotions, the awareness or intensity of experiences, the way in which emotional situations are appraised and reappraised, the expression of emotions, or the evaluation and subsequent regulation of emotions.

EMPIRICAL RESEARCH

Gendered emotional meaning systems

Though most cultures share the view that women are more emotional than men, this *general* cultural idea that women are (allowed to be) the more emotional sex must be modified in the light of current research (Brody and Hall, 1993; Shields, 1991). Not all emotions are taboo for men; the display of *powerful* emotions such as anger, disdain, contempt or hatred all imply one's dominant position over others, and are complementary to traditional male gender roles. It is emotions that imply powerlessness and vulnerability which are considered inappropriate for men, because these stand in opposition to male identity as defined by power, courage and strength (Fischer and Jansz, 1995).

Women, on the other hand, are supposed to be emotionally sensitive and to keep harmonious relationships with others. By implication, women's display of powerful emotions is expected to elicit negative reactions, whereas their expression of *powerless* emotions, such as sadness, fear, disappointment or insecurity, is relatively more acceptable. Prototypical of these gendered beliefs are ideas such as 'men who cry are cissies' and 'women who show anger are bossy'.

These gendered expectations and emotion norms are already implanted at a very young age through peer and family socialization. Parents appear to talk about emotions more frequently with their daughters than with their sons, and they also display a wider range of emotions with their daughters in comparison with their sons. In several studies parents were asked to construct a story for their children on the basis of a wordless storybook (for example, Fivush, 1989). The results showed that parents did not talk about anger and disgust to their daughters, and spoke more about sadness with their daughters than with their sons. Further, parents seemed to talk more about the causes and consequences of emotional events with their sons, but discussed the emotional feelings with their daughters. Thus, there is evidence that, from an early age, girls are more exposed to talk about emotions than are boys, and there are slight differences in the contents of this talk; whereas girls seem to talk more about powerless emotions, boys talk more about powerful emotions.

Playing in same-sex peer groups further encourages these differences. Boys and girls have different play styles, and boys' groups and girls' groups display different social interaction patterns. Whereas boys operate in relatively larger groups, characterized by a strong hierarchy and competition, girls play in smaller, more intimate settings, where they try to minimize hostility and where their interactions are characterized by close co-operation and agreement (Maccoby, 1988, 1990). These gender differences in interaction style have consequences for the emotional skills which boys and girls develop throughout childhood and adolescence. Men develop more competitive skills and are therefore more experienced in displaying anger, whereas girls enjoy more experience in displaying social-emotional skills by sharing emotions that increase intimacy and decrease hostility, such as joy, compassion, disappointment or empathy.

Gender differences in emotions

When reviewing current empirical research on gender differences in emotions, it is clear that gender differences are smaller and more complex than may be suggested by reference to traditional sex-role stereotypes. Much of the research literature consists of self-descriptions, where subjects have to indicate how frequently they feel angry, afraid, sad, happy, or, for example, how often they express these emotions. Many of these studies report gender differences in the sense that women describe more intense and more frequent emotions. However, these self-report measures differ in directness and specificity. When taking these differences into account, it appears that women report being more emotional than men especially in response to direct questions (for example, 'How often are you angry?') rather than indirect measures (for example, the number of emotion words used in a conversation), when the self-reported measure is concerned with emotion expressions rather than subjective feelings, when the context is interpersonal rather than impersonal, and when the measure is global rather than discrete (LaFrance and Banaji, 1992). Thus, to a large extent the types of question influence the results of self-report studies, suggesting that gendered beliefs influence the recollection and labelling of emotions.

The influence of emotion norms on the intensity of emotional experiences was neatly demonstrated by Grossman and Wood (1993). In a first study they asked men and women to rate the intensity and frequency of their experiences of fear, joy, sadness, anger and love. Women reported feeling these emotions more intensely and more frequently than men, anger being the exception. In a second study, subjects had to watch emotional slides under three different conditions. In the first, the participants were told that emotional expressions were appropriate and healthy, in the second condition the opposite was told, and in the third, control condition, no specific instructions were given. The results indicated that women generated more extreme emotions when no instructions were given but these differences disappeared when normative pressures were comparable for men and women. These findings support the assumption that gender differences in the intensity and frequency of emotions are influenced by the different normative beliefs which men and women hold.

There is also empirical support for the idea that women's emotions are in line with expectations concerning traditional female gender roles, characterized by vulnerability, low status and little power. The largest and most consistent differences in emotions appear for powerless emotions such as sadness, fear and depression, with women reporting experience of these emotions more often and with more intensity. In addition, and in comparison with men, women also experience more shame and guilt, emotions that imply self-blame for negative events, and more happiness and life-satisfaction, which are related to women's social role of emotional caretaker within the family (Wood et al., 1989). With respect to anger, not gender but gender roles appear to be associated with the frequency of anger reports; masculine respondents are found to be significantly more prone to anger than feminine or androgynous respondents (for example, Kopper and Epperson, 1991; Van Goozen, 1994).

In sum, there is no evidence that only women and few men experience emotions; instead it should be stressed that there are many similarities in the reported emotions of men and women. However, there are also differences which seem to derive from the fact that women more often report emotions that imply powerlessness, vulnerability or the encouragement of social cohesion. This difference may be explained by the fact that because of the different roles into which men and women are socialized, and the different statuses which they have, women appraise a greater variety of situations in terms of their powerlessness, leading to the experience of powerless emotions. Hence, perhaps simplifying matters a little, women are not angry but sad, they do not feel contempt but compassion, they do not aggress but withdraw. Obviously, in turn these expressions will depend on the context in which the emotions are felt. For example, the sex of the other person, and the social implications of the individual's expression of emotion, seem to affect not only what the person feels but also how s/he labels or expresses these feelings (Brody et al., 1995; Stoppard and Gunn Gruchy, 1993).

Gender differences in emotion expression

Gender differences in the expression of emotions generally appear to be larger than differences in subjective feelings (for example, Lafrance and Banaji, 1992; Manstead, 1992). Observational studies of non-verbal expressions have shown that women are generally more expressive; they show more overt facial expressions, they smile more, make more gestures, body movements, and so on (see Hall, 1984). A variety of studies has also shown that it is easier to 'read' an emotion from a woman's face than from a man's face. Further, women report that they express more fear, sadness, anger and joy than men, and also are more confident in expressing these emotions. Women are also more willing to discuss their emotional experiences with others (Dindia and Allen, 1992).

These differences in emotion expression can be accounted for in terms of gender-specific norms and expectations. The traditional female gender role permits the overt expression of emotions in general, and of powerlessness emotions in particular, whereas the male gender role mainly reinforces antagonistic responses. Women therefore tend to express powerless emotions, such as fear and sadness, with more confidence and more overtly. Gender differences in anger expressions can be similarly explained. For example, Baggio (1989) reports that, when asked to write down anger episodes, men more often describe antagonistic behaviours while women describe passive consent. Further, those sex-typed as masculine express their anger more often than feminine or androgynous types, and indeed those typed as feminine show a greater tendency to suppress their anger. Reviews on gender differences in aggression also suggest the normative pressure of gender-role expectations (Eagly and Steffen, 1986). One of the most influential factors associated with gender differences in aggression is that women feel more anxiety and guilt after aggressive acts. If the aggression is seen as justified, however, no gender differences are found. This not only demonstrates the general rule that aggression is inappropriate for girls, but also highlights the fact that women expect that they will be in danger or that their victim will be hurt if they behave aggressively. Thus negative implications for oneself and others lead women to transform or suppress their anger. This may also explain why women (tend to) cry so often when they are angry or disappointed.

Crying is the ultimate display of powerlessness. Women not only report crying more often than men when angry or disappointed but also when they are sad, afraid or moved (Lombardo et al., 1983). Only in the case of very serious incidents, such as the death of someone close, do there appear to be no significant differences in the crying behaviour of men and women. Thus crying appears to be appropriate only in extreme situations for men but women are allowed to cry in a wider variety of contexts. At the same time, in a recent study in which participants had to evaluate a crying, laughing and non-emotional man and woman (in response to a 'tear-jerking' movie clip), the crying man was liked more than the crying woman. While the crying man was evaluated more positively than the laughing or non-emotional man, the crying woman was evaluated more negatively than the non-emotional woman (Labott et al., 1991). This may point not only to changing cultural attitudes towards the expressions of feelings of vulnerability or helplessness by men but also to the idea that men's crying is attributed to different, and perhaps more serious, causes as compared to women.

In sum, gender differences in emotion expression follow the same pattern as those associated with emotion experience. They are in line with gender-specific expectations and rules, leading women to communicate their emotions relatively freely and overtly while men feel reluctant to show their vulnerability, powerlessness or concern with others.

Conclusions

This chapter has raised some critical questions concerning the use of the concept of emotionality as being the core characteristic of one gender, women. Emotionality generally refers to typical female emotions and therefore obscures the fact that men also experience and display emotions. The general claim that women are more emotional than men thus tells us more about Western cultural stereotypes than about the subtleties and complexities of men's and women's emotions. Empirical research on gender differences in emotions shows that differences are larger when global questions are asked. Hence the question should be raised as to whether these differences reflect actual differences in feelings or whether they merely reflect different emotional belief systems. Because women are expected to be at least more concerned with aspects of emotional lives than men are, and because discourse on emotions is more inherent in women's social lives, it may not surprise us that women recognize, remember and report more emotions, and more intense emotions, than do men.

The suggestion that gender differences in these studies reflect gender-specific expectations is further supported by the fact that many studies in which distinct emotions in specific situations were examined showed similarities between men's and women's emotional reactions. This does not mean that there are no differences. The differences that are found all point in the same direction; both men and women are more likely to experience and express emotions that are in line with their gender roles. Women more often experience and express emotions that display powerlessness and vulnerability, and which support social cohesion, whereas men seem much more reluctant to do so. At the same time men seem somewhat more likely to express emotions that enhance their status, assertiveness or dominance.

The chapter has reviewed several explanations for these differences, focusing on recent social psychological and feminist accounts. Although biological explanations may account for some of the variance, for example in crying or aggression, the support for the influence of social variables is much stronger. The different social roles into which men and women are socialized have several implications that may account for gender differences. First, gender roles imply differences in power and status. Thus, the greater tendency to experience and express powerless emotions by women and powerful emotions by men may be the direct result of these actual differences in power. This explanation has, for example, been offered for women's greater expressiveness in the non-verbal domain. Women, like other individuals with low status, pay more attention to non-verbal cues in social interaction than individuals with high status. Frequent smiling is also thought to be a characteristic of low-status individuals because they must maintain harmonious relationships with those higher in the hierarchy. A second implication of male and female roles is the difference in emotional and social commitments. Girls are socialized into roles which include emotional expressiveness and social bonding as integral components. In other words, gender differences in emotions can be largely seen as the result of emotions being elicited, experienced, expressed and regulated as a function of different social roles and socialization histories.

REFERENCES

Baggio, M.K. (1989). Sex differences in behavioral reactions to provocation of anger. *Psychological Reports* **64**, 23–6.

Brody, L.R. and Hall, J.A. (1993). Gender and emotion. In Lewis, M. and Haviland, J.M. (eds), *Handbook of emotions*. (pp. 447–61). New York: Guilford Press.

Brody, L.R., Lovas, G.S. and Hay, D.H. (1995). Gender differences in anger and fear as a function of situational context. *Sex Roles* **32**, 47–78.

Chodorow, N. (1978). *The reproduction of mothering: psychoanalysis and the sociology of gender.* Berkeley: University of California Press.

Chodorow, N. (1989). *Feminism and psychoanalytic theory.* New Haven: Yale University Press.

Deaux, K. and Major, B. (1987). Putting gender into context. *Psychological Review* **94**, 369–89.

Dindia, K. and Allen, M. (1992). Sex differences in self-disclosure: a meta-analysis. *Psychological Bulletin* **112**, 106–24.

Eagly, A.H. (1987). *Sex differences in social behavior: a social role interpretation.* Hillsdale, NJ: Erlbaum.

Eagly, A.H. and Steffen, V.J. (1986). Gender and aggressive behavior: a meta-analytic review of the social psychological literature. *Psychological Bulletin* **100**, 309–30.

Eichenbaum, L. and Orbach, S. (1983). *What do women want?* London: Fontana.

Fischer, A.H. (1993). Sex differences in emotionality: fact or stereotype? *Feminism & Psychology* **3**, 303–18.

Fischer, A.H. and Jansz, J. (1995). Reconciling emotions with Western personhood. *Journal for the Theory of Social Behaviour* **25**, 59–81.

Fivush, R. (1989). Exploring sex differences in the emotional content of mother–child conversations about the past. *Sex Roles* **20**, 675–91.

Frijda, N.H. (1986). *The emotions.* Cambridge: Cambridge University Press.

Gilligan, C. (1982). *In a different voice.* Cambridge, MA: Harvard University Press.

Grossman, M. and Wood, W. (1993). Sex differences in the intensity of emotional experience: a social role interpretation. *Journal of Personality and Social Psychology* **65**, 1010–22.

Hall, J.A. (1984). On explaining gender differences: the case of nonverbal communication. In Shaver, P. and Hendrick, C. (eds), *Review of personality and social psychology 7: sex and gender.* (pp. 177–201). Newbury Park, CA: Sage.

Heymans, G. (1910). *Psychologie der vrouwen.* (Psychology of women). Amsterdam: Wereldbibliotheek.

Jansz, J. and van Drunen, P. (eds.) (1996). *Met zachte hand. Opkomst en verbreiding van het psychologisch perspectief.* (With a gentle touch: emergence and generalization of psychological views.) Utrecht: De Tijdstroom.

Kenrick, D.T. and Trost, M.R. (1993). The evolutionary perspective. In Beall, A.E. and Sternberg, R.J. (eds), *The psychology of gender.* (pp. 148–73). New York: Guilford Press.

Kopper, B.A. and Epperson, D.L. (1991). Women and anger: sex and sex-role comparisons in the expression of anger. *Psychology of Women Quarterly* **15**, 7–14.

Kottler, J.A. (1996). *The language of tears.* San Francisco: Jossey-Bass.

Labott, S.M., Martin, R.B., Eason, P.S. and Berkey, E.Y. (1991). Social reactions to the expression of emotion. *Cognition and Emotion* **5**, 397–419.

LaFrance, M. and Banaji, M. (1992). Toward a reconsideration of the gender–emotion relationship. In Clark, M.S. (ed.), *Review of personality and social psychology 14: emotions and social behavior*. (pp. 178–202). Newbury Park, CA: Sage.

Lewin, M. (ed.) (1984). *In the shadow of the past: psychology portrays the sexes*. New York: Columbia University Press.

Lloyd, G. (1984). *The man of reason: 'male' and 'female' in Western philosophy*. London: Methuen.

Lombardo, W.K., Cretser, G.A., Lombardo, B. and Mathis, S. L. (1983). Fer cryin' out loud – there is a sex difference. *Sex Roles* **9**, 987–96.

Maccoby, E.E. (1988). Gender as a social category. *Developmental Psychology* **24**, 755–65.

Maccoby, E.E. (1990). Gender and relationships. *American Psychologist* **45**, 513–20.

Manstead, A.S.R. (1992). Gender differences in emotion. In Gale, M.A. and Eysenck, M.W. (eds), *Handbook of individual differences: biological perspectives*. (pp. 355–89). Chichester: Wiley.

Moir, A. and Jessel, D. (1989). *Brain sex: the real difference between men and women*. London: Mandarin.

Pott, H. (1992). *De liefde van Alcibiades. Over de retionaliteit van emoties.* (The love of Alcibiades. On the rationality of emotions). Amsterdam: Boom.

Shields, S.A. (1987). Women, men and the dilemma of emotion. In Shaver, P. and Hendrick, K. (eds), *Review of personality and social psychology 7: sex and gender.* (pp. 229–51). Newbury Park, CA: Sage.

Shields, S.A. (1991). Gender in the psychology of emotion: a selective research review. In Strongman, K.T. (ed.), *International review of studies on emotion.* (pp. 227–47). New York: Wiley.

Shields, S.A. and Koster, B.A. (1989). Emotional stereotyping of parents in child rearing manuals, 1915–1980. *Social Psychological Quarterly* **52**, 44–55.

Stoppard, J.M. and Gunn Gruchy, C.D. (1993). Gender, context and expression of positive emotion. *Personality and Social Psychology Bulletin* **19**, 143–50.

Van Goozen, S. (1994). Male and female: effects of sex hormones on aggression, cognition and sexual motivation. Unpublished doctoral dissertation, Amsterdam.

Williams, J.E. and Best, D.L. (1990). *Measuring sex stereotypes: a multi-nation study.* Newbury Park, CA: Sage.

Wood, W., Rhodes, N. and Whelan, M. (1989). Sex differences in positive well-being: a consideration of emotional style and marital status. *Psychological Bulletin* **106(2)**, 249–64.

Further reading

Brody, L.R. and Hall, J.A. (1993). Gender and emotion. In Lewis, M. and Haviland, J.M. (eds), *Handbook of emotions*. (pp. 447–61). New York: Guilford.

Deaux, K. and Major, B. (1987). Putting gender into context. *Psychological Review* **94**, 369–89.

Fischer, A.H. (1993). Sex differences in emotionality: fact or stereotype? *Feminism & Psychology* **3**, 303–18.

Grossman, M. and Wood, W. (1993). Sex differences in the intensity of emotional experience: a social role interpretation. *Journal of Personality and Social Psychology* **65**, 1010–22.

Shields, S.A. (1991). Gender in the psychology of emotion: a selective research review. In Strongman, K.T. (ed.), *International review of studies on emotion.* (pp. 227–47). New York: Wiley.

Discussion questions

1. What makes you cry? How acceptable is it for men to cry in public in the 1990s? In private?
2. What makes you angry? Are there differences in the ways in which men and women display anger in public? In private?
3. Is emotionality still associated with women more than with men? If so, which emotions?
4. Which emotions (if any) are associated more with men than with women? How does this reflect the male sex-role stereotype?
5. Why have feminists been critical of simplistic views that women are more emotional than men?
6. Are mothers responsible for the perpetuation of gender differences in emotion? What about fathers?

Part 2

The Life-span

8

CHILDHOOD

Jean Whyte

INTRODUCTION

From the moment of birth, our gender exerts a pervasive influence on both our physical and social development, and as we progress through childhood our gender and age combine to influence who we become. Gender development results in gender differences, and gender differences in turn lead to gender inequalities. An understanding of gender development is therefore central to our understanding of inequalities, and to begin to understand this process we must focus attention on the early years, on childhood. This chapter aims to consider gender development throughout this stage of life, in the context of the models of gender development which have dominated the psychological literature up to the present day.

Understanding of gender development within psychology has tended to be derived from three overarching explanatory models – the biological, the environmental and the mentalistic. For the sake of clarity and convenience, these are dealt with separately below, but in reality the lines of demarcation between them are not always so clear-cut. The models or conceptual frameworks are not mutually exclusive; instead, each places its primary emphasis on different facets of development – and indeed there are occasions when the three models are able to offer complementary insight into the process of human development through childhood.

THE BIOLOGICAL MODEL

In its most extreme version, those who subscribe to this model (including sociobiologists) would be likely to argue that individual differences have their roots primarily in our genetic code, with little role played by either the environment or cognitive factors. However, today even the most radical sociobiologist would acknowledge the part played by the environment, but would argue that it can only exert its influence within strict parameters as established by our genetic predispositions. Sociobiologists would maintain that the greater relative physical strength of men, together with their greater lung power, make them better adapted to be hunters. In contrast, women's childbearing and milk-production capacities predispose them to nurturant roles (Barash, 1982; Wilson, 1975; 1978), and these gender roles then act together in a complementary fashion as part of humankind's broader adaptation to the environment.

Some researchers have suggested that specific aspects of biological differences (for example, men's exclusive possession of the Y chromosome [Hutt, 1978; Ounstead and Taylor, 1972], men's greater amounts of testosterone, and women's experience of monthly hormonal changes [involving estrogens and progestins]) underlie gender differences in behaviour, abilities and aptitudes, rates of development and psychological functioning (Money and Erhardt, 1972). Despite early enthusiasm for such arguments, later writers have concluded that the relationship between biological functions (such as hormone levels) and social behaviour (for example, aggression) is far from straightforward or causal. While there may be complex feedback loops involving, for example, testosterone and assertiveness, there remains little by way of firm evidence (Mazur, 1985).

If there were biologically given sex differences in behaviour and in psychological functioning we would expect to find some sign of them before we feel the impact of social experiences in early childhood. Research has failed to find conclusive and consistent psychological differences between young boys and girls, for example in temperament or activity levels. In addition, a biological model would find it difficult to explain how one gender came to be socially dominant; social dominance does not necessarily follow from superior physical strength but rather it is oriented around culturally determined values (Sayers, 1982). Nor does this theory give credit to the non-physical attributes which we bring to our roles and to the transforming nature of these other characteristics (Bem, 1993).

Environmental models

Psychoanalytic theory

According to Freudian theory, females are both sexually and morally inferior to males and their psychological functioning is essentially different. Women's inferiority is seen to stem from biological givens (primarily the fact that males have a penis and females do not), but the environment in the form of relationships also contributes to differentiate the psychological make-up of girls and boys. The development and later repression of sexual feelings at the unconscious level in the early years, the Oedipus and Electra complexes, results in boys having no problems identifying with their father and internalizing his attitudes whereas girls see their mother as weak and ineffectual because she and they lack a penis and so girls cannot fully identify with their mothers; this has consequences for the development of girls' superego and hence for their psychological functioning and self-concept.

The controversial notion of penis envy (see Chapter 11) has been interpreted as the girl's awareness not simply of not having a penis, but of not having the power and control that appears to go with it from an early age (see Rutenbeek, 1967). The issue of feelings of 'inferiority/superiority' versus 'difference' was taken further by Erikson (1968) in relation to the different bodily experiences of males and females, the former being seen as projecting and outward, the latter as inner-directed, more contained. He also proposed that the biological differences may result in womb envy for males. Since men cannot create life in the same way as women, men may substitute career achievement as an alternative means of creation.

The origins of women's self-image, and the image that others have of them, as caring, sacrificing and relational, were explored by Nancy Chodorow (1978), following on from Freud and Erikson. She saw this as beginning at the breastfeeding stage and setting the scene for later notions of femaleness. According to Chodorow, girls have no problems identifying with their mother, and their self-concept is dependent on mutuality and relatedness, thus preparing them in turn to be related to others. Boys, on the other hand, soon learn to separate from their mother and to identify themselves in terms of differences from her. In the process they learn to repress any feminine tendencies. Thus, men's self-concept depends on their being able to suppress aspects of their identity in order to establish an identity as a separate and independent individual.

As you may expect, psychoanalytic theories have not been without their critics. For example, while it may be generally accepted that biology plays an important part in how cultures come to define gender, culture will also dictate what is acceptable practice with regard to mothering and interactions with babies. Also, while early experiences do seem to matter, whether they matter quite as much as the psychoanalysts would like to have us believe is still not proven. In addition, while it does seem to be the case that a strong emotional bond is normally formed between a mother and her baby (Sroufe, 1985), there is no evidence that this hinges on the sex of the child (Golombok and Fivush, 1994).

On a more positive note, Chodorow's ideas are in sympathy with much of what is now believed about gender differences in adults, namely that females are more relationally oriented than males and males are more oriented towards autonomy and independence than females (see Chapter 1). These ideas also link in with the proposals of Carol Gilligan (1982) in relation to the origins of gender differences in moral development (see Chapter 3). Gilligan found that while males and females can use both care-based and justice-based reasoning when discussing moral problems, females appear to use more care-based reasoning. Also, when asked to discuss personal moral dilemmas, females focus more on interpersonal dilemmas and use care-based moral reasoning, whereas males focus on abstract impersonal problems and use justice-based moral reasoning.

BEHAVIOURIST THEORIES

Social learning

Local norms and social pressures, rather than innate determinants, are seen by social learning theorists to have the most significant influence on gender development. Socializing agents such as parents, teachers, peers and the mass media convey repetitive messages about the importance of gender-role-appropriate behaviour. They also provide examples of what is expected and attempt to shape behaviour by reinforcing what is considered appropriate and acceptable.

Working from within a social learning perspective, observational learning and modelling have received considerable attention, with observational learning of gender-appropriate behaviours seen to result from modelling. Different models become more prominent at an early age and are differentially reinforced according to the sex of the child (Fagot, 1978). This is especially true for boys and their relationship with their fathers (Fagot and Hagan, 1991). There is also evidence that parents tend to encourage their same-sex children to join them in traditionally sex-typed activities (Lytton and Romney, 1991). At the same time, there is little research which suggests that parents differentially reinforce their sons and daughters for social and personal aspects of gender-typed behaviour, such as aggression and dependency. However, in our culture it is considered more appropriate for females to express emotion than it is for males, and indeed the Adams et al. (1995) review of studies of early childhood demonstrated that parents did have different expectations of sons and daughters in this respect. In line with social learning theory, parents were found to use more frequent and varied emotional language in conversation with daughters than with sons, and that daughters in their turn used more terms associated with emotion than sons.

The types of toys provided, and the type of play that is stimulated, also lead to different problem-solving experiences, affecting cognitive development (Block, 1983). This could have a knock-on effect for self-esteem when children are faced with similar tasks. They may approach tasks differently and hence have differential rates of success. Girls seem to need more approval from others and to have less confidence than boys and this could be linked to the findings that boys receive more praise and positive evaluation from parents and teachers (Whyte, 1974) than do girls for equivalent levels of ability and achievement (see Chapter 10). In turn girls have lower expectations for success and are more likely than boys to attribute their failure to a general lack of personal ability. In contrast, boys have been found to attribute success to personal ability and failure to external influences (Alessandri and Lewis, 1993).

This theory is confirmed in the case of children who inhabit a social environment which tries not to encourage gender-stereotyped behaviour. Hoffman and Kloska (1995) reported that parents who have less stereotypical attitudes to gender roles have daughters who have a more internal locus of control, usually more common in males than in females. More typically, girls adopt an extrinsic locus of control, which can result in greater vulnerability to a sense of helplessness and depressive symptoms than is the case with intrinsically motivated individuals (Boggiano and Barrett, 1992). The need to seek approval which is associated with an extrinsic locus of control leads to stress. Van Aken and Riksen-Walraven (1992) found that parental support to sons facilitated a sense of self-efficacy (that is, the experience and expectation of being an effective agent in one's life), and they suggested that a lack of continuity in parental supportive behaviour towards daughters could result in a low sense of self-efficacy among girls.

The mass media, and in particular television, is regarded as a source of highly stereotyped gender role models. For example, males have been found to outnumber females in a ratio of 7:3 on television (Durkin, 1985), and are often seen in more dominant roles associated with higher occupational status. Conversely, females are portrayed as more subordinate and occupying a narrow range of traditional female roles (Durkin, 1986). Clear differences are identifiable even in the commercials which are directed at children (Welch et al., 1979).

Some studies have reported associations between the amount of television which children watch and the degree to which they adhere to traditional sex-role beliefs (Morgan, 1982), yet on the other hand there is some evidence that television can contribute to promoting more open and egalitarian beliefs and attitudes (Johnston and Ettema, 1982). However, correlation does not imply causation and the evidence for and against either argument is neither consistent nor persuasive.

Looking across the literature derived from social learning approaches, consistent differences have been found in the socialization of the two genders with regard to the encouragement of independence and autonomy, with boys more likely to be encouraged to show independence than girls. At the same time, boys are more likely to be punished for aggression and to receive physical punishment for misdeeds. Fathers are generally more sensitive than mothers to gender-role properties, to the extent that they discourage cross-gender play and especially for boys (Fagot, 1978). However, in honesty, even when considering the encouragement of gender-typed activities, the effects which have been found are best described as modest.

These reservations aside, other factors undoubtedly do affect the extent to which children learn from social models. It seems likely that children's social experiences interact with their developing concepts of gender to determine which particular gender-related characteristics will be exhibited on a given occasion. Unfortunately, social learning theories are not able to account for the fact that children's gender-role beliefs appear to change over time and sometimes are even more rigid than those of their parents (Stagnor and

Ruble, 1987). It has also been found that children attend selectively to models (a consoling finding with regard to the impact of television and other media) and that, for example, they take into account both the gender of the model and the gender typicality of the actions, and they do not necessarily imitate a same-sex model (Masters et al., 1979). Their choice will be based on factors including stereotypes and gender-schematic processing biases, thus bringing a cognitive element into play.

MENTALISTIC MODELS

In contrast with social learning approaches, which tend to downplay the active role played by cognition (other than through the process of identification), cognitive developmental theories propose that the individual knows which gender identity is appropriate through his or her active construction of the world within which s/he interacts. For example, Kohlberg (1966) saw the origin of this understanding in the child's concept of physical things. This begins with his/her own body which in turn is related to a social order which makes functional use of gender categories in culturally universal ways.

According to Kohlberg, understanding of gender and a gender identity develops in stages:

- Gender labelling (2–$3\frac{1}{2}$ years). At this stage the child sees him/herself and others as being in the same category but not necessarily for life.
- Gender stability ($3\frac{1}{2}$–$4\frac{1}{2}$ years). During this stage awareness of the durability of one's own gender grows, but this is seen to be dependent on the physical concept of gender. For example, McConaghy (1979) study found that clothing was important in young children's defining of gender, although whether this result would be replicated in the 1990s (with more evidence of unisex dressing) is debatable.
- Gender consistency ($4\frac{1}{2}$–7 years). Understanding of the permanency of gender and constancy, regardless of activities or clothes, occurs at this stage (at around the same age as the Piagetian concept of conservation is accomplished).

Kohlberg considers that as conceptual understanding increases, the child is motivated to seek out more information about the details of gender roles, for example by looking for potential models of gender-appropriate behaviour. Children then organize their own behaviour to ensure mastery of their own gender role; in other words, they are seen as engaging in self-socialization rather than being passive recipients of information. While Kohlberg's work remains influential, it has not been without its critics. Most notably, Carol Gilligan has branded Kohlberg's general theory of moral development as androcentric as it appears to place greater value on forms of masculine moral reasoning (see Chapter 3).

More recently, gender-schematic processing theory (Martin, 1991) has stressed the active processing of gender-related information from the time when the child discovers his or her own sex. According to this theory, once children have developed a gender label for their identity, they look increasingly to the environment for information with which to build and enrich the appropriate gender schema. Children select data which are consistent with their schemata (their organized mental representations of the world), and disregard data that are inconsistent with them, before selecting appropriate forms of behaviour. Early in life they acquire a sense about the gender-appropriateness of certain activities and if they encounter an adult who is engaged in some activity which is stereotypically associated with the opposite sex, they may fail to take the information on board (Carter and Levy, 1988). It has been suggested that gender schemata are concerned with the organization of information and affect cognitive processes such as memory, whereas gender constancy is associated with motivationally relevant variables such as activity choice and the distortion of gender-related information (Stagnor and Ruble, 1987).

While these cognitive approaches have been valuable in acknowledging that universal cognitive structures develop to promote the acquisition of information and the ordering of that information in a gendered way, they have little to say about the relationship between the child's development and the surrounding culture, or about why the sexes should be differentially valued. The environment is taken as given and it is not recognized that the construction of social-role knowledge is a collective activity. Hence the bases of gender differentiation may not lie solely in the child's mind but also in the child's socially organized experiences – the ways in which the culture organizes gender differentiation. It has been found that relationships between the strength of gender concepts and gender-typed preferences for behaviour and identity are not strong, except that boys have stronger stereotypes and greater resistance to opposite-sex activities, as is true of their fathers. It has been found to be very difficult to get children to change their minds, to dissuade them from subscribing to traditional stereotypes and especially to change their behaviour (Huston, 1985). Yet, if the child was constructing his/her reality from the social world around him/her, and that world had started to promote a changed message, then we would expect that schemata and hence stereotypes would be affected. This finding once more points to the complexities associated with studying gender development and a tacit acknowledgement that each perspective must not be viewed in glorious isolation but must be considered in a complementary and comparative fashion in order that an inclusive analysis can eventually be completed.

Conclusions

Whichever perspective is afforded greatest prominence, the research consistently demonstrates that powerful forces serve to shape and differentiate girls from boys. However, in the postmodern years of the late 1990s, will gender differentiation in childhood continue to persist in the face of considerable social changes? In a fascinating study, Sharpe (1994) revisited schools in the 1990s where she had first interviewed girls in the 1970s to record changes over two decades. While she found that in some ways the two generations were not so far apart, they also showed striking differences. For example, the 1990s girls were more assertive and were less willing to conform to a conventional 'feminine role'; they had a strong sense of equality and independence and they stressed the importance of obtaining education and pursuing a career. This is encouraging when placed alongside research cited above which shows that, in the context particularly of gender development, the relations between biology and social behaviour are dynamic and are capable of modification across time and place.

REFERENCES

Adams, S., Kuebli, J., Boyle, P.A. and Fivush, R. (1995). Gender differences in parent–child conversations about past emotions: a longitudinal investigation. *Sex Roles* **33(5/6)**, 309–23.

Alessandri, S.M. and Lewis, M. (1993). Parental evaluation and its relation to shame and pride in young children. *Sex Roles* **31(5/6)**, 335–43.

Barash, D.P. (1982). *Sociology and behavior.* 2nd edn. London: Heinemann.

Bem, S.L. (1993). *The lenses of gender: transforming the debate on sexual inequality.* New Haven, CT: Yale University Press.

Block, J.H. (1983). Differential premises arising from differential socialization of the sexes: some conjectures. *Child Development* **54**, 1335–54.

Boggiano, A.K. and Barrett, M. (1992). Gender differences in depression in children as a function of motivational orientation. *Sex Roles* **26(1/2)**, 11–17.

Carter, D.B. and Levy, G.D. (1988). Cognitive aspects of early sex-role development: the influence of gender-schemas on preschoolers' memories and preferences for sex-typed toys and activities. *Child Development* **59**, 782–92.

Chodorow, N. (1978). *The reproduction of mothering: psychoanalysis and the socialization of gender.* Berkeley: University of California Press.

Durkin, K. (1985). *Television, sex roles and children: a developmental social psychological account.* Milton Keynes and Philadelphia: Open University Press.

Durkin, K. (1986). Sex roles and the mass media. In Hargreaves, D.J. and Colley, A.M. (eds), *The Psychology of Sex Roles.* (pp. 201–14). London: Harper and Row.

Erikson, E.H. (1968/1974). Womanhood and the inner space. Reprinted in J. Strouse (ed.), *Women and analysis.* (pp. 291–319). New York: Grossman.

Fagot, B.I. (1978). The influence of sex of child on parental reactions to toddler children. *Child Development* **49**, 459–65.

Fagot, B.I. and Hagan, R. (1991). Observations of parent reactions to sex-stereotyped behaviours. *Child Development* **62**, 617–28.

Gilligan, C. (1982). *In a different voice: psychological theory and women's development.* Cambridge, MA: Harvard University Press.

Golombok, S. and Fivush, R. (1994). *Gender development.* Cambridge: Cambridge University Press.

Hoffman, L.W. and Kloska, D.D. (1995). Parents' gender-based attitudes towards marital roles and child rearing: development and validation of new measures. *Sex Roles* **32(5/6)**, 273–95.

Huston, A. (1985). The development of sex-typing: themes from recent research. *Developmental Review* **5**, 1–17.

Hutt, C. (1978). Sex-role differentiation in social development. In McGurk, H. (ed.), *Issues in childhood social development*. (pp. 171–202). London: Methuen.

Johnston, J. and Ettema, J.S. (1982). *Positive images: breaking stereotypes with children's television*. Beverly Hills and London: Sage.

Kohlberg, L. (1966). A cognitive-developmental analysis of children's sex-role concepts and attitudes. In Maccoby, E.E. (ed.), *The development of sex differences*. (pp. 82–173). Stanford, CA: Stanford University Press.

Lytton, H. and Romney, D.M. (1991). Parents' differential socialization of boys and girls: a meta-analysis. *Psychological Bulletin* **109**, 267–96.

Martin, C.L. (1991). The role of cognition in understanding gender effects. *Advances in Child Development and Behaviour* **23**, 113–49.

Masters, J.C., Ford, M.E., Arendt, R., Grotevant, H.D. and Clark, L.V. (1979). Modeling and labeling as integrated determinants of children's sex-typed imitative behaviour. *Child Development* **50**, 364–71.

Mazur, A. (1985). A biosocial model of status in face-to-face primate groups. *Social Forces* **64**, 377–402.

McConaghy, M.J. (1979). Gender performance and the genital basis of gender: stages in the development of constancy of gender identity. *Child Development* **50**, 1223–6.

Money, J. and Erhardt, A.A. (1972). *Man and woman, boy and girl*. Baltimore, MA: Johns Hopkins University Press.

Morgan, M. (1982). Television and adolescents' sex-role stereotypes: a longitudinal study. *Journal of Personality and Social Psychology* **43**, 947–55.

Ounstead, C. and Taylor, D.C. (1972). The Y-Chromosome message: a point of view. In Ounstead, C. and Taylor, D.C. (eds), *Gender differences: their ontogeny and significance*. (pp. 241–62). London: Churchill.

Rutenbeek, H.M. (ed.) (1967). *Psychoanalysis and female sexuality*. New Haven, CT: College and University Press.

Sayers, J. (1982). *Biological politics: feminist and anti-feminist perspectives*. London: Tavistock.

Sharpe, S. (1994). *Just like a girl: how girls learn to be women*. London: Penguin Books.

Sroufe, L.A. (1985). Attachment classification from the perspective of infant–carer relationships and infant temperament. *Child Development* **56**, 1614.

Stagnor, C. and Ruble, D.N. (1987). Development of gender role knowledge and gender constancy. In Liben, L.S. and Signorella, M.L. (eds), *Children's gender schemata: new directions for child development* (No. 38, pp. 5–22). San Francisco: Jossey-Bass.

Van Aken, M.A.G. and Riksen-Walraven, J.M. (1992). Parental support and the development of competence in children. *International Journal of Behavioural Development* **15(1)**, 101–123.

Welch, R.L., Huston-Stein, A., Wright, J.C. and Plehal, R. (1979). Subtle sex-role cues in children's commercials. *Journal of Communication* **29**, 202–9.

Whyte, J. (1974). Behavioural styles and teachers' estimations of intelligence. *Irish Journal of Education* **8(1/2)**, 62–77.

Wilson, E.O. (1975). *Sociobiology: the new synthesis*. Cambridge, MA: Harvard University Press.

Wilson, E.O. (1978). *On human nature*. Cambridge, MA: Cambridge University Press.

Further reading

Brannon, L. (1996). *Gender: psychological perspectives.* London: Allyn and Bacon.

Feldman, S. and Elliott, G. (1990). *At the threshold: the developing adolescent.* Cambridge, MA: Harvard University Press.

Golombok, S. and Fivush, R. (1994). *Gender development.* Cambridge, MA: Cambridge University Press.

Lytton, H. and Romney, D.M. (1991). Parents' differential socialization of boys and girls: a meta-analysis. *Psychological Bulletin* **109**, 267–96.

Sharpe, S. (1994). *Just like a girl: how girls learn to be women.* London: Penguin Books.

Discussion questions

1. Thinking back to your time at primary school, or even earlier, to what extent was gender significant in terms of your choice of friends?
2. Again thinking of your childhood, around the age of 11 years, try to remember your favourite toys. How sex-typed were these toys? In more general terms, how sex-typed was your play at that age?
3. Can you recall incidents where your parent(s) or significant others punished you for 'gender-inappropriate behaviour'? Were these sanctions more or less severe for girls than for boys?
4. How significant do you believe television to be in reinforcing traditional gender roles among young children?
5. In terms of your own childrearing practices, either present or planned, to what extent do you or will you endeavour to teach or condition gendered behaviour?

9

ADOLESCENCE

Carol Curry

INTRODUCTION

Traditionally, the period of life known as adolescence has been characterized by what Freud termed *Sturm und Drang* (storm and stress), a time when young people are seen to be breaking away from the strictures of parental influence and values, and moving towards autonomy and the establishment of their own identity. Over recent years, this characterization has been challenged, with an alternative formulation charting an altogether less stormy passage through adolescence. For many adolescents, social competence as an independent adult may be attained not through unavoidable conflict and acrimony but within the context of a secure family environment where exploration of alternative ideas, identities and behaviour is allowed and actively encouraged (Barber and Buehler, 1996).

In this respect, 'normal' adolescence can be viewed as a period of positive development rather than a time of turmoil. At the same time, this is not to deny that for some adolescents, problems do arise, and there is a considerable literature devoted to the problems of adolescence. These problems include depression (Petersen et al., 1993), substance abuse (Leventhal and Keeshan, 1993), unplanned pregnancies and sexually transmitted diseases (Brooks-Gunn and Paikoff, 1993), and even the growing problem of suicide. In Western societies, while some adolescents may display affective disturbances, it is a relatively small minority who will show clinical depression or report 'inner turmoil' (Compas, et al., 1995). Instead, the majority worry about everyday issues such as school and examination performance, finding employment, family and social relationships, self-image, conflicts with authority, and their future generally (Gallagher et al., 1992). Hence, it is on these issues that the chapter will tend to focus, paying particular attention to gender in relation to identity formation, parental relationships and relationships with peers.

Defining adolescence

Various definitions of adolescence have been proposed over the years but most focus on the biological changes that occur to make reproduction possible, normally between the ages of 10 and 17 years. Research on this period of the life-cycle has moved from using main-effect models (emphasizing basic biological change) towards transactional models which consider the relationship of pubertal development to behaviour, cognition and social relationships. For example, research has considered hormonal changes associated with mood state and behaviour (Paikoff and Brooks-Gunn, 1991), and the timing of the onset of puberty in relation to both peer-group acceptance and emotional adjustment (Petersen et al., 1991), and parent–child relationships (Holmbeck and Hill, 1991).

In terms of basic biological development, gender differences during adolescence are marked. Boys typically reach puberty two years after girls and, in behavioural terms, there is a similar two-year lag between boys and girls in shifting from same-sex towards opposite-sex relationships (Abrams, 1989). More generally, issues such as attractiveness, desirability and sexuality have been shown to be less salient for boys during adolescence than girls. Overall, girls tend to achieve developmental milestones earlier than boys, but their earlier maturity is not an artefact related to superior intellectual abilities. Instead it seems likely to reflect the fact that adolescent girls, for whatever reason, are less egocentric and less concrete in their thinking, and generally are more self-reflective and self-aware (Cohn, 1991).

The search for identity

Alongside the obvious biological changes, cognitive changes are clearly occurring during adolescence. The emphasis in thought processes transfers from the real to the possible, with more consideration of abstraction characterized by 'if . . . then' questions and a developing sense of self (Elkind, 1967). Much research has been concerned with the process of identity formation during this stage of life, as the establishment of a firm sense of ego identity is seen as providing a crucial bridge between childhood and adulthood, and beyond that, the basis for the successful formation of stable intimate relationships.

Erikson (1968) has suggested that the fifth of his eight stages of development (which coincides with adolescence) centres around a functional identity crisis. The adolescent moves towards the development of his/her own ego identity (the integration of new physical appearance, abilities, feelings and roles of childhood, together with a consistent identity as an adult) but is simultaneously battling with identity diffusion (where a firm identity is never attained because s/he is so overwhelmed by changes and possibilities). Identity development has been found to be strongly and consistently related to the capacity to experience and resolve this identity crisis and become 'identity achieved' (Allen et al., 1994). According to Erikson, some adolescents avoid this identity crisis by 'foreclosure', that is unquestioning and ongoing acceptance of parental values and beliefs (Marcia, 1996). Foreclosure has been found to be most frequent in relation to sex-role attitudes, vocational choice and religious beliefs while in the area of political beliefs, identity diffusion is more apparent (Noller and Callan, 1991).

Self-concepts at this time shift progressively from the concrete (where I live; what I look like; what I do) to the abstract (my beliefs; my attitudes; my personality characteristics), producing a picture of the self which is differentiated and unique. Not surprisingly, adolescents have been found to maintain a complex web of selves to help accommodate the complexities of modern living – with different 'selves' featuring in the family, at school or with friends. According to the social identity perspective on identity formation, identity is made up of both the personal and the social, and the salience of either shifts according to context (Turner, 1987). As the adolescent moves between these different social worlds, so clearly different facets of self and of identity will take precedence.

In terms of gender differences, the core of identity itself has been found to differ between the genders, with male identity centring on 'individual competence and knowledge' while female identity centres on 'relating to others' (Kahn et al., 1985). Consistency in terms of gender-role identity at this time is associated with higher levels of self-esteem (Benson and Mullins, 1990), and the basis of self-esteem may also be gender differentiated. Women are more likely to have a socio-centric or connected self-schema in which relationships with other people are crucial elements, while men are more likely to have an individualistic, distinct schema with 'other' set apart from the self (Josephs et al., 1992). These differences are thought to arise from different sources:

- from boys' early experience of having to differentiate themselves from their mother, while girls experience similarity and continuance with their mother
- from an imbalance in social power, with women having to be attuned to dominant others who control their fate
- from a difference in social roles assigned to men and women from birth which gives rise to different concerns and commitments (connecting and relating for women, separating and individuating for men).

Therefore it follows that when adolescents are considering their future, girls and boys have different cognitions about their most probable self and most promising selves, and in turn these may influence their career aspirations. For example, given sex-role expectations, the career choices made by young women may be underpinned with concern for a wider range of life domains than those made by boys (Curry et al., 1994), with girls attaching greater importance to good interpersonal relationships and the family while boys emphasize the importance of their own social prestige and career (Macek, 1994).

RELATIONSHIPS WITH PARENTS: TOWARDS AUTONOMY

One component of adolescent development, and the concomitant search for identity, is a move towards autonomy. This requires a process of individuation/separation from, and a re-appraisal of, relationships with parents. Steinberg and Silverberg (1986) give the following examples of how autonomy has been interpreted:

- a growing sense of detachment
- the outcome of individuation
- resistance to peer or parental pressure
- a subjective sense of independence
- self-reported confidence in decision-making and self-governance
- the use of principles or independent reasoning in moral, political and social problem-solving.

Part of the problem for both parents and their children in coping with adolescence in the 1990s is perceived to be an absence of 'rites of passage' in Western society, with a related lack of consensus as to where adolescence begins and ends, and precisely what are adolescents' rights, privileges and responsibilities (Erdheim, 1995). The term 'maturity gap' has been used to describe the incongruity of achieving biological maturity at adolescence without simultaneously being awarded adult status. Indeed, having personal discretion in decision-making fosters positive psychological development in adolescence just as it does in adulthood (Owens et al., 1996). For example, it has been suggested that delinquency in adolescence could actually be adaptive as a way of facilitating self-definition and of expressing autonomy (Compas et al., 1995). Furthermore, if adolescents fail to negotiate new relationships with parents, and their parents are highly critical and rejecting, then adolescents are likely to adopt a negative identity. In addition, parents who rated their own experience of adolescence as stormy and stressful reported more conflict in their relationships with their children and were less satisfied with their family (Scheer and Unger, 1995).

It should not be forgotten that during the period of adolescence, the adolescent's parents are also going through a time of transition, reappraising their life goals, career and family ambitions, and assessing whether they have been able to live up to their expectations as parents. Thus parents may also require the security of a close and supportive family, and the potential for interpersonal conflict within the family unit at this time should not be underestimated. Where such conflict does occur, it has been found to be more strongly associated with negative mother–son relationships than with same-gender dyads (Osborne and Fincham, 1996).

Communication

The quality of communication between parents and adolescents is crucial in maintaining good family relationships, but unfortunately it is one aspect of the adolescent–parent relationship which is at greatest risk during this time. Barnes and Olson (1985) view communication as one of the three major dimensions in the circumplex model of marital and family systems, acting to aid cohesion and adaptability. Families where communication is good are often close and loving and have a more flexible approach to family problem-solving. Indeed the quality of family communication has been associated with successful adolescent identity formation and role-taking ability, and with helping adolescents' individuation from the family, along with higher levels of moral maturity (Walker and Taylor, 1991).

Areas of conflict

If the adolescent is not to suffer foreclosure, in Marcia's terms, then some questioning of, and possible rejection of, parental authority must occur. However, research suggests that there may be a mutual shying away from topics which have the potential to cause the greatest degree of conflict, topics such as sex, drugs, religion and politics. Instead, conflicts with parents tend to be persistent and arise over the everyday details of family life, including schoolwork, home chores, disobedience, choice of activities, social life and friends, fighting with and teasing siblings, failure to finish tasks, and personal hygiene (Barber, 1994).

Changing perceptions of power

A power struggle between adolescents and their parents can arise from the parents' desire for authority alongside their child's desire to maintain jurisdiction over his/her life (Allen et al., 1996). Style of parenting and parental use of power in the family has been found to be a crucial determinant in identity formation and well-being of adolescents (Wentzel and Feldman, 1996). Authoritarian and coercive parenting often results in adolescents who are less likely to explore identity alternatives, and are more likely to adopt external rather than internal moral standards and to have lower self-confidence and self-esteem. Authoritative parents who expect mature behaviour while setting clear standards, encouraging independence, individuality and openness, and recognizing the rights of both parents and children have been found to be more effective than either permissive or authoritarian parents (Radziszewska et al., 1996). The effects of authoritative parenting appear to extend beyond the home, also influencing the quality and behaviour of peer relationships (Fletcher et al., 1995).

Interestingly, adolescents tend to report fairly high levels of both personal well-being and affection for their parents, with mothers generally held in higher regard than fathers (Paterson et al., 1994). Yet, with hindsight, individuals tend to look back on their adolescence as a time of dissatisfaction and disrupted relations with parents. In other studies, adolescents have been found to present a more negative picture of their family than do their parents, possibly because they are less concerned with creating a good impression and therefore perhaps rate the family more accurately. Absence does appear to make the heart grow fonder, as adolescents who have left home for college express increased affection, communication, satisfaction and independence in comparison with those who have remained in the parental home.

As discussed earlier, males and females have different bases for their identity, with male identity based more on instrumental competence and knowledge about the external world and female identity based around interpersonal concerns. Accordingly, adolescent males spend less time with parents and an increasing amount of time engaged in hobbies, sports, work and school. In contrast, females base their identity on interpersonal competence, which is more easily and appropriately achieved through interaction with peers rather than with parents. Montemayor (1986) concluded from his research that adolescents prefer to be with peers because peers form egalitarian relationships that centre around age-specific interests, making this type of association considerably more attractive than the hierarchical, task-oriented relationships that adolescents have with their middle-aged parents.

Gender differences are also evident in communication styles involving adolescents and their parents. For example, there is better communication between daughters and mothers than between daughters and fathers (Noller and Callan, 1991) and daughters reveal more personal information while sons disclose more about work and their attitudes and opinions. In addition, sons often experience greater conflict with their mothers than with their fathers, but both sons and daughters enjoy greater openness with their mothers than with their fathers (Field et al., 1995).

Parents' expectations about the division of labour, rules of behaviour and beliefs about their adolescents have likewise been shown to be related to gender. Indeed, adolescence has been characterized as a developmental phase involving a certain rigidity in beliefs about gender-appropriate roles and an intolerance of deviations from the norm, especially among females. Just as appropriate sex-typed behaviour is reinforced by parents of younger children, the family continues to be the main provider of sex-role stereotypes during adolescence. Parents, for example, have been found to criticize adolescent boys for being lazy, impulsive, unsociable and having undesirable friends, whereas girls are criticized for being disobedient, foolish, unappreciative, quarrelsome and stubborn. Additionally, parents' perceptions of their child's ability in various domains are gender-related, and these beliefs influence the children's self-concepts about their own abilities (Updergraff et al., 1996).

Adolescents too have been found to hold stereotypic views of their parents. Females tend to rate their mothers as significantly higher on femininity, emotionality and awareness of the feelings of others. Mothers are also perceived to have a greater involvement with parenting (Paulson and Sputa, 1996) and in particular when dealing with behavioural problems (Phares, 1993). Fathers are perceived to be more independent and better able to cope with pressure. Given these traditional belief structures, social learning theory would suggest that adolescents may actually be less likely to challenge stereotypical views of male and female gender roles than adults.

Adolescent girls are clearly aware of the dual expectation of having a career and carrying the main responsibilities for homes and families (Greene and Wheatley, 1994). Teenage girls are still socialized into accepting the main household burden by doing more housework than boys, even when they are preparing for higher education courses and future careers. Sex roles are also emphasized through the segregation of tasks by sex, with adolescent males more likely to take responsibility for chores such as mowing the lawn, washing the car or taking out the rubbish while girls tend to do more general house cleaning (Peters, 1994).

Peer relationships

As adolescents' relationships with parents are changing, so peer relationships become increasingly important and often seem to exert an even greater influence on adolescents' attitudes and behaviour than relationships with parents, and this is especially true for females (Urberg et al., 1995). It has been proposed that adolescents turn to peers for the companionship and emotional support which they would welcome from their parents but which is not forthcoming. However, a more common argument is that continual parent–adolescent bickering eventually leads adolescents to accept the norms, values and standards of peers and to reject those of parents. As already mentioned, not all researchers propose conflict-based models of separation from parents. An alternative is a model of synergy between parent and peer systems during adolescence, where the role of the family is not replaced by peers but rather the adolescent moves quite comfortably between the two (Brown et al., 1993).

Conclusions

While not ignoring the considerable research which has charted the problems of adolescence, for a great many young people the teenage years can be looked upon as a time of positive change and growth. Development from childhood through adolescence to adulthood is best achieved within a supportive family which encourages the exploration of alternative ideas and behaviour, with adolescents seeking to establish a separate identity at the same time as negotiating changes in the power balance between themselves and their parents. Gender differences in adolescence are evident in the earlier maturity of girls, not just in biological terms but also in terms of cognition, affect and behaviour. The basis of identity has been found to differ by gender, with females' identity centred on issues relating to others, while males' identity is based on issues of individual competence and knowledge.

Gender differences are also apparent in the relationships between parents and their adolescents and as regards parental expectations – for example, in terms of the segregation of household chores and tasks. Peer relationships become of greater importance during adolescence, but there is also evidence that adolescents, rather than rejecting parents, often move easily between family and peer groups, although those aspects of self which are presented in each context may be quite different. Finally, whether adolescence is best represented as a sea of tranquillity or a storm of conflict appears to depend crucially on a combination of personal and contextual variables, within which gender and family relationships are central. At the very least, while conflict between life domains and value systems is inevitable during this time of change, this conflict may just as easily be seen as a positive force for good as a negative force driving the adolescent from the family nest.

References

Abrams, D. (1989). Differential association: social developments in gender identity and intergroup relations during adolescence. In S. Skevington and D. Barker (eds), *The social identity of women.* (pp. 59–83). London: Sage Publications.

Allen, J.P., Hauser, S.T., Bell, K.L. and O'Connor, T.G. (1994). Longitudinal assessment of autonomy and relatedness in adolescent–family interactions as predictors of adolescent ego development and self-esteem. *Child Development* **65(1)**, 179–94.

Allen, J.P., Hauser, S.T., O'Connor, T.G., Bell, K.L. and Eickholt, C. (1996). The connection of observed hostile family conflict to adolescents' developing autonomy and relatedness with parents. *Development and Psychopathology* **8(2)**, 425–42.

Barber, B.K. (1994). Cultural, family and personal contexts of parent–adolescent conflict. *Journal of Marriage and the Family* **56(2)**, 375–86.

Barber, B.K. and Buehler, C. (1996). Family cohesion and enmeshment: different constructs, different effects. *Journal of Marriage and the Family* **58(2)**, 433–41.

Barnes, H.L. and Olson, D.H. (1985). Parent–adolescent communication and the circumplex model. *Child Development* **56**, 438–47.

Benson, D.E. and Mullins, E. (1990). Consistency of role identity and self-esteem. *National Journal of Sociology* **4(2)**, 158–73.

Brooks-Gunn, J. and Paikoff R.L. (1993). Sex is a gamble, kissing is a game: adolescent sexuality and health promotion. In Millstein, S.G., Petersen, A.C. and Nightingale, E.O. (eds), *Promoting the health of adolescents: new directions for the twenty-first century* (pp. 180–208). New York: Oxford University Press.

Brown, B.B., Mounts, N., Lamborn, S.D. and Steinberg, L. (1993). Parenting practices and peer group affiliation in adolescence. *Child Development* **64**, 467–82.

Cohn, L.D. (1991). Sex differences in the course of personality development: a meta-analysis. *Psychological Bulletin* **109(2)**, 252–66.

Compas, B.E., Hinden, B.R. and Gerhardt, C.A. (1995). Adolescent development: pathways and processes of risk and resilience. *Annual Review of Psychology* **46**, 265–93.

Curry, C., Trew, K., Turner, I. and Hunter, J. (1994). The effect of life domains on girls' possible selves. *Adolescence* **29**, 133–50.

Elkind, D. (1967). Egocentrism in adolescence. *Child Development* **38**, 1025–34.

Erdheim, M. (1995). Is there an end of adolescence? Reflections from an ethnopsychoanalytic perspective. *Praxis der Kinderpsychologie und Kinderpsychiatrie* **44(3)**, 81–5.

Erikson, E.H. (1968). *Identity: youth and crisis.* London: Faber and Faber.

Field, T., Lang, C., Yando, R. and Bendell, D. (1995). Adolescents' intimacy with parents and friends. *Adolescence* **30**, 133–40.

Fletcher, A.C., Darling, D.E., Steinberg, L. and Dornbusch, S.M. (1995). The company they keep: relation of adolescents' adjustment and behaviour to their friends' perceptions of authoritative parenting in the social network. *Developmental Psychology* **31(2)**, 300–10.

Gallagher, M., Millar, R., Hargie, O. and Ellis, R. (1992). The personal and social worries of adolescents in Northern Ireland: results of a survey. *British Journal of Guidance and Counselling* **30(3)**, 274–90.

Greene, A.L. and Wheatley, S.M. (1994). I've got a lot to do and I don't think I'll have the time: gender differences in late adolescents' narratives of the future. *Journal of Youth and Adolescence* **21(6)**, 667–86.

Holmbeck, G.N. and Hill, J.P. (1991). Conflictive engagement, positive affect, and menarche in families with seventh grade girls. *Child Development* **62**, 1030–48.

Josephs, R.A., Markus, H. and Tarforodi, R.W. (1992). Gender differences in the source of self esteem. *Journal of Personality and Social Psychology* **63**, 391–402.

Kahn, S., Zimmerman, G., Csikszentmihalyi, M. and Getsels, J.W. (1985). Relations between identity in young adulthood and intimacy at midlife. *Journal of Personality and Social Psychology* **49**, 1316–422.

Leventhal, H. and Keeshan, P. (1993). Promoting healthy alternatives to substance abuse. In Millstein, S.G., Petersen, A.C. and Nightingale, E.O. (eds), *Promoting the health of adolescents: new directions for the twenty-first century.* (pp. 260–84). New York: Oxford University Press.

Macek, P. (1994). Future expectations and self-esteem of adolescents. *Ceskoslovenska Psychologie* **38(6)**, 489–502.

Marcia, J.E. (1996). Development and validation of ego identity status. *Journal of Personality and Social Psychology* **3**, 551–8.

Montemayor, R. (1986). Family variation in parent–adolescent storm and stress. *Journal of Adolescent Research* **1**, 15–31.

Noller, P. and Callan, V.J. (1991). *The adolescent in the family.* London: Routledge.

Osborne, L.N. and Fincham, F.D. (1996) Marital conflict, parent–child relationships, and child adjustment – does gender matter? *Journal of Developmental Psychology* **42(1)**, 48–75.

Owens, T.J., Morimer, J.T. and Finch, M.D. (1996). Self-determination as a source of self-esteem in adolescence. *Social Forces* **74(4)**, 1377–404.

Paikoff, R.L. and Brooks-Gunn, J. (1991). So do parent–child relationships change during puberty? *Psychological Bulletin* **110**, 47–66.

Paterson, J.E., Field, J. and Pryor, J. (1994). Adolescents' perceptions of their attachment relationships with their mothers, fathers and friends. *Journal of Youth and Adolescence* **23(5)**, 579–600.

Paulson, S.E. and Sputa, C.L. (1996). Patterns of parenting during adolescence – perceptions of adolescents and parents. *Adolescence* **31**, 369–81.

Peters, J.F. (1994). Gender socialization of adolescents in the home – research and discussion. *Adolescence* **29**, 913–34.

Petersen, A.C., Compas, B.E., Brooks-Gunn, J., Stemmler, M., Ey, S. and Grant, K.E. (1993). Depression during adolescence. *American Psychologist* **48**, 155–68.

Petersen, A.C., Sarigiani, P.A. and Kennedy, R.E. (1991). Adolescent depression: why more girls? *Journal of Youth and Adolescence* **20**, 247–71.

Phares, V. (1993). Perceptions of mother's and father's responsibility for children's behaviour. *Sex Roles* **29(11/12)**, 839–51.

Radziszewska, B., Richardson, J.L., Dent, C.W. and Flay, B.R. (1996). Parenting style and adolescent depressive symptoms, smoking and academic achievement – ethnic, gender and SES differences. *Journal of Behavioural Medicine* **19(3)**, 289–305.

Scheer, S.D. and Unger, D.G. (1995). Parents' perceptions of their adolescence – implications for parent–youth conflict and family satisfaction. *Psychological Reports* **76(1)**, 131–6.

Steinberg, L. and Silverberg, S.B. (1986). The vicissitude of autonomy in early adolescence. *Child Development* **57**, 841–51.

Turner, J.C. (1987). *Rediscovering the social group: a self-categorisation theory.* Oxford: Blackwell.

Updergraff, K.A., McHale, S.M. and Crouter, A.C. (1996). Gender roles in marriage – what do they mean for girls' and boys' school achievement. *Journal of Youth and Adolescence* **25(1)**, 73–88.

Urberg, K.A., Degirmencioglu, S.M., Tolson, J.M. and Halliday-Scher, K. (1995). The structure of adolescent peer networks. *Developmental Psychology* **31(4)**, 540–7.

Walker, L.J. and Taylor, J.H. (1991). Family interactions and the development of moral reasoning. *Child Development* **62**, 264–83.

Wentzel, K.R. and Feldman, S.S. (1996). Relations of cohesion and power in family dyads to social and emotional adjustment during early adolescence. *Journal of Research on Adolescence* **6(2)**, 225–44.

Further reading

Barber, B.K. (1994). Cultural, family and personal contexts of parent–adolescent conflict. *Journal of Marriage and the Family* **56(2)**, 375–86.

Compas, B.E., Hinden, B.R. and Gerhardt, C.A. (1995). Adolescent development: pathways and processes of risk and resilience. *Annual Review of Psychology* **46**, 265–93.

Fletcher, A.C., Darling, D.E., Steinberg, L. and Dornbusch, S.M. (1995). The company they keep: relation of adolescents' adjustment and behaviour to their friends' perceptions of authoritative parenting in the social network. *Developmental Psychology* **31(2)**, 300–10.

Josephs, R.A., Markus, H. and Tarforodi, R.W. (1992). Gender differences in the source of self-esteem. *Journal of Personality and Social Psychology* **63**, 391–402.

Noller, P. and Callan, V.J. (1991). *The adolescent in the family.* London: Routledge.

Discussion questions

1. Thinking back to your own adolescence, would you naturally characterize that time as a period of *Sturm und Drang*? If not, how would you characterize it and how different would it have been if you had been born a member of the opposite sex?
2. Drawing comparisons with members of the opposite gender, how would you describe the development of your own gendered identity during adolescence?

3. At what age were you aware of making plans about your future? Which life domains did you take into account when making those plans and how significant was your gender identity?
4. How significant are peers and parents in attitude formation and change during adolescence?

10

EDUCATION

Ann Colley

Introduction

Two areas within education have been the primary focus of interest driven by concern that women and girls may be presented with different opportunities to those enjoyed by their male peers. The first of these is in the choice of pathway through the educational system. Girls' and boys' subject choices and enrolments vary according to the perceived femininity or masculinity of particular disciplines, and, in the case of girls, much attention has been focused upon their lower interest and enrolments in mathematics and physical sciences in particular. Related to such issues, a second broad area of interest has been in the educational contexts and practices which encourage or discourage female achievement. Issues such as single-sex versus mixed-sex teaching, classroom interactions, curriculum design and delivery, and methods of assessment have all been found relevant to gender differences in choice or achievement in particular subject areas.

Theoretical perspectives

The theoretical perspectives which have been brought to bear on this area are those which explain differences in stereotypes of male and female behaviour, and stereotypes of academic subject areas and their occupational links. Two main approaches from developmental psychology, social learning theory (Mischel, 1966; 1970; Bandura, 1977) and cognitive developmental theory (Kohlberg, 1966) provide explanations of how our stereotypes of masculinity and femininity are learned and enacted. Both place considerable emphasis upon the socialization process. The former stresses the centrality of positive and negative reinforcement of acceptable and unacceptable gender-role behaviour through interactions with parents and significant others, whereas the latter places emphasis on the interaction between the individual and the environment while the individual actively attempts to form internal representations of information crucial to behaving appropriately in social contexts.

Approaches in social psychology, which emphasize the importance of information present in our social environment and interactions with others, provide a basis for understanding the content of our internal representations of gender-related behaviour. The social role theory expounded by Eagly (1987) is particularly helpful in understanding the link between perceptions of subject areas in education and later occupational roles. Eagly proposed that social roles and the abilities and attributes linked to them provide expectations of male and female behaviour. The effects of observed social roles upon stereotypes of normative masculine and feminine behaviour are inevitably strongly related to reproductive roles and the division of labour between females as caregivers and males as providers. While this strict division of labour is increasingly less prevalent, the assumption still remains that women are the main caregivers, and the nurturant attributes associated with such roles are ascribed to them. The content of stereotypes of masculinity and femininity is the foundation for measures of gender-role identity such as those of Bem (1974), and Spence and Helmreich (1978). It is also reflected in the attributes necessary for enactment of occupational roles associated with a predominance of males or females, which stress instrumental or agentic versus nurturant or communal qualities. In an educational context it forms the basis for perceptions of academic subject areas as masculine or feminine, related to the degree to which they are about things or about people.

It would not be appropriate to discuss the theoretical background to differences in the educational pathways taken by women and men without mentioning possible biological bases for stereotypes of masculine and feminine attributes and abilities. Eagly makes the point that any influence of biological differences is translated through the social environment and is necessarily indirect. Nevertheless, the evidence of sex differences in cognitive abilities (for example, Halpern, 1992) has been used to explain differences in choice and in achievement. There is a growing and substantial literature on sex differences in spatial, mathematical and verbal skills, the most recent contributions to which are meta-analyses of empirical studies (see Chapter 6). The conclusions of the meta-analytic studies have challenged the size of the sex differences assumed on the basis of piecemeal studies, but have themselves been subject to criticisms of methodology and of conclusions concerning the practical significance of effects of particular sizes (for example, see Hyde and Plant, 1995).

On a common-sense basis it is clear that the link between performance on subscales of psychometric tests of cognitive abilities and performance in academic subject areas is far from straightforward, and male and female public examination results indicate that the basis for academic choices and performance requires a more complex analysis than simply relating them to psychometric test scores. The effects of gender apparently vary at different stages of the educational system. The picture emerging from the UK National Curriculum Assessments (SATs) at the ages of 7, 11 and 14 years is somewhat mixed; girls have performed better than boys in English and in some areas of mathematics but boys are ahead in science. Girls have outperformed boys in national academic qualifications at the age of 16 years since the introduction of the GCSE in the 1980s (Elwood, 1995; Arnot et al., 1996), with the 1995 results showing that girls equal or better boys' performance in the majority of subjects. The picture again changes at 18 years, when A-level results have been better for boys.

It would be difficult to explain such data without examining the role of educational factors including the nature of the curriculum and assessments used at these educational stages. For example, A-levels and SATs are more traditional in their assessment; A-levels use examinations of various kinds and SATs use standardized testing procedures. GCSEs, however, use a variety of assessment methods, with a tendency to use more continuous assessment and fewer multiple choice tests than A-levels, and multiple choice tests have been found to have a gender bias in favour of boys (Murphy, 1982).

Any debate concerning gender inevitably has a political context which drives research questions. With respect to the apparent tendency for females to feel excluded from parts of the school curriculum, feminist approaches have been significant in setting part of the agenda for studies in a variety of areas, from the study of sex differences in cognitive abilities through to observations of interactions within the classroom and the hidden curriculum which undervalues girls' performance in male-dominated areas. Given the diverse backgrounds and research traditions in social psychology and beyond from which feminist psychologists are drawn (see Chapter 3), it is not surprising that they do not adopt a uniform approach to understanding gender differences in general, and those relevant to educational issues in particular (Eagly, 1995; Hyde and Plant, 1995). Feminist empiricists (for example, Hyde and Linn, 1988) have used conventional empirical and statistical methods, including the meta-analyses already mentioned in Chapter 6, to investigate the robustness of reported sex differences, and have attempted to demonstrate that these are weaker than previously reported, or are non-existent. The political impetus underlying this approach is that unless sex differences are significant and relevant to participation and performance in male-dominated areas in education and occupations, then strategies for equal access must have a high priority. In effect the approach is attempting to counter the 'differences are female deficiencies' position, in which differences can be used to the disadvantage of women.

A second approach which has emerged from feminist writing more generally (for example, Gilligan, 1982) seeks to demonstrate that stereotypical attributes of women can be at least as valuable as those of men in male-dominated areas; for example, in organizational contexts a person-oriented approach to management may serve better than one which stresses competition (see Chapter 12). This latter approach seeks to restructure the environments in which women are under-represented in order that their participation is encouraged and valued. A third approach has emphasized the historical, cultural and political context of the notion of gender, stressing the variations in its meaning and questioning the acceptance that gender is a stable universal category. This postmodernist approach views gender as socially constructed, and challenges the objectivity of scientific empirical approaches because they too are influenced by dominant cultural and political perspectives. Using qualitative methodologies, it therefore seeks to understand how accepted truths about gender are constructed, and how these are used within education (for example, Walden and Walkerdine, 1982).

All of these theoretical approaches have contributed to our understanding of how choices for women in education are moulded and constrained. The remainder of this chapter will focus upon studies of academic subject stereotyping and choice, and the learning environment, in order to provide an overview of some of the most important issues which bear upon the educational paths taken by males and females.

CONTEMPORARY RESEARCH

Subject choice and preferences

Empirical studies over the last two decades have consistently found that the pattern of female academic subject preferences differs from that of males (for example, Weinreich-Haste, 1979; 1981; Colley et al., 1994a; 1994b). At secondary school girls show stronger preferences than boys for English, modern languages and religious education, while the reverse is true for mathematics, the physical sciences, physical education and craft subjects such as woodwork and metalwork. Enrolments on courses, not surprisingly, show the same pattern as reported preferences. For example, the male:female ratio for enrolment for physics A-level in 1995 was roughly 4:1, while that for English, French and German was roughly 3:7. Applications for university courses show a similar pattern.

Interestingly, lack of female interest in physical science and mathematics has attracted substantially more attention than the lack of male interest in English and modern languages. Both physics and modern languages are regarded as important subject areas for employment, but problematic for recruitment. Inevitably the educational agenda is heavily influenced by political considerations, and the impetus for greater female participation in male-dominated educational and occupational areas, prompted by the rise of feminism, continues to attract attention and drive research effort. The large literature on female under-representation in physical science, mathematics and technology encompasses a variety of approaches from traditional empirical quantitative research to qualitative analyses which have highlighted the importance both of our stereotypes of subject areas and of the learning environment.

Stereotypes of academic subject areas

Weinreich-Haste (1981) examined the stereotypes of secondary school subjects using pupils' ratings on seven bipolar scales: feminine–masculine, boring–interesting, simple–complicated, useless–useful, easy–difficult, involves thought–involves feelings, about people–about things. The feminine–masculine ratings of different subjects reflected the preferences of girls and boys found more generally. More interestingly, the inter-correlations between the scales throw some light on the stereotypes held by male and female pupils. For girls, masculine, difficult and complicated inter-correlated while for boys, masculine, interesting and about things inter-correlated. Weinreich-Haste's findings have more recently been replicated by Archer and Macrae (1991).

What do these stereotypes tell us? Archer and Macrae suggested that in particular they confirm the notion that masculine areas are perceived as being of higher status. The most striking link is with occupational stereotypes. Technical jobs associated with machines, or those associated with complex financial or economic systems, are dominated by men, while people-oriented occupations, particularly in the caring professions, are dominated by women. With a few exceptions, there is a clear status and salary differential between the two. The career aspirations of secondary school pupils have been found to reflect the status quo (Kelly, 1989) and mirror the traditional domestic caregiver roles of women and provider roles of men.

The learning environment

Gender stereotypes have a powerful effect upon our perceptions of ourselves and others, but like any other stored knowledge are used only when relevant, either because they are invoked by some salient feature of the environment or because they are relevant to our current motives and goals (Bodenhausen and Wyer, 1985; Deaux and Major, 1987). One determinant of the degree of salience of gender in educational environments may be the presence of one or both sexes in the classroom. Single-sex teaching most commonly takes place in secondary schools with a single-sex intake, but educators at a variety of levels have also experimented with single-sex classrooms or single-sex teaching groups within coeducational schools.

In evaluating the effects of single-sex schools upon the choices and achievement of pupils, a further agenda emerges in addition to gender politics, that of educational reform, which of course has its own cultural and political context. The debate on the benefits of single-sex schools for girls, boys, both or neither has continued since the 1960s, being revitalized in England recently by the publication of school league tables which show single-sex schools to achieve the best public examination performance. There is an obvious confound in using these tables to support any position on the issue, however, because the high-achieving schools also tend to select their intake on the basis of academic performance, usually at age 11 years. Within the state system single-sex schools have tended to represent remnants of the single-sex grammar school system, while the majority of mixed ability comprehensive schools are coeducational. Educational research on the relative benefits of single-sex versus mixed education has covered social development, academic performance and subject preferences. Initial findings from the work of Dale (1969; 1971; 1974) stressed the social benefits of a mixed-sex social environment. Boys appeared to derive benefits, including better academic performance, while there appeared to be little effect of school type upon girls. The detail of these findings has since been challenged, however, and methodological problems, particularly that of controlling for variables relating to the selection of pupils or other factors relating to school intake has dogged comparisons of single-sex and mixed education here, in the USA and in Australia (for example, Lee and Bryk, 1989; Marsh, 1989).

One issue which has continued to attract attention has been the academic achievement of girls in mixed classrooms in subject areas stereotyped as masculine. Comparisons of subject preferences in single-sex and mixed schools have indicated that greater gender polarization occurs in mixed-sex environments, such that preferences conform more readily to gender stereotypes (for example, Ormerod, 1975; Stables, 1990). The single-sex classroom may, therefore, offer greater opportunity for girls to acquire confidence in subjects such as physical science, mathematics and technology. Lawrie and Brown (1992) compared the perceptions of subjects and A-level enrolments in the two school types and obtained findings consistent with the notion of less gender polarization in single-sex schools. Enjoyment of mathematics was lower among girls in the mixed school in comparison with both their male peers and girls in the single-sex school. Enrolments for A-level mathematics for girls in the single-sex school were double that of those in the mixed school, while those for English were strikingly lower. Such trends showing less gender stereotyping in the single-sex school were also present in the enrolments of the boys.

The tendency for less gender stereotyping of preferences to occur in a single-sex environment can be at least partially explained in terms of the lack of salience of issues relating to gender when only one sex is present. Comparisons of self with others within the classroom will be less likely to include expectations of relative ability relating to gender expectations, although broader expectations of what males and females do will inevitably be present. These expectations may in some situations be extremely important, so that the variation in the salience of gender in the environment reduces in importance. Colley et al. (1994b) compared the subject preference rankings of single-sex and coeducational school pupils in two age groups: 11–12 years and 15–16 years. There was clear evidence of gender polarization among the older pupils in coeducational schools, but this was not present in the data from the younger pupils. The explanation offered was in terms of the strengthening of gender stereotypes of behaviour in the older group, who were more likely to spend leisure time in mixed groups and for whom the pressures of adult role adoption during adolescence will have encouraged the greater use of gender stereotypes in all areas of behaviour.

Science has been a particular focus of interest with respect to single-sex versus mixed teaching because of concerns about apparent female reluctance to take courses in the physical sciences, mathematics and IT. Harvey and Stables (1986) examined attitudes to science in general, and to physics, chemistry and biology separately, among pupils in mixed and single-sex secondary schools. Attitudes to science were more positive among girls in single-sex schools than those in mixed schools, while no school type differences were found among boys. For attitudes to physics, which is the most male-dominated of the three sciences, girls in single-sex schools were again more positive than their peers in mixed-sex schools while the reverse was true for boys. For chemistry no differences emerged. For biology, which attracts a substantial number of girls, the reverse effect to that for physics occurred.

Experiments with single-sex teaching of science and mathematics have yielded some positive results (Smith, 1986; Whyte, 1986), but at least part of the effect seems to arise from changes in teachers' expectations of girls' potential and preferred learning styles. The importance of the teacher's role in combating gendered behaviour in the mixed classroom has also been supported by the results of an intervention project by Rennie and Parker (1987), who compared single-sex and mixed-sex groups of Year 5 primary schoolchildren working on activities associated with the learning of an area of physical science – electricity. Their field study used two groups of teachers (with equal numbers of men and women in each), matched on biographical factors, attitudes to science, and teaching methods. The experimental group were given inservice training on both teaching the topic and strategies for minimizing gender differences in attitude and achievement. The control group received topic-based training only. All teachers then taught six lessons on the topic based on the training they had received, while the researchers made structured observations of teachers and pupils. In the classrooms of the experimental group teachers there were no observable differences in the way in which the mixed and single-sex groups behaved, and the girls were actively involved in the groupwork activities. In the classrooms of the control group teachers, however, girls in the mixed-sex groups spent less time being actively involved in experimenting, while the boys used the equipment. Rennie and Parker concluded that single-sex groups may result in greater active involvement by girls when a teacher's awareness of gender issues is low. Strategies for encouraging girls were identified: ensuring that groups are small and that the children work with friends or those they are familiar with, and offering additional support and encouragement to girls to use equipment that they are generally less familiar and confident with than boys.

The differential behaviour of teachers to boys and girls has also been highlighted by Walden and Walkerdine (1982), who observed different approaches taken by mathematics teachers to explaining good and poor performance by girls and boys. Girls' good performance was seen as the product of industry rather than ability, while boys' poor performance was attributed to bad behaviour within the classroom and lack of concentration.

Girls therefore were assumed not to have ability in the face of evidence to the contrary, while boys were assumed to have hidden ability when no evidence was forthcoming. Such observations are illustrative of more general findings in the literature on attributions for male and female success and failure. For example, Swim and Sanna (1996) conducted a meta-analysis of attributional studies and found evidence for gender-based attributions when male-stereotyped tasks are being undertaken (the evidence for such effects for female-stereotyped tasks was less strong). Success was attributed to high ability in males and high effort in females, while failure was attributed to low effort or bad luck for males and low ability in females. It is hardly surprising that masculine-stereotyped academic subject areas are perceived as difficult and complicated by females and that they are reluctant to participate.

Findings such as those of Rennie and Parker (1987), in addition to evidence from other intervention studies including the GIST (Girls Into Science and Technology Initiative – see, for example, Whyte, 1986), indicate that teachers have a significant role to play in encouraging increased participation in masculine areas of the curriculum by girls. Studies of curriculum content (for example, Sjoberg, 1988), and delivery (for example, Arch and Cummins, 1989; Toh, 1993) indicate that making the content of courses more relevant to the person-oriented concerns of girls, and providing greater structure and support for learning in areas in which they do not feel confident and with which they are unfamiliar, can also encourage greater participation.

Conclusions

The educational system inevitably reflects broader cultural beliefs and concerns. Gender, whether viewed as a dichotomous category or as a set of constructed truths, has far-reaching consequences in influencing the skills we acquire and choices we make during a long period of learning and development. Participation by girls in male-dominated areas such as physical science, mathematics and technology is constrained both by our internal representations of female abilities and attributes and by educational environments which vary in the degree to which gender is salient and to which the needs of females are addressed. The picture which emerges from contemporary studies is complex, but it is clear that the immediate learning environment can, to some extent at least, moderate the effects of gender stereotypes and truths.

References

Arch, E.C. and Cummins, D.E. (1989). Structured and unstructured exposure to computers: sex differences in attitude and use among college students. *Sex Roles* **20**, 245–51.

Archer, J. and Macrae, M. (1991). Gender-perceptions of school subjects among 10–11 year olds. *British Journal of Educational Psychology* **61**, 99–103.

Arnot, M., David, M. and Weiner, G. (1996). *Educational reforms and gender equality in schools.* Manchester: Equal Opportunities Commission.

Bandura, A. (1977). *Social learning theory.* Englewood Cliffs, NJ: Prentice-Hall.

Bem, S.L. (1974). The measurement of psychological androgyny. *Journal of Consulting and Clinical Psychology* **45**, 155–62.

Bodenhausen, G.V. and Wyer, R.S. (1985). Effects of stereotypes on decision making and information-processing strategies. *Journal of Personality and Social Psychology* **48**, 267–82.

Colley, A., Comber, C. and Hargreaves, D.J. (1994a). Gender effects in school subject preferences. *Educational Studies* **20**, 13–19.

Colley, A., Comber, C. and Hargreaves, D.J. (1994b). School subject preferences of pupils in single sex and coeducational secondary schools. *Educational Studies* **20**, 379–85.

Dale, R.R. (1969). *Mixed or single sex school? Volume 1: A research study about pupil–teacher relationships.* London: Routledge & Kegan Paul.

Dale, R.R. (1971). *Mixed or single sex school? Volume 2: Some social aspects.* London: Routledge & Kegan Paul.

Dale, R.R. (1974). *Mixed or single sex school? Volume 3: Attainment, attitudes and overview.* London: Routledge & Kegan Paul.

Deaux, K. and Major, B. (1987). Putting gender into context: an interactive model of gender-related behavior. *Psychological Review* **94**, 369–89.

Eagly, A.H. (1987). *Sex differences in social behavior: a social role interpretation.* Hillsdale, NJ: Erlbaum.

Eagly, A.H. (1995). The science and politics of comparing women and men. *American Psychologist* **50**, 145–58.

Elwood, J. (1995). Undermining gender stereotypes: examination performance in the UK at 16. *Assessment in Education* **2**, 283–303.

Gilligan, C. (1982). *In a different voice: psychological theory and women's development.* Cambridge, MA: Harvard University Press.

Halpern, D.F. (1992). *Sex differences in cognitive abilities.* (2nd edn). Hillsdale, NJ: Erlbaum.

Harvey, T.J. and Stables, A. (1986). Gender differences in attitudes to science for third year pupils: an argument for single sex teaching groups in mixed schools. *Research in Science and Technology Education* **4**, 163–70.

Hyde, J.S. and Linn, M.C. (1988). Gender differences in verbal ability: a meta-analysis. *Psychological Bulletin* **104**, 53–69.

Hyde, J.S. and Plant, E.S. (1995). Magnitude of psychological gender differences: another side to the story. *American Psychologist* **50**, 159–61.

Kelly, A. (1989). When I grow up I want to be . . .: a longitudinal study of the development of career preferences. *British Journal of Guidance and Counselling* **17**, 179–200.

Kohlberg, L. (1966). A cognitive-developmental analysis of children's sex-role concepts and attitudes. In Maccoby, E.E. (ed.), *The development of sex differences.* (pp. 82–173). London: Tavistock.

Lawrie, L. and Brown, R. (1992). Sex stereotypes, school subject preferences and career aspirations as a function of single/mixed schooling and presence/absence of an opposite sex sibling. *British Journal of Educational Psychology* **62**, 132–8.

Lee, V.E. and Bryk, A.S. (1989). Effects of single-sex schools: response to Marsh. *Journal of Educational Psychology* **81**, 647–50.

Marsh, H.W. (1989). Effects of attending single-sex and coeducational high schools – achievement, attitudes, behaviors and sex differences. *Journal of Educational Psychology* **81**, 70–85.

Mischel, W. (1966). A social learning view of sex differences. In Maccoby, E.E. (ed.), *The development of sex differences.* (pp. 56–81). London: Tavistock.

Mischel, W. (1970). Sex typing and socialisation. In Mussen, P.H. (ed.), *Carmichael's Manual of Child Psychology.* Vol. 2. (pp. 3–72). New York: Wiley.

Murphy, R. (1982). Sex differences in objective test performance. *British Journal of Educational Psychology* **52**, 213–19.

Ormerod, M.B. (1975). Subject preference and choice in co-educational and single-sex secondary schools. *British Journal of Educational Psychology* **45**, 257–67.

Rennie, L.J. and Parker, L.H. (1987). Detecting and accounting for gender differences in mixed-sex and single-sex groupings in science lessons. *Educational Review* **39**, 65–73.

Sjoberg, S. (1988). Gender and the image of science. *Scandinavian Journal of Educational Research* **32**, 49–60.

Smith, S. (1986). *Separate tables.* London: HMSO.

Spence, J.T. and Helmreich, R.L. (1978). *Masculinity and femininity: their psychological dimensions, correlates and antecedents.* Austin: University of Texas Press.

Stables, A. (1990). Differences between pupils from mixed and single sex schools in their enjoyment of school subjects and in their attitudes to science and to school. *Educational Review* **42**, 221–30.

Swim, J.K. and Sanna, L.J. (1996). He's skilled, she's lucky: a meta-analysis of observers' attributions for women's and men's successes and failures. *Personality and Social Psychology Bulletin* **22**, 507–19.

Toh, K.-A. (1993). Gender and practical tasks in science. *Educational Research* **35**, 255–61.

Walden, R. and Walkerdine, V. (1982). *Girls and mathematics: the early years.* London: Heinemann.

Weinreich-Haste, H. (1979). What sex is science? In Hartnett, O., Boden, G. and Fuller, M. (eds), *Women: sex role stereotyping.* (pp. 168–81). London: Tavistock.

Weinreich-Haste, H. (1981). The image of science. In Kelly, A. (ed.), *The missing half: girls and science education.* (pp. 216–29). Manchester: Manchester University Press.

Whyte, J. (1986). *Girls into science and technology: the story of a project.* London: Routledge & Kegan Paul.

Further reading

Deaux, K. and Major, B. (1987). Putting gender into context: an interactive model of gender-related behavior. *Psychological Review* **94**, 369–89.

Hyde, J.S. and Plant, E.S. (1995). Magnitude of psychological gender differences: another side to the story. *American Psychologist* **50**, 159–61.

Walkerdine, V. and the Girls and Mathematics Unit (1989). *Counting girls out.* London: Virago.

Weinreich-Haste, H. (1981). The image of science. In Kelly, A. (ed.), *The missing half: girls and science education.* (pp. 216–29). Manchester: Manchester University Press.

Whyte, J. (1986). *Girls into science and technology: the story of a project.* London: Routledge & Kegan Paul.

Discussion questions

1. Discuss the gender truths which apply to girls in education.
2. How can women be attracted to science?
3. Why has there been so little effort to attract boys into modern languages?
4. Discuss why so many women are attracted to psychology.
5. Is it reasonable to expect education to make a difference to the status quo?

11

PARENTING AND THE FAMILY

Nuala Quiery

INTRODUCTION

Historically there have been two broad strands to the psychological study of gendered development within the family. The first is the psychoanalytic tradition. This account of the development of male and female gender identity focuses on *why* development is gendered. The second strand consists of those approaches which focus on *how* male and female gender identity develops and differs, and how these gender roles are maintained. This second strand is more recent and reflects the growing interest in cognitive approaches within psychology.

The chapter will begin with an introduction to the ideas of Sigmund Freud, who was the first to present a theory of gendered development and the consequences for adult personality. Of particular interest is his account of the origins of masculine and feminine gender identity within the family and the gender stereotypes which emerge from this process – the male as the instrumental, emotionally distant ambassador of the wider world and the female as expressive, nurturing and embedded in relationships. I will then outline the findings of cognitive-developmental approaches before illustrating how recent developments in this field of psychology have come to incorporate something of both of these strands.

PSYCHOANALYTIC APPROACHES

Sigmund Freud presented the world with a psychological theory of personality which located childhood experience as central to individual development. Moreover, he presented a theory of gendered development in which sexuality and gender identity are paramount. Freud's theory is as contentious now as it was then, although for very different reasons. While it is not relevant here to enter into the details of this debate (see Chapter 4), it is appropriate when setting the historical context for approaches to gendered development to acknowledge Freud's theoretical contribution as the first. Any attempt to trace the history of psychological approaches to parenting and gender development must acknowledge that this history arose initially and fundamentally from his work, and many of the concepts he first elucidated are still grappled with today.

Freud located early childhood experience in the relationship initially with the mother and later within the mother–father–child triangle. He maintained that psychological development is by definition psychosexual: 'For all psychoanalysts the development of the human subject, its unconscious and its sexuality go hand-in-hand, they are causatively intertwined' (Mitchell and Rose (eds), 1982, p. 2). To the psychoanalyst, gender is not something that is simply ascribed to a child by adults, or adopted by a child in a culturally appropriate and socially defined manner. Rather, a person is formed through his or her sexuality (ibid.), and this is a process in which the child is actively engaged. External reality has to be acquired, and we are quite literally forged by this experience or process of acquisition. According to Freud, sexuality assumes its form by means of the negotiation of a long and tortuous path by the individual boy or girl – this is the process of gender development. In stating this, Freud made a radical departure from accepted thinking of his time which held that sexuality is an instinct and is therefore preadapted to reality.

Central to Freud's theory was his belief in the existence and importance of the unconscious. In his view the unconscious is energized by instinctual drives which motivate behaviour. The individual seeks an outlet for this energy and the fulfilment of a need, for example hunger, at a particular point in time, by means of an object (i.e. a person). Freud thus asserted both the impact and relevance of the individual's social environment. Instincts do not exist in isolation but in the context of our relations with others. For example, an infant's hunger provides the energy and motivation to seek consummation for this need, that is, the satisfaction of receiving nourishment. Through socialization, we each learn that our needs can only be met in socially acceptable ways made available to us by existing social relations. This is nowhere more true than in the phallic stage of childhood when our gender identity is forged.

For Freud, gender and sexuality are thus not separate aspects of psychological development but are intrinsic to one another. He proposed that the infant goes through three stages, or prisms, of experience, seeking gratification of psychosexual urges by whatever means are at his/her disposal. These stages are:

- The Oral Stage (birth–1 year). The infant seeks gratification of instinctual psychosexual urges by means of sucking, etc.
- The Anal Stage (1–3 years). The infant seeks gratification by means of holding on to or letting go of faeces.

- The Phallic Stage (3–5 years). This culminates in the emotional crisis known as the Oedipus Complex.

At each stage instinctual urges aim to achieve gratification by means of a different part of the body. The body is the instrument of the drive and another person is the object of this drive. Together, they are the means to the satisfaction of this drive. In the oral and anal stages the infant strives to meet his/her needs in the only way available to him/her, that is, using his/her body parts over which s/he has physical control or capability. This s/he does in relationship with one or more caretakers. In the phallic stage gender identity is said to be consolidated and it is in this stage that the experiences of boys and girls diverge.

Male gender identity formation

According to Greek legend, Oedipus was a man who unwittingly murdered his father, married his mother and had children of his own by her. Freud likened the predicament of the young male child during the phallic stage to that of Oedipus. That is, fundamentally the son is in competition with his father for the love of his own mother. The male child consequently feels threatened by his more powerful rival, and resolves this dilemma by identifying with the father. The son's reward is that he comes to inherit the culturally superior position of the male in patriarchal society.

The mother thus becomes the object of the child's sexual drive or libidinal energy during the Oedipal stage, and the father becomes the son's rival for the mother's attention and affection. The son, threatened by this powerful figure, and fearing castration, ultimately relinquishes his claim to an exclusive relationship with his mother by identifying with the father. In this way he adopts a male gender identity.

Female gender identity formation

Freud was never able to satisfactorily account for how women negotiate the Oedipal phase. The son is rewarded for his deference to his father, as he too will eventually come to inherit the father's powerful position when he reaches manhood. The closest a woman will come to sharing or participating in the father's power is by giving birth to a son.

> A mother is only brought unlimited satisfaction by her relation to a son; this is altogether the most perfect, the most free from ambivalence of all human relationships. A mother can transfer to her son the ambition which she has been obliged to suppress in herself, and she can expect from him the satisfaction of all that has been left over in her of her masculinity complex. Even a marriage is not made secure until the wife has succeeded in making her husband her child as well and in acting as a mother to him.
>
> (Freud, 1964, p. 168)

The daughter is said to develop an ambivalent relationship with her mother, with whom she identifies as a woman but whom she resents for her lack of a phallus. Freud's theory of psychosexual development was to give credence to the notion that women rear children and men rule the world. The subservience of women in our culture was thus validated by this account of development. More recently, feminist psychoanalytic theorists have sought to make more palatable Freud's theory in relation to female development by engaging with this problematic account of gender development. Some have done this by returning to the original tale of Oedipus and tracing the fate of the female characters in the story, that is his mother Jocasta and daughter Antigone, noting the fact that they are portrayed only in relation to the needs of Oedipus, and are thus seen only from a male perspective.

> Freud was accurate in observing that anatomy is destiny, but erred in his explanation... Anatomy given meaning in our society becomes destiny, for this is the meaning that it is given... Once assigned, it is gender, as the basic psychological organising principle in the family (along with age) and in larger society (along with race and class), that determines and organises development and identity
>
> (Kaschak, 1992, p. 42)

Ellyn Kaschak (1992), who retells and examines the myth of Oedipus, describes how it is only by self-definition and leadership on the part of Antigone (the daughter of Oedipus) that the Oedipal stage can be resolved for her as a woman. Only in this way can she be defined as anything other than solely in relation to her father, and only in this way can she come to see herself from any other perspective. This conflict between the self-denial of caring for others, and being a person in one's own right, is a familiar one to women raised to value nurturing qualities and the maintenance of intimate relationships above everything else. Freud thus elucidated the stereotypical male and female gender roles still recognizable today, namely the instrumentality of the male and the connectedness of the female.

The legacy of psychoanalysis: mother-blaming

The belief that mothering is the essential childhood condition for adult adjustment led to models of psychological development which sought to track the effects of single events in early childhood on later outcome. John Bowlby, as a trained psychoanalyst and medical doctor, had the appropriate qualifications to become an accepted expert in this field. Bowlby asserted that not only is the mother–child bond unique, but also that it alone is essential to adult emotional well-being and adjustment, the desired ultimate outcome of development. This insistence on the importance of mothering over and above all other conditions of childhood experience excluded fathers and confined women with children to this role (often referred to as the motherhood mandate). In 1952 Bowlby declared to the World Health Organisation that his work on the role of mothering in mental health was nothing short of a discovery comparable in magnitude to that of the role of vitamins in physical health (Woodhead et al. (eds), 1991, p. 64).

Evidence in support of Bowlby's views on mother–infant bonding as instinctive has drawn heavily on animal research, in which bonding is regarded as an imprinting event rather than an emotional process. Other evidence to support his proposition that maternal deprivation (as he termed inadequate maternal attachment) leads to irreparable emotional damage was drawn from outcome studies of children reared in orphanages or separated from parents as a result of traumatic wartime experiences in Europe during World War II. The conclusions drawn from this work were transposed onto any childhood experience of separation so that in 1951 a World Health Organisation report stated that day nurseries would cause permanent damage to the emotional health of a future generation (Tizard, 1991, p. 64).

It was to be two decades before the dubious relevance of Bowlby's theory and research to working mothers and their children was to be acknowledged. Beyer (1995), in her recent review of the impact of maternal employment on children, made two points about this historical legacy. First, that in the 1950s maternal employment was considered deviant and induced guilt and overprotective maternal behaviour, and second, that the result of this focus has been that: 'Although there has been an increase in research on fathers, more such research is urgently needed. Researchers' preoccupation with putative deleterious effects of maternal employment on children but virtual absence of interest in the effect of paternal employment is a case in point' (Beyer, 1995, p. 241). Maternal employment has since been found to enhance the well-being of mothers and daughters. This focus on the mother as the chief determinant of child outcome led also to a large body of research which attempted to identify and quantify the specific characteristics of this early relationship which optimize child outcome. However, despite good intentions, this approach served to reinforce the view of mothers as the source of developmental difficulty, since termed mother-blaming. It also excluded fathers, and failed to acknowledge the role of the child as an active agent in his/her social environment. Traditionally, the study of child development and the family has been male dominated both in terms of the focus of interest and theoretical perspective. This has changed somewhat in recent years, and there has been a shift in focus away from mother-blaming and towards more realistic and meaningful approaches to the understanding of both psychopathology (Caplan and Hall-McCorquodale, 1985) and normal development. This is attributable both to the rise in the number of women and mothers now working in this field, and in particular to the impact of feminist scholarship.

COGNITIVE DEVELOPMENTAL APPROACHES TO PARENTING AND GENDER

In comparison to approaches which find their roots in psychoanalysis, the North American contribution to the study of gender and development has been of a very different kind. As Eleanor Maccoby observed, 'Historically, the way we psychologists think about the psychology of gender has grown out of our thinking about individual differences' (Maccoby 1990, p. 513). This has certainly been true of the surge of interest in gender and development in the 1970s and early 1980s, much of which was undertaken in the USA. Some of these studies, for example, compared mothers' and fathers' reactions to their newborn sons and daughters and testify to the fact that gendered development begins at birth, if not before. White and Woollett (1991) provide an overview of observational studies of fathers and their neonates. What parents typically say, and the different patterns of contact between mothers, fathers and their infants, have all been the subject of this study of difference.

Other areas which have been the focus of interest have been, for example, the effect of parental discord and divorce on sons and daughters (Emery, 1982). In the 1990s a number of researchers have continued this tradition by revisiting, as it were, the research interests of these earlier studies and replicating their work in order to see if the experience of gendered development has changed. Coats and Overman (1992), for example, cover similar ground to that of Hennig and Jardim (1977) when reporting that successful professional women report having had fathers with whom they had a close relationship in childhood, and who encouraged them in non-traditional roles. Peirce (1993) carried out a content analysis of teenage girls' magazines and, finding that there has been little change since the earlier study by McRobbie (1982), concluded, 'Through the stories, a teenage girl learns that male–female relationships are more important than just about anything, that she is not supposed to act or be aggressive or solve problems – others will do that for her – and that there really are male and female professions' (Peirce, 1993, p. 65). Similarly, Etaugh and Liss (1992) replicated the findings of Langlois and Downs (1980), and also Fagot (1978), that parents reward gender-typical play. There are some studies, however, which indicate change in fathers' attitudes and behaviours in the last 15–20 years.

THE ROLE OF FATHERS

The meaning we attach to words reflects both our understanding and our experiencing. Consequently, the verb 'to mother' means to nurture or care for some person or animal, not only a son or daughter, whereas 'to father' is to engender.

It is a consistent and persistent finding that fathers treat sons and daughters in a more gendered way than do mothers (Maccoby, 1990). Typically, fathers' interactions with their children are more instrumental and achievement-oriented than those of mothers (Collins and Russell, 1991), and they give more attention to sons, whereas mothers attend equally to sons and daughters (Crouter et al., 1993). Moreover, fathers have been found to reward compliant behaviour in girls and assertiveness in boys (Kerig et al., 1993). While there have been some changes in the behaviour of fathers in the last 15–20 years, they are less than dramatic, and the burden of childrearing and homemaking still falls on mothers. Major (1993) observes that inequality between men and women in the distribution of family work is still the norm in families. Wille (1995) comments that changes in parental roles are appearing primarily as a result of the increase in dual-wage-earning families. Evidence suggests that parents still engage in stereotypical gender-typing from birth. Karraker et al. (1995), for example, repeated the work of Rubin et al. (1974) to explore whether the strong gender stereotyping of infants at birth, particularly by fathers (girls being viewed as finer featured, more delicate, softer and smaller than boys), is still prevalent. The authors concluded that while gender-stereotyped perceptions of newborns have not disappeared, they have declined and, more interestingly, that fathers did not display greater gender stereotyping than mothers in their study.

Not surprisingly, children's awareness of gender stereotypes is apparent in pre-school years, and the more traditional the parents' attitudes, the earlier children demonstrate this knowledge (Fagot et al., 1992). Gender-stereotypical behavioural styles in interaction with playmates are also evident in the pre-school years (Cramer and Skidd, 1992), boys being more aggressive and competitive, and girls more co-operative and facilitative in relating to others.

Fathers' espousal of traditional or egalitarian attitudes has been found to correlate with young children's knowledge of sex roles among 4-year-olds. Fagot et al.'s (1995) study found that fathers with egalitarian attitudes spent as much time interacting with their children as mothers. In addition, fathers in couples who espouse egalitarian beliefs are more likely to be supportive in a range of family activities including housework and childcare (Weisner et al., 1994), and the children of egalitarian couples have less rigid gender-role knowledge. This is attributed to differences in the behaviour of fathers in traditional and egalitarian couples. Changes are clearly taking place and some men are finding this change difficult to accept. Kerry Daly expesses some of the difficulty men encounter as fathers who seek to refashion fatherhood in the absence of appropriate role models: 'In the resonant silence of their own fathers' voices, they seek to proclaim a new expression of fatherhood' (Marsiglio (ed.), 1995, p. 20).

Recent developments

The stereotypical male role as instrumental and distant, and the female as relationship- and intimacy-oriented, as portrayed by Freud, is still very real today. The apparent connectedness–separatedness dichotomy, once regarded as expressing the two poles of a female–male gender continuum, is still at the core of this issue (Maccoby, 1990; Hops, 1995). Recent work in the theory and research of gender identity concludes that it is the psychologically androgynous individual who enjoys the greatest well-being in our culture. In this view, female and male psychological characteristics are no longer the two poles of one continuum, but rather are attributes and aspects of identity which can and do coexist within an individual. Hunt (1993) demonstrated that 'both instrumentality and expressiveness are equally, independently related to several major components of well-being including depression, positive affect, affect balance and life satisfaction' (p. 162).

In an attempt to explore the link between gender identity and psychological androgyny, Grimmell and Stern (1992) present a social-conflict model of the influence of gender role on psychological well-being. In this model it is the degree of congruence between one's ideal gender role and the demands of an individual's life situation that determines psychological well-being. As parents, men are more likely then women to have a gender ideal which is not in conflict with their day-to-day experiencing; to quote, 'the highest psychological well-being (is) among those individuals whose personal gender role ideals closely match both their personal behaviour and their life demands' (Grimmell and Stern, 1992, p. 496).

Psychological androgyny and gendered development

How do gendered socialization processes in the family link to the development of an androgynous personality and optimum psychological well-being? Psychologists are now beginning to address this issue. In our culture it is considered more appropriate for females to express emotion than it is for males, and indeed Adams et al. (1995) have reviewed studies of early childhood which demonstrate that parents do have different expectations of sons and daughters in this respect. Mothers and fathers have been observed to use more frequent and varied emotional language in conversation with daughters than with sons. Similarly, daughters are found to use more terms associated with emotion than sons. Clearly, girls are taught to value emotions more than boys and to share them with others (see Chapter 7).

Girls often emerge from childhood having low self-esteem, seeking approval from others and having less confidence than boys. One reason may be that boys still receive more praise and positive evaluations from parents than do girls, for equivalent levels of ability and achievement. In turn, girls have lower expectations for success and are more likely than boys to attribute their failure to a general lack of personal ability. Boys, on the other hand, are found to attribute success to personal ability, and failure to external influences (Alessandri and Lewis, 1993). In the words of Hops (1995), 'Interactional research suggests that differential parenting practices shape more instrumental achievement oriented and aggressive behaviour in boys and more dependent emotional and socially appropriate behaviour in girls' (p. 428).

This statement echoes Freud's portrayal of gender identity formation within the family, and in fact recent researchers have attempted to detect the mechanisms at work in parenting socialization processes which reproduce masculine and feminine gender identity. In the past, the study of gender identity formation has traditionally remained very separate from psychological theories of child development but there is a growing trend towards bringing these two approaches together by drawing upon both European and North American traditions to undertake work which is both theoretically and empirically rigorous. Three recent studies serve to illustrate how this is happening.

Haigler et al.'s (1995) study, for example, examines the role of the key child development issue of attachment in gender identity formation among adolescents. Working from the premise that secure attachment leads to the development of competence, they predicted that androgynous adolescents in their study would report stronger attachment to parents than other gender-role groups. What they found was that adolescents in the feminine and androgynous gender-role groups reported higher attachment to parents than those in the masculine or undifferentiated gender-role groups.

Boggiano and Barrett (1992) similarly explored whether approval-seeking in girls is attributable to parental socialization practices. Hoffman and Kloska (1995) report that parents who have less stereotypical attitudes to gender roles have daughters who have a more internal locus of control. Girls have been found to be more extrinsically motivated than boys – that is, they approach tasks for extrinsic reasons such as to gain approval or please someone else. Parents prefer the behaviour of children who are extrinsically motivated and encourage this orientation, particularly in girls. Boggiano and Barrett (1992) suggest that children who are extrinsically motivated are much more vulnerable to experiencing a sense of helplessness and depressive symptoms than their intrinsically motivated, and generally male, peers. Approval-seeking has thus been found to be a source of stress, low self-esteem and depressive symptoms in girls. In their study of 127 8-year-old boys and girls, the authors found girls to be more extrinsic and more susceptible to feelings of helplessness and depression. They suggest that deficits in the attachment relationship with a child's primary caretaker(s) may be the source of this problem.

Van Aken and Riksen-Walraven (1992) explored the role of parental support in the development of competence among young children aged from nine months to 12 years. In an observational study of young children and their parents they reported that parental support to sons facilitated a sense of self-efficacy, that is, the experience and expectancy of being an effective agent in one's life. In this way parents are thought to contribute more to their sons' than their daughters' growing sense of competence. Van Aken and Riksen-Walraven suggest that a lack of continuity in parental supportive behaviour towards daughters results in a low sense of self-efficacy among girls. The findings of this and other studies indicate how parenting practices may contribute to approval-seeking behaviour in girls, and greater confidence and intrinsic motivational orientation among boys, and thus help specify some of the mechanisms at work in developing a distinct gender identity.

Conclusions

Psychologists who are interested in parenthood and the family are now combining an understanding of parenting practices together with a theoretical understanding of the development of sex-typed gender identities, so as to explore the relationship between gender identity formation and childhood experiences. Studies of this kind combine elements of both European and North American traditions, and in so doing they provide fresh insight into parenting attitudes and practices. While these studies remain few and far between, the potential of this work not only to further our knowledge of the parenting correlates of aspects of gender-role identity formation but also advance our understanding of underlying theoretical concepts is clear.

References

Adams, S., Kuebli, J., Boyle, P.A. and Fivush, R. (1995). Gender differences in parent–child conversations about past emotions: a longitudinal investigation. *Sex Roles* **33(5/6)** 309–23.

Alessandri, S.M. and Lewis, M. (1993). Parental evaluation and its relation to shame and pride in young children. *Sex Roles* **31(5/6)**, 335–43.

Beyer, S. (1995). Maternal employment and children's academic achievement: parenting styles as mediating variable. *Developmental Review* **15**, 212–53.

Boggiano, A.K. and Barrett, M. (1992). Gender differences in depression in children as a function of motivational orientation. *Sex Roles* **26(1/2)**, 11–17.

Caplan, P.J. and Hall-McCorquodale, I. (1985). Mother-blaming in major clinical journals. *American Journal of Orthopsychiatry* **55**, 345–53.

Coats, P.B. and Overman, S.J. (1992). Childhood play experiences of women in traditional and non-traditional professions. *Sex Roles* **26(7/8)**, 261–71.

Collins, W.A. and Russell, G. (1991). Mother–child and father–child relationships in middle childhood and adolescence: a developmental analysis. *Developmental Review* **11**, 99–136.

Cramer, P. and Skidd, J.E. (1992). Correlates of self-worth in preschoolers: the role of gender-stereotyped styles of behavior. *Sex Roles* **26(9/10)**, 369–90.

Crouter, A.C., McHale, S.M. and Bartko, W.T. (1993). Gender as an organising feature in parent–child relationships. *Journal of Social Issues* **49(3)**, 161–74.

Daly, K.J. (1995). Reshaping fatherhood: finding the models. In Marsiglio, W. (ed.), *Fatherhood: contemporary theory, research and social policy.* (pp. 21–40). London: Sage.

Emery, R.E. (1982). Interparental conflict and the children of discord and divorces. *Psychological Bulletin* **92(2)**, 310–30.

Etaugh, C. and Liss, M.B. (1992). Home, school, and playroom: training grounds for adult gender roles. *Sex Roles* **26(3/4)**, 129–47.

Fagot, B.I. (1978). The influence of sex of child on parental reactions to toddler children. *Child Development* **49**, 459–65.

Fagot, B.I., Leinbach, M.D. and O'Boyle, C. (1992). Gender labelling, gender stereotyping, and parenting behaviors. *Developmental Psychology* **28(2)**, 225–30.

Fagot, B.I. and Leinbach, M.D. (1995). Gender knowledge in egalitarian and traditional families. *Sex Roles* **32(7/8)**, 513–26.

Freud, S. (1964). *New introductory lectures on psycho-analysis.* Trans. by J. Strachey. Harmondsworth: Penguin.

Grimmell, D. and Stern, G.S. (1992). The relationship between gender role ideals and psychological well-being. *Sex Roles* **27(9/10)**, 487–97.

Haigler, V.F., Day, H.D. and Marshall, D.D. (1995). Parental attachment and gender-role identity. *Sex Roles* **33(3/4)**, 203–20.

Hennig, M. and Jardim, A. (1977). *The managerial woman.* New York: Anchor Press/ Doubleday.

Hoffman, L.W. and and Kloska, D.D. (1995). Parents' gender-based attitudes toward marital roles and child rearing: development and validation of new measures. *Sex Roles* **32(5/6)**, 273–95.

Hops, H. (1995). Age- and gender-specific effects of parental depression: a commentary. *Developmental Psychology* **31(3)**, 428–31.

Hunt, M.G. (1993). Expressiveness does predict well-being. *Sex Roles* **29(3/4)**, 147–69.

Karraker, K.H., Vogel, D.A. and Lake, M.A. (1995). Parents' gender-stereotyped perceptions of newborns: the eye of the beholder revisited. *Sex Roles* **33(9/10)**, 687–701.

Kaschak, E. (1992). *Engendered lives: a new psychology of woman's experience.* New York: Basic Books.

Kerig, P.K., Cowan, P.A. and Cowan, C.P. (1993). Marital quality and gender differences in parent-child interaction. *Developmental Psychology* **29(6)**, 931–9.

Langlois, J.H. and Downs, A.C. (1980). Mothers, fathers, and peers as socialization agents of sex-typed play behaviours in young children. *Child Development* **51**, 1237–47.

Maccoby, E. (1990). Gender and relationships. *American Psychologist* **45**, 513–20.

McRobbie, A. (1982). Jackie: an ideology of adolescent femininity. In Waites, B., Bennett, T. and Martin, G. (eds), *Popular culture: past and present.* (pp. 263–83). London: Croom Helm.

Major, B. (1993). Gender, entitlement, and the distribution of family labor. *Journal of Social Issues* **49(3)**, 141–59.

Marsiglio, W. (ed.) (1995). *Fatherhood: contemporary theory, research and social policy.* London: Sage.

Mitchell, J. and Rose, J. (eds) (1982). *Feminine sexuality.* London: Macmillan.

Peirce, K. (1993). Socialization of teenage girls through teen-magazine fiction: the making of a new woman or an old lady? *Sex Roles* **29(1/2)**, 59–68.

Rubin, J.Z., Provenzano, F.J. and Luria, Z. (1974). The eye of the beholder: parents' views on sex of newborns. *Americal Journal of Orthopsychiatry* **44**, 512–19.

Tizard, B. (1991). Working mothers and the care of young children. In Woodhead, M., Light, P. and Carr, R. (eds), *Growing up in a changing society: a reader. Child development in social context 3.* (pp. 61–77). London: Routledge.

Van Aken, M.A.G. and Riksen-Walraven, J.M. (1992). Parental support and the development of competence in children. *International Journal of Behavioral Development* **15(1)**, 101–23.

Weisner, T.S., Garnier, H. and Loucky, J. (1994). Domestic tasks, gender egalitarian values and children's gender typing in conventional and non-conventional families. *Sex Roles* **30(1/2)**, 23–54.

White, D.G. and Woollett, E.A. (1991). The father's role in the neonatal period. In Woodhead, M., Carr, R. and Light, P. (eds), *Becoming a person: a reader. Child development in social context 1.* (pp. 74–106). London: Routledge.

Wille, D.E. (1995). The 1990s: gender differences in parenting roles. *Sex Roles* **33(11/12)**, 803–17.

Woodhead, M., Carr, R. and Light, P. (eds) (1991). *Becoming a person: a reader. Child development in social context 1.* London: Routledge.

Further reading

Daly, K.J. (1995). Reshaping fatherhood: finding the models. In W. Marsiglio (ed.), *Fatherhood: contemporary theory, research and social policy.* (pp. 21–40). London: Sage.

Jacklin, C.N. and McBride-Chang, C. (1991). The effects of feminist scholarship on developmental psychology. *Psychology of Women Quarterly* **15**, 549–56.

Kaschak, E. (1992). *Engendered lives. a new psychology of woman's experience.* New York: Basic Books. [Chapter 3: Oedipus and Antigone revisited: the family drama. pp. 55–89].

Lips, H. (1993). *Sex and gender: an introduction.* 2nd edn. Mountain View, CA: Mayfield Publ. [Chapter 2: Theoretical perspectives on sex and gender. pp. 37–71].

Tizard, B. (1991). Working mothers and the care of young children. In Woodhead, M., Light, P. and Carr, R. (eds), *Growing up in a changing society: a reader. Child development in social context 3.* (pp. 61–77). London: Routledge.

Discussion questions

1. Picture one of your parents at the school gate when you were 8 years of age. How would this parent describe you to another parent?
2. What is a good father? A good mother?
3. How important is parenthood to you in relation to other identities you have?
4. Devise a means to explore among parents the assertion that 'Gender roles may act to reduce psychological well-being by setting up conflicts between social and organismic demands' (Grimmell and Stern, 1992, p. 494).
5. Do egalitarian attitudes translate into behaviour within the family? Discuss with particular reference to parenting.

12

WORK

John Kremer

Introduction

In contrast with many topics covered in this text, gender and the labour market has attracted widespread interest across a number of disciplines, and for a considerable period of time. Economists, sociologists, social and economic historians and social anthropologists have all made a substantial contribution to debate and more recently, psychologists have also begun to play a part in proceedings.

While psychology's role has the potential to be extremely significant, a glance through contemporary texts on gender and psychology often reveals a reliance on official statistics and demographic data to describe gender segregation and discrimination in the labour market, with relatively little by way of theoretical explanation or of a focus on matters which are strictly definable as psychological. For example, only relatively recently have psychologists begun to look systematically within organizations in order to determine how gender inequality is created and perpetuated (for example, Itzin and Newman (eds), 1995; Nicolson, 1996). This chapter will aim to pull together this emerging literature, with the emphasis primarily on the psychological factors which impact on gender in the labour market.

The gendered history of paid employment

In Western societies, from the time of the industrial revolution to the present day, the labour market has been characterized by gender divisions, with women normally portrayed as the losers and men the winners. Explanations as to why inequality exists have tended to rely heavily on feminist analyses (see Chapter 3). These are in general agreement that Western societies are overtly patriarchal, characterized by an imbalance of power between men and women and by mechanisms which serve to perpetuate this male hegemony.

Historically, the roots of gender inequality in the workplace are often traced to the division of labour (and the division between work and home) which were associated with industrialization and the growth of capitalism. According to the social historian Sheila Rowbotham (1973), prior to the mid-nineteenth century, there were a variety of means of production which often allowed women and men to work, if not side by side, certainly in close proximity and often from home. Industrialization effectively removed paid employment from the home but at the same time encouraged reliance on the nuclear family as the primary and most cost-effective unit of production underpinning capitalism. This served to place the burden of homecare, childcare and domestic organization squarely on the shoulders of women. In the words of Blau and Winkler (1989): 'The broad thrust of industrialisation diminished the relative status of women by creating a gender division of labour in which, after marriage, women were responsible for home work and men were responsible for market work' (p. 266). In relation to paid employment, this historical process is seen as creating and sustaining the dual labour market (Barron and Norris, 1991). Traditionally, men have been seen as dominating the primary employment sector, with their employment histories often remaining unbroken from school to retirement. In contrast, women predominate in the secondary employment sector, a sector marked by greater instability, fewer career prospects and poorer working conditions. Women's employment histories have been described in terms of an 'M' profile, with the dip or gap in paid employment being associated with the child-rearing years spanning the mid-20s and early 30s.

As we approach a new millennium, employment profiles for men and for women are changing rapidly and it is always important to acknowledge this evidence of rapid change. Mothers are now less likely to leave paid employment to care for young children, and women's significance in the labour market continues to grow apace. For example in October 1997, women made up 49.5 per cent of those currently in paid employment in the UK and estimates suggest that by the year 2000 women will outnumber men in the labour market, albeit with a far higher percentage in part-time employment (currently, 47 per cent of working women are part-timers in comparison with 12 per cent of working men; *Labour Market Trends*, 1997).

From the psychological perspective, individual behaviours and attitudes do not always coincide with social trends. In the post-industrial and post-modern world of the 1990s we still continue to wrestle with the legacy of gendered employment profiles which have been inherited from an earlier time. One example is the motherhood mystique or motherhood mandate, first identified by Lena Hollingworth in the early years of this century but still very much in evidence today. That is, the notion created and perpetuated by our culture that women are born and reared to be, first and foremost, mothers. The role of fathers in procreation cannot be denied but the fatherhood mandate receives far less prominence, if any mention at all.

Set against these historical trends, the remainder of the chapter will endeavour to give a flavour of the current literature, first considering attitudes and motivations of men and women to paid employment, and towards those in employment, before looking at the impact of childcare on work and finally how gender impacts on organizational life.

Attitudes and motivations

Given the dual labour market model, and traditional attitudes towards women's rights and roles in society, a stereotype persists that men are inherently more committed to work than women and that women's attitudes to work are generally less positive than are men's. One important task for the applied psychologist is to look behind and beyond such stereotypes, to identify the true picture of men's and women's responses to work and thus perhaps to challenge the foundations on which stereotypes are constructed and perpetuated.

To begin, are women more or less willing or committed to work than men? The answer which data consistently show is simply no. A succession of surveys in the 1980s and 1990s have demonstrated that although fewer women are in paid work than men, and their working conditions are often inferior, the overwhelming majority of those women who do work prefer to be in paid employment. In addition, the majority of those not in work, and particularly those aged under 50 years, would prefer to be in employment. For example, in 1983 across the European Community (EC) it was found that only one third of women were working but that two thirds would have preferred to be working (Commission of the European Communities, 1983). Further, a fascinating story was revealed when the preferences (and presumed preferences) of husbands and wives to the wife working were compared. Across Western Europe, husbands assumed that their wives were less willing to work than was the case, and what is more, they were also convinced that their wives were of the same opinion. The majority of men (61 per cent) preferred that their wives did not work yet 63 per cent of wives said that they would prefer to work. It is also significant that European wives were more accurate in guessing their husband's preference for wife working than was true of husbands guessing wives' preference.

While the number of men wanting their partners to remain at home is declining, a significant minority of men remain to be convinced that women wish to work and they are also unaware of or deliberately blinkered to women's aspirations. Other international surveys (Scott and Duncombe, 1991; Scott et al., 1993) have revealed continued and widespread scepticism that women can work without detrimental costs to family life, but beyond this have argued that 'gender-role attitudes are more complex than any overall summary "egalitarian versus traditional" scale might imply' (Scott and Duncombe, 1991, p. 11). This is a finding that those involved with attitudinal research should never disregard; there is always a temptation to generalize from specific measures of attitudes to global statements about attitudinal predispositions, and as recent theorizing on social cognition suggests, this is not only dangerous but is an inaccurate portrayal of the complexity of our schemata or cognitive representations of the social world.

That traditional stereotypes persist and present hurdles to many women's career aspirations is beyond dispute, but how do women's attitudes and orientations tally with this stereotype? Do men and women differ with regard to their feelings about work? Again the answer is no. When working men and women are asked to rate the importance which they attach to various factors at work then gender differences are rare and normally only extend to items where work commitments may clash with domestic responsibilities (Martin and Roberts, 1984; Kremer and Montgomery (eds), 1993). In line with these findings, research has generally failed to reveal major gender differences in terms of attitudes to work, and especially among the young (Dex, 1988). In terms of reasons for working, financial considerations are cited most often by both women and men, followed by intrinsic rewards including the stimulation of work and feeling useful.

Attitudes aside, given women's poorer working conditions (Beechey, 1986), it may be assumed that working women should be less content than men. Paradoxically, research has consistently found higher levels of job satisfaction among women, and even higher satisfaction among part-time workers and those working from home. Controversially, the British sociologist Catherine Hakim (1991) has argued that the similarities in work-orientation scores between women and men do not reflect upon underlying similarity between the genders but instead upon women and men's different life goals. This, she argues, comes through most clearly when comparing men's and women's commitment to work, as measured by questions asking if the person would wish to continue working irrespective of financial necessity. For a substantial proportion of women, their main concern is identified as a 'marriage career', with their career at work assuming secondary importance. Thus it is argued that, for many women, expectations are lower and satisfaction rates are consequently higher as these expectations are more easily met.

This argument is premised upon a notion of 'commitment' which is psychologically invalid. It ignores our sophistication as information processors, and our ability to maintain a strong 'commitment' to more than one life domain simultaneously. To develop our understanding of these issues it is important to examine precisely what is behind terms such as work motivation. According to psychological research dating back to the 1960s, work motivation is best described as a cognitive-behavioural process involving a wide range of personal and situational variables which mediate the relationship between effort, performance, reward and finally, job satisfaction or the degree of satisfaction with the entire process and hence the amount of effort likely to be put into work in the future (Porter and Lawler, 1968). Working with these more elaborate models of the process of work motivation, differences between the genders are hard to unearth and hence we must accept the null hypothesis, that men and women have similar motivations and commitment to work.

Childcare and attitudes to women at work

While attitudes of men and women towards their own work are very similar and generally positive, looking back over this century, societal attitudes to working mothers have been less positive. For example, in the 1930s, fewer than 20 per cent of women in the USA agreed that married women should be in full-time work. In the UK, a 1943 women at work survey revealed that 30 per cent of women did not believe in a woman working after marriage, and in total, 58 per cent considered that a woman's place was at home, notwithstanding financial necessity. It is also noteworthy that at that time many professions, including teaching, banking and the civil service, operated 'marriage bars' which required women to leave work when they married. By 1965, marriage bars had virtually disappeared and at that time fully 89 per cent of women approved of a married woman working if she had no children, but only 20 per cent gave their support if children were of preschool age. To consider shifts in attitude over time, direct comparisons can be made between surveys carried out in Great Britain in 1965, 1980 and 1987, together with a Northern Ireland survey in 1990. As can be seen, the significance of pre-school-age children remains a very important factor in the determination of replies.

Witherspoon (1988) has described the shift in attitudes to working mothers during the 1980s as tantamount to a sea-change, and it would appear that the tide is continuing to run strongly although a significant minority of women continue to believe that mothers with pre-school children should remain at home.

One factor which has helped to change attitudes has been the steady rise in women's overall involvement in the labour market over time. At the same time, it would be wrong to assume that the relationship between economic

TABLE 12.1 Attitudes towards women working

per cent agreeing that the woman ought to remain at home				
	1965	**1980**	**1987**	**1990**
Married, no children	1	1	1	1
Married, children all at school	20	11	7	10
Married, children all under school age	78	60	45	41
per cent agreeing that it is up to the woman to decide				
	1965	**1980**	**1987**	**1990**
Married, no children	75	62	69	92
Married, children all at school	35	50	61	67
Married, children all under school age	5	15	26	40

Source: Kremer and Montgomery (eds), 1993

activity and attitudes is either linear or causal; allowance must be made for economic and political fluctuations which may halt or even reverse the tide. During periods of recession or war, for example, female employment rates may rise but this will reflect increasing numbers in part-time and seasonal work or work based on short-term contracts. In addition, when male unemployment rates increase, for example in peace time, men may feel that their 'right to work' is threatened by women working, and attitudes towards women working may become less positive as a consequence. Equally, where childcare services are limited and women have few choices other than to leave work then this trend may reflect in more traditional attitudes towards working mothers. In the words of Scott and Duncombe,

> It is unlikely that women will reap the benefits of employment unless there are substantial changes in female labour market conditions and substantial shifts in normative beliefs about gender roles.... Moreover, unless beliefs about gender roles change, and women stop being defined as primarily responsible for family care, women who are in paid work will have to struggle to do a double shift of employment and family care whilst still fearing that their families may suffer.
>
> (Scott and Duncombe, 1991, p. 20)

When considering attitudes towards the rights and roles of women, the shortened, twenty-two-item version Attitudes to Women Scale (Spence and Helmreich, 1972) remains one of the most popular devices. Kremer and Curry (1987) divided the scale into those items dealing with work and non-work/social domains, and discovered that it was the work items which accounted for almost all differences in scores between women and men. That is, men were prepared to accept equal rights outside the workplace but not when employment was the focus of attention. Given such resistance towards equality among many men, it remains important to continue to prioritize equal opportunities campaigns and challenge any misplaced notion that things have 'gone too far'.

Domestic life and paid employment

Over recent years, much has been made of the emergence of new or modern man (the antithesis of traditional man who, when asked if he took sugar in his tea, remarked, 'I don't know, you'd better ask the wife'!). Unfortunately, hard evidence of new man, the partner who is prepared to share the burden of family life and play a significant role in childrearing, is difficult to find. In one recent survey in the UK, it was found that 82 per cent of husbands had never ironed, 73 per cent had never washed clothes and 24 per cent had never cooked (Montgomery, 1993). Hence, there is little evidence to suggest that domestic responsibilities have been lifted from the shoulders of women. Instead, women's dual roles (homecarer and worker) persist. Indeed, even in situations where both partners are not in paid employment, or where the woman is the primary wage earner, then this pattern often still endures.

An additional caring burden is being added to women as the population grows older (see Chapter 13). That is, caring responsibility for elderly relatives is seen primarily as women's work. In the past, the maintenance of domestic responsibilities, including informal care, alongside paid employment was associated with lowered self-esteem and feelings of guilt and anxiety, most especially among working mothers with young children. Research in the 1990s is starting to show that these feelings are no longer as prevalent and that instead successful multi-tasking can be linked with enhanced self-esteem where adequate support from the family, the employer and the state are all available. A growing body of work is also highlighting the negative effects on psychological well-being of being 'trapped' in a role which is seen as unfulfilling or lacking in challenge, with particular attention focusing on the role of full-time homecarer.

Gender in organizations

While attitudes, aspirations and employment legislation have made a considerable impact on the sexual division of the labour market in the 1990s, the gendered nature of many work organisations continues to cause disquiet (Cockburn, 1991). Attention has therefore shifted to the barriers, both structural and personal, which impede women's progress within work organizations (Maddock and Parkin, 1993; Reskin and Padavic, 1994). These barriers include traditional attitudes and stereotypes towards working women, a shortage of family-friendly policies, inadequate or uneconomic childcare services for working women, and various structural devices which generally contrive to make organizations gender unfriendly and which reinforce glass ceilings and glass walls, including sexual and gender harassment alongside less overt forms of discrimination (see Collier, 1995; Davidson and Cooper, 1992; Reskin and Padavic, 1994).

One area of research which continues to demand attention concerns the perceptions, behaviour and attitudes of men and women in management. Earlier research tended to suggest that, in order to succeed in a man's world, women managers were obliged to cloak their femininity. It was argued that this could lead to role conflict as their work roles could be in conflict with the traditional female stereotype based on caring and nurturance. The model of the successful manager was essentially defined in masculine terms at that time, and for this reason many women were seen to be leaving behind their gender as they climbed the managerial ladder – hence terms such as 'queen bee' entered the business lexicon. To be successful in a man's world required women to be more masculine than the men, and this was seen to bring inevitable social and psychological consequences. More recently, this picture has changed, and change has been driven by two forces.

First, the model of the effective manager has changed, and hence expectations about what is appropriate managerial behaviour have altered. In modern organizations the 'macho manager', perhaps better described as bully

(Randall, 1997), is increasingly seen as dysfunctional. Instead organizations are coming to recognize that qualities traditionally associated with femininity are to be encouraged among managers. At the same time, the old notion of 'jobs for life' is disappearing fast from most organizations. For both genders, single-track career paths are much shorter, and the expectation that a good manager must be a 'company man' to the exclusion of all other life domains is seen as outdated. Accordingly, opportunities for women and men to engage in this brave new world on a more equal footing have increased.

Second, over recent years gender-role stereotypes have changed dramatically, most notably with the introduction in the late 1980s of the 'superwoman' role model for young women. Multi-roling and coping with multiple demands are now seen as positive attributes to be aspired to by men and women alike. In this climate it may be men who feel themselves under greatest threat and feel most defensive. The rise of men's groups and the reaction or backlash to the development of equal opportunities programmes may bear witness to this trend. From the woman's perspective, there is now less evidence to suggest that women managers in the 1990s suffer lowered self-esteem related to role conflict because of the dual demands of work and primary responsibility for looking after the home. However, it is those women who still aspire towards traditional sex roles, defined primarily by feminine attributes, who remain the most vulnerable (Kirrane and Kremer, 1994).

Structural factors which stand in the way of women's progress are most often identified by women themselves as the most important hurdles to their advancement. The construction of glass ceilings is taken to be associated most strongly with the patriarchal nature of many organizations, where male managers may dwell comfortably in a men-only world and either actively resist change or find it difficult to see how that world may change. Burke and Davidson (1994) offer three related hypotheses as to why glass ceilings remain impenetrable. First, it could be argued that it is because women are 'different' from men and are less suited to positions of leadership or responsibility. This hypothesis remains unsubstantiated. Second, it is argued that the more powerful majority (men) actively discriminate against the minority (women) and hence perpetuate inequality. Third, it is maintained that policies, practices and procedures, sometimes unwittingly, support the status quo, for example women's lack of influence, existing under-representation of women, tokenism, lack of mentors and sponsors, and denial of access to challenging work.

A social exchange analysis would suggest that because men are those who have occupied the most powerful positions in organizations and because these men have most to lose if the status quo is disturbed, then a male hegemony within an organization is naturally quite resistant to change. Change will not occur automatically but requires positive actions which provide women with the opportunity to break the glass ceilings to advancement and the glass walls to equality of access (Kremer et al., 1996). At the risk of sounding overly optimistic there are signs that the cracks are starting to appear and that the merit principle is beginning to hold sway in public- and private-sector organizations alike. For women, for men and for efficient management this has to be a good thing.

Conclusions

In the face of continuing inequality of opportunity, and the smokescreen of traditional stereotypes, there is little evidence to suggest that women see themselves as permanently consigned to the margins. This is revealed by the increasing number of women breaking through into management roles, the significance which working women attach to their employment and the commitment they give to their work, irrespective of relatively poorer conditions of employment. According to Hakim (1991), these high levels of job satisfaction must not be taken at face value, because for many women their primary life goals and interests are away from work. Using such a gender-related model to describe women's work commitment while at the same time implicitly using a job-related model to interpret men's commitment is a temptation which must be avoided. Instead each individual's life experiences, priorities and circumstances (which in turn may be influenced by gender and including childcare responsibilities) are likely to determine motivations and attitudes to work.

Research has described large shifts in attitudes towards women working during the 1980s and there is little to suggest that this change is not continuing apace (Thomson, 1995; Trewsdale and Kremer, 1996). At the same time, the single most significant factor which continues to dominate perceptions of gender at work is childcare (Brannen et al., 1994). Successive surveys have revealed that among women and men alike, there continues to be ambivalence towards accepting that mothers with pre-school children should be in paid employment. How far this finding reflects a principled stand concerning the responsibilities associated with motherhood within the nuclear family (the motherhood mandate), and how far it is a rationalization or reflection of the practicalities and cost of childcare arrangements must remain a matter for conjecture.

Research dealing with causal attribution has traditionally described gender differences such that men are more likely to assume personal agency than are women; men say they choose but women say they have choices imposed upon them. Could it be that women's external attribution bias is becoming less powerful, and consequently women may now be more willing to define themselves as controllers of their destiny; as agents rather than puppets? This is not to deny that considerations such as pay are still very important in terms of day-to-day existence, nor that the inequitable division of labour within the home continues to exert a massive impact on women's employment opportunities. Instead, it is to recognize that women's own perception of their capacity for influence and change within organizations may be shifting. In terms of long-term goals of equality of opportunity at work, such evidence is certainly cause for optimism and is likely to be a powerful force for social change.

REFERENCES

Barron, R.D. and Norris, G.M. (1991). Sexual divisions in the dual labour market. In Leonard, D. and Allen, S. (eds), *Sexual divisions revisited.* (pp. 153–77). Basingstoke: Macmillan Press.

Beechey, V. (1986). Women's employment in contemporary Britain. In Beechey, V. and Whitelegg, E. (eds), *Women in Britain today.* (pp. 77–131). Milton Keynes: Open University Press.

Blau, F.D. and Winkler, A.E. (1989). Women in the labour force: an overview. In Freeman, J. (ed.), *Women: a feminist perspective.* (pp. 265–86). Mountain View, CA: Mayfield Publishing Co.

Brannen, J., Meszaros, G., Moss, P. and Poland, G. (1994). *Employment and family life: a review of research in the UK (1980–1994).* Research Series No. 41. Sheffield: Employment Department.

Burke, R.J. and Davidson, M.J. (eds) (1994). *Women in management: current research issues.* London: Paul Chapman.

Cockburn, C. (1991). *In the ways of women: men's resistance to sex equality in organisations.* London: Macmillan Press.

Collier, R. (1995). *Combating sexual harassment in the workplace.* Buckingham: Open University Press.

Commission of the European Communities (1983). *European women and men in 1983.* Brussels: CEC.

Davidson, M.J. and Burke, R.J. (eds) (1994). *Women in management: current research issues.* London: Paul Chapman.

Davidson, M.J. and Cooper, C. (1992). *Shattering the glass ceiling.* London: Paul Chapman.

Dex, S. (1988). *Women's attitudes towards work.* Basingstoke: Macmillan Press.

Hakim, C. (1991). Grateful slaves and self-made women: fact and fantasy in women's work orientations. *European Sociological Review* **7(2)**, 101–21.

Itzin, C. and Newman, J. (eds) (1995). *Gender, culture and organizational change: putting theory into practice.* London: Routledge.

Kirrane, M. and Kremer, J. (1994). The attitudes, aspirations and career orientations of women in junior management. *Irish Journal of Psychology* **15(4)**, 540–58.

Kremer, J. and Curry, C. (1987). Attitudes towards women in Northern Ireland. *Journal of Social Psychology* **127(5)**, 531–4.

Kremer, J., Hallmark, A., Berwick, S., Clelland, J., Duncan, J., Lindsay, W. and Ross, V. (1996). Gender and equality of opportunity in public sector organisations. *Journal of Occupational and Organizational Psychology* **69**, 183–98.

Kremer, J. and Montgomery, P. (eds) (1993). *Women's working lives.* Belfast: HMSO.

Labour Market Trends (Oct. 1997). London: Office for National Statistics.

Maddock, S.J. and Parkin, D. (1993). Gender cultures: women's choices and strategies at work. *Women in Management Review* **8(2)**, 3–9.

Martin, J. and Roberts, C. (1984). *Women and employment: a lifetime perspective.* London: HMSO.

Montgomery, P. (1993). Paid and unpaid work. In Kremer, J. and Montgomery, P. (*Women's working lives*) (pp. 15–42). Belfast: HMSO.

Nicolson, P. (1996). *Gender, power and organisation: a psychological perspective.* London: Routledge.

Porter, L.W. and Lawler, E.E. (1968). *Managerial attitudes and performance.* Homewood, IL: Dorsey Press.

Randall, P. (1997). *Adult bullying: perpetrators and victims.* London: Routledge.

Reskin, B. and Padavic, I. (1994). *Women and men at work.* Thousand Oaks, CA: Pine Forge Press.

Rowbotham, S. (1973). *Hidden from history: 300 years of women's oppression and the fight against it.* London: Pluto Press.

Scott, J., Braun, M. and Alwin, D. (1993). The family way. In Jowell, R., Brook, L. and Dowds, L. (eds), *International social attitudes: the 10th BSA report.* (pp. 23–47). Aldershot: Dartmouth.

Scott, J. and Duncombe, J. (1991). A cross national comparison of gender-role attitudes: is the working mother selfish? *Working papers of the ESRC Research Centre on Micro-social Change.* Paper 9. Colchester: University of Essex.

Spence, J.T. and Helmreich, R.L. (1972). The Attitudes Towards Women Scale: an objective instrument to measure attitudes towards the rights and roles of women in contemporary society. *JSAS Catalogue of Selected Documents in Psychology* **2**, 66.

Thomson, K. (1995). Working mothers: choice or circumstance? In Jowell, R., Curtice, J., Park, A., Brook, L. and Ahrendt, D. (eds), *British social attitudes: the 12th report.* (pp. 61–90) Aldershot: Gower.

Trewsdale, J. and Kremer, J. (1996). Women and work. In Breen, R., Devine, P. and Dowds, L. (eds), *Social attitudes in Northern Ireland: the 5th report.* (pp. 70–93). Belfast: Appletree Press.

Witherspoon, S. (1988). Interim report: a woman's work. In Jowell, R., Witherspoon, S. and Brook, L. (eds). *British social attitudes: the 5th report.* (pp. 175–200). Aldershot: Gower.

Further reading

Campbell, D.J., Campbell, K.M. and Kennard, D. (1994). The effects of family responsibilities on the work commitment and job performance of non-professional women. *Journal of Occupational and Organizational Psychology* **67**, 283–96.

Itzin, C. (1995). The gender culture in organizations. In Itzin, C. and Newman, J. (eds), *Gender, culture and organizational change: putting theory into practice.* (pp. 30–53). London: Routledge.

Kremer, J., Hallmark, A., Berwick, S., Clelland, J., Duncan, J., Lindsay, W. and Ross, V. (1996). Gender and equality of opportunity in public sector organizations. *Journal of Occupational and Organizational Psychology* **69**, 183–98.

Maddock, S. and Parkin, D. (1994). Gender cultures: How they affect men and women at work. In Davidson, M. and Burke, R. (eds), *Women in management: current research issues.* (pp. 29–40). London: Paul Chapman.

Montgomery, P. (1993). Paid and unpaid work. In Kremer, J. and Montgomery, P. (eds), *Women's working lives* (pp. 15–42). Belfast: HMSO.

Discussion questions

1. How do marriage and motherhood impact on employment prospects? Why was this the case and why is this the case?
2. Domestic responsibilities: where is new man when the ironing needs to be done?
3. Can or should men and women ever experience equality at work?
4. What techniques are best able to promote a genuine equal opportunities culture?
5. Glass walls and glass ceilings in the workplace – fact or fantasy for women?
6. Looking ahead, in your opinion who will be best equipped to deal with work organizations in the twenty-first century, men or women, and why?

13

OLD AGE

Norma Rainey

INTRODUCTION

When discussing gender, developmental psychologists have normally been inclined to focus attention on the early years of life. However, as the population becomes ever older (Craig, 1983), and a growing body of knowledge charts life beyond the childrearing years, then it has become increasingly apparent how gender exerts its influence across the entire life-span, up to and including old age. For example, research consistently has shown that Western cultures operate what is known as a 'double standard' of ageing in relation to gender. Age has been shown to be more salient, more value-laden and generally more negative for women than it is for men who, by way of contrast, may often enjoy increased status with age (Etaugh, 1993). What is more, women are more likely to be labelled as being 'middle-aged' or 'old' by men at an earlier age than vice versa. Being categorized as both old *and* female brings to bear a double-edged sword in terms of negative stereotypes; older women not only have to contend with age-related stereotypes but also with those used to categorize women.

The chapter aims to show the impact which ageing has on the lives of older adults, and in particular on the lifestyles and social behaviour of those men and women who are euphemistically referred to as being in 'the twilight years', or, less charitably, as having 'one foot in the grave'. While no rigid age limits are set when defining old age, for the purposes of the chapter the focus will tend to be on those years beyond the statutory retirement age of 65 years.

HEALTH AND CAREGIVING

To begin, two apparently contradictory observations about gender and health in old age are well established. First, women have a substantial and continuing advantage in terms of life expectancy. The current male to female ratio for the world's aged population (that is, aged over 65 years) is estimated to be three males to every four females, and globally, elderly women represent the fastest-growing section of the population. Second, indicators of healthcare utilization consistently reveal that older women use healthcare services more frequently than older men (Etaugh, 1993); hence the expression, 'Women get sick but men die'.

A number of researchers have considered these figures (for example, Gove and Hughes, 1979) and concluded that older women's poorer health rates are predominantly explained by their contracting milder types of disease, with lower risk of mortality, than men. Therefore, women's higher rates of complaints about illness, and their greater use of care resources, reflect the fact that women need more medical help than men but their medical complaints (rheumatism, arthritis and osteoporosis, for example), while often very painful, are not as immediately life-threatening as those suffered by men (for example, heart disease). Hence, more correctly, it is the case that women report sickness more often, but are more likely to live; men report sickness less often, but are more likely to die.

In line with these findings, older women's healthcare needs have been shown to be different from those of older men. For example, they are more likely than men to suffer from chronic and debilitating conditions that require long-term home healthcare and assistance with the upkeep of their homes. At the same time, the financial, emotional and physical burden of caring for infirm elderly people at home is more likely to fall upon elderly and middle-aged women than upon men. In fact, about 72 per cent of the caregivers of infirm, older people are women. Of these women caregivers, 33 per cent (with a mean age of 69 years) provide care for their husbands, and 40 per cent (with a mean age of 52 years) provide care for a parent (Special Committee on Ageing, 1987–8). The unfortunate consequence of these social trends is that these female caregivers are left in old age with little by way of financial or emotional resources to help cope with their own increasing medical and social needs.

An additional fact in relation to caregiving is that women are increasingly entering the labour market and remaining in work, even during the years of childrearing (McLaughlin, 1993). Of particular significance is the increase in working women aged 45–64 years – the very group who traditionally provide the majority of hours to voluntary service agencies and informal support for elderly people. At the moment, there is no indication that today's women, even those who do work, are abandoning their filial responsibilities. In fact, these so-called 'women in the middle' appear to be assuming multiple roles – caring for their own families, for aged parents, and perhaps for parents-in-law, in addition to working. How long this pattern will continue is unknown, but clearly the strain involved for those caught in the caring trap is considerable and must have long-term implications for both younger families and older people.

Socio-economic class

When considering the effect of socio-economic class on old age, the necessity for dealing with gender issues is shown starkly in the way in which pension and insurance schemes often serve to discriminate against women. For example, in the UK, if a woman has taken time away from paid employment to raise a family or to care for an elderly or disabled dependant (and has not maintained her national insurance contributions voluntarily), then she may well find that by the age of retirement she has not accumulated sufficient national insurance credits to qualify for a state pension.

As women outlive men by an average of seven years (Lopata, 1979), most married women face the prospect of widowhood at the end of their lives. An elderly widow is in a particularly vulnerable position because she usually faces a sharp reduction in income after her husband's death. In the USA, Lopata (1979) reported that the incomes of widows in Chicago were about half of what they had been before widowhood, and a similar position exists in the UK and Ireland. In addition, most widows usually choose not to move to less expensive housing so they are then burdened with the problem of maintaining a house on a greatly reduced income. Therefore, many elderly widows become what is termed 'house poor' (Struyk and Soldo, 1980). What is more, as Lawton (1980) has stated, often elderly women do not have the physical ability, strength or experience to perform necessary repairs to their homes. Hence, they must pay to have such functions carried out, which in turn adds yet another drain on their already stretched budget.

Aside from the financial problems, there are considerable status implications associated with widowhood (Lopata, 1973). After the death of their husbands, many widows are reluctant to maintain community and neighbourhood friendships and ties. Many withdraw from social life, and particularly from events which they would have attended as one half of a couple. When reflecting on the lower status she experienced as a result of this withdrawal, one woman said that she felt as though she had become a 'second-class citizen'. Additionally, many better-educated women found that widowhood threatened their self-identities because their activities and outlook on life were often constructed around their husbands' lives and their husbands' work associates. In contrast, working-class women were less involved in the lives of their husbands; these couples communicated less with each other, and a husband's death was not as damaging to his wife's self-identity. Having to give up their own home and go to live with their children, for example, represents a further loss in status for older widows. This is perceived as a loss both in the eyes of the community and in the widow's own self-perception. The fact that she is no longer mistress of her own home, and is no longer surrounded by the possessions that she has accumulated over a lifetime, can represent a traumatic erosion of status in the microenvironment of her home.

Hence, in many Western societies not only is there a reduced financial position but the elderly widow must also cope with a considerable shift in roles. As Lopata (1979) stated, 'Her identity as a wife is shattered and there is no comfortable role of widow available to her as to widows in other parts of the world' (p. 31). For example, in some non-Western countries, such as Russia and China, the older woman has a role assigned to her – she takes care of grandchildren while her daughter(s) works. In Western societies, either this may not be feasible due to greater geographical mobility, or older women may deliberately avoid this role. Many widows state that they prefer to live by themselves and to be independent of the constraints of regular childcare, but this independence may entail feelings of uselessness.

LIFE EXPERIENCES

From a social psychological perspective, Young (1965) suggested that, in addition to encountering different transitions into old age, men and women may also align themselves to different levels of group membership. He suggested that the immediate social environment, and kin groups in particular, structure women's lives whereas men's lives are typically shaped by more diverse social units. With this in mind, two themes have emerged in discussions of men's and women's life courses:

- The family is the main force shaping the course of women's adult lives, while work is the key influence on men's lives.
- Women's lives are characterized by 'discontinuity' (rather than 'regularity') and form no 'orderly' patterns in comparison with men's.

Triple jeopardy

At this juncture, introduction of the concept of jeopardy is relevant. In 1956, Talley and Kaplan (cited in Rodeheaver and Datan, 1988) first applied this concept to the circumstance of being simultaneously old and black. Those who were old and black were regarded as doubly jeopardized because they carried into old age 'a whole lifetime of economic and social indignities' caused by racial prejudice and discrimination. The concept of double jeopardy was subsequently extended to include triple jeopardy or even quadruple jeopardy, with triple jeopardy being a term most often applied to older women. In this context, the term encapsulates neatly the three separate but interacting conditions faced by many women who are growing older. These conditions are poverty, widowhood and caregiving.

First, there is a higher risk of older women falling into poverty at some time in their lives than is the case for men. This is because of the inequalities in social security benefits, reduced pensions when a woman's husband dies, and, for those who were in employment before retirement, inequalities in male and female salaries. In addition, there are those women who have had life-long financial dependency on their husbands.

Second is widowhood. The most significant effects of poverty are often revealed in widowhood. Gender in itself does not predict stress following the death of a spouse, but inactivity, isolation, poor health and diminished financial resources do, and all of these conditions are common among elderly women.

Finally, with regard to caregiving, older women constitute the bulk of both recipients and providers of care. It has been estimated that for every one resident of a nursing home, there are between two and three older people receiving extensive care from family members (Brody, 1985). As you may imagine, this can create a number of problems, but especially with conflicting familial expectations and values. This problem is made yet worse by the common notion that families should do more for elderly relatives to relieve the burden of care that is shouldered by the state. However, perhaps of greatest significance for older women is the increasing likelihood that they will become caregivers for their elderly parents, more of whom are living longer and with more chronic health problems than at any other time in history. In addition, there is the assumption that women are naturally gifted, or predisposed, towards caregiving. As a consequence, this can mean that they are offered less help than men in similar circumstances. Hence the term triple jeopardy captures the indignities arising from social, economic and psychological conditions surrounding both ageing and being female, with particular emphasis on poverty, widowhood and caregiving.

At the same time, there is general consensus that at a personal or psychological level, women age with less difficulty than men; but there is less agreement as to why. As many Western women live their entire lives within the domestic domain, some researchers have argued that women are faced with less dramatic and difficult transitions in old age (Keith, 1985), such as coping with the transition from paid employment to retirement. The actual physical demands associated with tasks traditionally performed by women are also seen as more adaptable to the constraints of ageing. For example, in societies where hunting and heavy agricultural work is necessary, old men are noticeably less efficient than younger men in performing these tasks. However, it is much easier for older women to continue to prepare the food and to look after the children, thus freeing the younger, stronger women for the more productive work of gathering and gardening. This large investment in childcare has a further compensation for these women; the bonds of affection created between women and their children and grandchildren are often a guarantee of both material and emotional comfort in later years.

Another explanation as to why women may age with less difficulty than men is that, throughout their lives, they have had to cope with the physical constraints of pregnancy, lactation, menstruation and menopause. These experiences may predispose women to adapt to the bodily changes associated with ageing more easily than men. In this way, underlying many of the arguments about women's relatively successful adaptation to ageing is the premise that discontinuity is difficult and that women are seen as better able to adjust, either because they experience less discontinuity throughout their working lives or because they experience more physical discontinuities and therefore are more skilled in adaptation than men.

Other research on retired working women has shown that they have more versatile social networks than men, and these do not necessarily suffer with retirement (Antonucci, 1994). Retirement often triggers an increase in social activities for these women. It seems that they use their newly acquired leisure time to engage in social interactions that their previous working status constrained. In fact, many of these women define leisure as 'freedom to do what you like'.

Overall, it is becoming apparent that women's work histories and life expectancies are sufficiently different from men's to ensure that retirement takes on a different meaning for each gender. Unlike men in the labour force, employed women retire at an earlier age and tend to base their plans for retirement around those of their spouse. In addition, a woman's marital status has implications for her retirement and what it means in her life. For example, a married woman who stayed in the domestic domain tends to set the boundary of retirement according to that of her husband, despite the fact that her own work life changes little as long as she has household duties to perform. However, should a married woman have been in the paid workforce, some marital conflict may ensue as to when each partner will retire and how they will spend their time during the years of retirement. The majority of single women are in the labour force and hence they tend to define retirement in much the same way as men – the same economic and personal decisions have to be confronted (Liang, 1982). For this reason, it is the relationship between marital status and gender which is significant in retirement and not simply gender acting alone.

The gender differences in health and life expectancies also influence men's and women's attitudes towards retirement. On reaching retirement age, how a person plans for the future greatly depends on the person's anticipated life expectancy. At age 65 years, there is a high probability that women will live for at least another 18 years and that the last 17 years of their lives will be spent in widowhood. For a man, however, the chances are that he will live another 14 years, during which time he will remain married (Dreyer, 1989). Such biological criteria are an integral part of older men's and women's life space and become important constituents in their approaches to retirement and feelings about post-retirement satisfaction.

Social networks

Implicit in the discussion so far has been the influence and importance of social networks in the lives of older women. For example, in one study, a group of elderly people were asked, 'What is most important to you today?' The majority answered, 'Family and friends' (Novak, 1983). This finding was confirmed by Argyle in 1987, who noted that money, career and religion were relatively less important for older people than were personal relationships.

Reflecting on such findings, a major area of interest among those concerned with understanding and promoting successful ageing is the informal support provided by close personal relationships (particularly involving family, friends and intimates) rather than the formal support provided by agencies and the helping professions. Maintaining close relationships with other people is often a significant factor in determining whether older men and women feel a sense of belonging to the social system (Duck, 1991). This importance may be intensified with age because society withdraws from older adults on two levels. First, it withdraws behaviourally, in the form of enforced retirement. Second, it withdraws attitudinally, in the form of attributing diminishing powers, qualities and abilities to those who are old.

Family members and friends are of prime importance in older people's informal support networks and are pivotal in how life is experienced towards the latter part of the individual life-cycle. Overall, individual adaptation to old age on all levels has been shown to be highly dependent on personal tolerance to stress and life events and on the availability of informal social support networks (Duck, 1991).

Friendship

When discussing social networks and contacts, the issue of friendship, most especially in the lives of older women, is significant. But why friendship? Growing older is associated with the diminution of roles and of choices, with retirement and loss of spouse particularly predominant in these losses. What is more, most of these role losses are beyond the older person's control. In addition, with retirement older people often regard their contribution to society as being devalued because age has altered their status to that of 'non-participant', pensioner or just simply 'old person' (Rosow, 1985). Friendship is a voluntary, non-institutionalized and relatively enduring relationship, and therefore it is extremely important in offering succour, constancy and stability in the lives of most older people. It has been shown that friendships positively influence older people's well-being and morale, and the support of friends (and other primary relationships) has been shown to decrease dependency on social security agencies and other formal organizations (Duck, 1991).

Psychologically, it appears to be the element of choice that differentiates friendships from other types of relationship (Baltes and Baltes, 1986). Older people can choose to make friends or not and they can choose to continue a friendship or they can choose to dissolve it. Accordingly, choice in friendship is one life domain over which older people can continue to exercise a sense of control.

Friendship is as important in later life as it is during adolescence and young adulthood. However, people do report a decline in the number of their friends as they grow older and in their social interactions with them. Obviously, death is a major reason for this but other reasons include declining health, relocation, transportation difficulties, and loss of social contacts made at work (Argyle and Henderson, 1985).

Regarding gender differences in patterns of friendship, Winstead (1986) stated that different friendship patterns between men and women have been reported so often that she hesitates to question their validity. While it has been shown that both men and women are 'better off' when they socialize in a meaningful way, the factors underlying socializing differ between the genders. Studies have shown that men report having a greater number of casual friends than women while women tend to have more intense long-term relationships than men. Frequently, male friendships involve married couples; men report having few (if any) close friends, especially in middle age, and have less frequency of contact with their friends than younger men. Interestingly, most older men name their wife as their best friend (Wright, 1989).

There are also gender differences in the behavioural patterns of male and female friendships. For example, it has been shown repeatedly that women value close, intimate relationships with other women, based on mutual help and support. For women, conversation is an important aspect of friendships. Women friends spend a great deal of time in self-disclosure, giving and receiving advice and social support, and discussing personal problems and intimate details of their lives. Conversely, male friendships are less intimate and are centred around shared activities and interests (Winstead, 1986). Indeed, older men are more likely to turn to women friends for intimate conversation, or to romantic partners, and especially wives (Wright, 1989).

Traditionally, in Western societies, and particularly during marriage, men's roles are characterized as career- or work-oriented, and men are seen as the primary providers for home and family. Women, on the other hand, are assumed to have greater responsibility for maintaining the marital home and childrearing (Montgomery, 1993). For women, childrearing responsibilities may limit interactions with friends and yet the significance of women's friendships throughout the life-span has been well documented. For example, the advice and support of friends is reported to enhance a woman's relationship with her husband (Rubin, 1986), while female friends reinforce one another in the performance of childrearing responsibilities (Hess, 1979). Even in the workplace, friendships between women help to promote their performance in professional roles, especially in male-dominated settings (Hunter et al., 1983).

In the light of these findings, it is surprising to learn that elderly men actually report having more friends and more social contact with their friends than do elderly women (Roberto and Kimboko, 1989). However, older women's friendships normally involve more long-term, intense and highly intimate relationships whereas men's friendships often operate at a more superficial level, with low levels of intimacy. It has been suggested that older women's networks consist of 'friends as friends', but elderly men's 'friends' are best categorized as 'associates or acquaintances' (Argyle and Henderson, 1985). This hypothesis has been supported many times, suggesting that older men may have a less stringent definition of friendship than older women.

In general, therefore, there are both behavioural and psychological differences in men's and women's same-sex friendships and these differences carry through into later life. Men report having more casual friends than women while women engage in more intense, intimate relationships. Men are more likely to do things together, such as participating in sports or other hobbies, while divulging personal information is rare. For women, conversation is important. Having a close, personal, confidential relationship with another woman has important reinforcing properties in the lives of most women.

Other researchers have looked at friendship differences between the socio-economic classes. Elderly widows and widowers who would be classified as working class consistently report feeling isolated, and this is particularly so in the case of widows: 'An indication that other factors that are unique to working class people, and especially women, prevent individuals from taking advantage of the social opportunities created by the prevalence of widowhood among peers' (Blau, 1973, p. 84). Blau explained these findings in terms of the differences in social interaction with friends which were in existence before the onset of old age. That is, through necessity working-class women may have had to limit their social contacts mostly to family, along with 'dropping in' on neighbours who lived close by. Middle-class women, on the other hand, had the opportunity to develop more extensive and geographically dispersed social lives, with frequent contacts with peers who were neither family nor neighbours. When their husbands die, the larger social network surrounding these middle-class women presents greater possibilities for establishing closer relationships with old friends, or forming closer ties with past acquaintances. In contrast, working-class women are less likely to have such an extensive or heterogeneous social network to draw upon.

Once more, the impact of financial considerations on life chances in old age is seen to be highly significant. In addition, women's financial position during widowhood itself is also likely to affect opportunities for maintaining or forming social contacts. Having less money than her middle-class counterpart can adversely affect the working-class woman's opportunities for travelling to visit friends or relatives, or, if she should wish, to engage in leisure activities.

Friendship and loneliness

These socal trends aside, fundamentally what is it about friendship which makes it so important in the lives of older people? As already mentioned, friendship allows choice and agency which promotes psychological well-being but alongside this, in a very practical sense, friends represent a potential shield against loneliness. The maintenance of a network of social relationships which provide varying degrees of emotional contacts, as well as more personal, satisfying and mutually shared relationships is seen to be of crucial importance in alleviating loneliness.

With regard to gender differences in loneliness, it has been suggested that men and women have different relational needs which may account for noted gender differences in the causes of loneliness (Duck, 1991). For men, the perceived quality of at least one relationship has been seen as the key factor in preventing loneliness; often, the presence of a female confidante (often partner) was strongly associated with men not feeling lonely. On the other hand, women assessed the impact of all their relationships, both same and opposite sex, on feelings of loneliness. It has been concluded that male socialization precludes the formation of same-sex, intimate friendship bonds which are so highly valued by women, and yet it is these types of relationship which appear to offer men the greatest protection from becoming lonely. Ironically, on a more positive note, given the higher mortality rates among men than among women, those men who do survive into old age are likely to have an increased opportunity for finding such a partner.

Conclusions

The evidence presented here suggests that gender differences and old age are intricately associated, and the many factors which serve to socialize and differentiate the two genders throughout life come to exert a profound effect on the lives and well-being of older men and women. While women are likely to suffer materially in old age (reflecting the triple jeopardy of widowhood, poverty and caregiving), socially and psychologically women generally would appear to be better adapted to life beyond retirement.

Many people have stated that studying women as a separate entity in the ageing literature is misleading, because they believe that the psychology of ageing *is* the psychology of women. They would argue that the problems of old age are essentially women's problems; though it can be argued equally that the problems of old age are not the preserve of one gender. Nevertheless, the problems and issues related to ageing may differ qualitatively between older men and older women. There is the inescapable fact that women, on average, tend to outlive men and also tend to marry men older than themselves. Consequently, studies of negative events in old age, such as bereavement or loss of social support, naturally involve far more women than men. However, to see the problems of old age as exclusively the problems of womankind is misleading. Statistically, women may well represent more than half the full picture but it is unlikely that their story alone will ever complete the portrait of old age.

References

Antonucci, T. (1994). A life-span view of women's social relations. In Turner, B.F. and Troll, L.E. (eds), *Women growing older.* (pp. 239–69). Thousand Oaks, CA: Sage.

Argyle, M. (1987). *The psychology of happiness.* London: Methuen.

Argyle, M. and Henderson, M. (1985). *The anatomy of relationships.* London: Penguin.

Baltes, M.M. and Baltes, P.B. (eds) (1986). *The psychology of control and ageing.* Hillsdale, NJ: Lawrence Erlbaum.

Blau, Z.S. (1973). *Old age in a changing society.* New York: New Viewpoints.

Brody, E.M. (1985). Parent care as a normative family stress. *The Gerontologist* **25,** 19–29.

Craig, J. (1983). The growth of the elderly population. *Population Trends, No. 32.* London: OPCS.

Dreyer, P.H. (1989). Postretirement life satisfaction. In Spacapan, S. and Oskamp, S. (eds), *The social psychology of ageing.* (pp. 109–33). Newbury Park, CA: Sage.

Duck, S. (1991). *Friends for life.* 2nd edn. New York: Harvester Wheatsheaf.

Etaugh, C. (1993). Women in the middle and later years. In Denmark, F.L. and Paludi, M.A. (eds), *Psychology of women: handbook of issues and theories.* (pp. 213–46). Westport, CT: Greenwood.

Gove, W.R. and Hughes, M. (1979). Possible causes of the apparent sex differences in physical health: an empirical investigation. *American Sociological Review* **44,** 126–46.

Hess, B. (1979). Sex roles, friendship and the life course. *Research on Ageing* **1,** 494–515.

Hunter, M.S., Saleebey, D. and Shannon, C. (1983). Female friendships: joint defense against power inequity. *Psychology, A Quarterly Journal of Human Behaviour* **20,** 14–20.

Keith, J. (1985). Age in anthropological research. In Binstock, R.H. and Shanas, E. (eds), *Handbook of ageing and the social sciences.* 2nd edn. (pp. 231–63). New York: Van Nostrand Reinhold.

Lawton, M.P. (1980). *Environment and ageing.* Monterey, CA: Brooks Cole.

Liang, J. (1982). Sex differences in life satisfaction among the elderly. *Journal of Gerontology* **37,** 100–8.

Lopata, H.Z. (1973). The effect of schooling on social contacts of urban women. *American Journal of Sociology* **79,** 604–19.

Lopata, H.Z. (1979). *Women as widows: support systems.* New York: Elseview-North Holland.

McLaughlin, E. (1993). Informal care. In Kremer, J. and Montgomery, P. (eds), *Women's working lives.* (pp. 175–90). Belfast: HMSO.

Montgomery, P. (1993). Paid and unpaid work. In Kremer, J. and Montgomery, P. (eds), *Women's working lives.* (pp. 15–42). Belfast: HMSO.

Novak, M. (1983). Discovering a good age. *International Journal of Ageing and Human Development* **16,** 231–9.

Roberto, K.S. and Kimboko, P.J. (1989). Friendships in later life: definitions and maintenance patterns. *International Journal of Ageing and Human Development* **28,** 9–19.

Rodeheaver, D. and Datan, N. (1988). The challenge of double jeopardy: towards a mental health agenda for ageing women. *American Psychologist* **43(8),** 648–54.

Rosow, I. (1985). Status and role change through the life cycle. In Binstock, R.H. and Shanas, E. (eds), *Handbook of ageing and the social sciences.* 2nd edn. (pp. 62–93). New York: Van Nostrand Reinhold.

Rubin, L.B. (1986). On men and friendship. *Psychoanalytic Review* **73**, 165–81.

Special Committee on Ageing, US Senate (1987–8). *Ageing America: trends and projections.* Washington, DC: U.S. Department of Health and Human Services.

Struyk, R.J. and Soldo, B.J. (1980). *Improving the elderly's housing.* Cambridge, MA: Ballinger.

Winstead, B.A. (1986). Sex differences in same-sex friendships. In Derlega, V.J. and Winstead, B.A. (eds), *Friendship and social interaction.* (pp. 81–97). New York: Springer-Verlag.

Wright, P.H. (1989). Gender differences in adults' same- and cross-gender friendships. In Adams, R.G. and Blieszner, R. (eds), *Older adult friendship: structure and process.* (pp. 197–221). Newbury Park, CA: Sage.

Young, F.W. (1965). *Initiation Ceremonies.* Indianapolis: Bobbs-Merrill.

Further reading

Antonucci, T. (1994). A life-span view of women's social relations. In Turner, B.F. and Troll, L.E. (eds), *Women growing older.* (pp. 239–69). Thousand Oaks, CA: Sage.

Etaugh, C. (1993). Women in the middle and later years. In Denmark, F.L. and Paludi, M.A. (eds), *Psychology of women: handbook of issues and theories.* (pp. 213–46). Westport, CT: Greenwood.

Roberto, K.S. and Kimboko, P.J. (1989). Friendships in later life: definitions and maintenance patterns. *International Journal of Ageing and Human Development* **28**, 9–19.

Rubin, L.B. (1986). On men and friendship. *Psychoanalytic Review* **73**, 165–81.

Wright, P.H. (1989). Gender differences in adults' same- and cross-gender friendships. In Adams, R.G. and Blieszner, R. (eds), *Older adult friendship: Structure and process.* (pp. 197–221). Newbury Park, CA: Sage.

Discussion questions

1. Draw up lists of words commonly used to refer to older men and older women. What do these lists have in common and what distinguishes the two lists? Can you offer any explanations as to why these differences exist?
2. Can you recollect talking to older relatives, for example grandparents? Were you aware that your grandfather appeared more or less content than your grandmother during retirement? What were the differences, if any, and why do you believe they existed?
3. With reference to older people that you know, what social networks are they part of and how do these networks impact on their well-being?
4. Looking forward to your own old age, what difficulties can you see psychologically, socially and materially? How can you buffer yourself against those difficulties?

Part 3

Health, Well-being and Society

14

HEALTH AND ILLNESS

Anneke van Wersch

INTRODUCTION

Psychologists have long been interested in people's illness and well-being but have focused greatest attention on their mental rather than their physical health. Recently, ideas about physical health and illness have shifted from a simple medical to a more comprehensive biopsychosocial perspective or model (Mann and Kato, 1996). In line with this shift, symptoms which were once regarded as purely physical, such as ulcers, tumours and cardiovascular problems, are nowadays not only treated by medication but are also dealt with holistically, seen as part of the individual's life as a whole and including their social environment, their psychological state and their lifestyle.

When endeavouring to identify and label symptoms as physical or psychological, problems are immediately encountered (Cohen and Rodriguez, 1995). For example, should headaches or diarrhoea be classified as physical problems or as psychological when they are based on tension or stress? Are cardiovascular diseases or cancers simply physical illnesses or could they be psychological as well? With these questions in mind, the criteria used to distinguish between physical and mental health become significant, but unfortunately no easy answers are available. Undoubtedly this reflects the complex relationship between the cognitive and the somatic, a complexity which has not always been acknowledged in the history of psychology, going back to Descartes' philosophy of mind/body dualism.

For the purpose of the present chapter, which offers an overview of gender differences in physical health and illness as seen by psychology and health-related disciplines, the criteria which will be employed will be those utilized by the researchers themselves. For example, some use 'physical health' in their title, others operationalize physical health in their text. The chapter will follow their lead. Likewise, when defining the term health itself, the most common definition is simply the absence of illness (Shifren and Bauserman, 1996) with certain variations depending on the aims, sample and instruments reported (Wech, 1983). Again, the chapter will follow the lead of existing literature.

As regards our propensity to label disorders as cognitive or somatic, Mechanic (1995) has argued that we are more inclined to attribute physical symptoms to an illness. This is primarily because physical illness is seen as more socially acceptable and less stigmatizing than when symptoms are attributed to psychiatric or psychological disorders. In addition, physicians find a physical illness easier to deal with because it gives them a greater feeling of control. The same is true for patients: a physical illness is more something that 'happens' to them, somehow outside 'their' control; people will feel sorry for them, send them cards or flowers, telephone or visit them. However, if they are suffering from a mental problem, it is regarded as 'their' responsibility; they are likely to receive little sympathy and people are less sure how to respond.

To consider these and related issues, the chapter has been divided into two sections. The first section overviews the gender differences in physical health and illness which are reported in the literature, while the second discusses the deficiencies of social-psychological theory in the research, and provides an overview of the social-psychological explanations given for such gender differences. By the end of the chapter it is hoped that the reader will have gained a greater understanding of the role which psychology can play in analysing and interpreting gender effects in physical health and illness.

Gender differences

When considering gender differences in relation to physical health, three points of view will be considered: looking healthy, feeling healthy and healthy behaviour.

Looking healthy

The commonsense idea of physical health refers to the way a person looks. The tanned, slim, athletically built person, as opposed to the pale, overweight individual, is generally seen as healthy. However, the emphasis on healthy looks does not always reflect healthy behaviour (Hayes and Ross, 1987). Sunbathing or tanning can lead to skin cancer, the incidence of which has increased by 3% per year over the last 30 years (Leary et al., 1994). No gender differences in tanning behaviour have been reported. Most gender research on 'looking healthy' has focused on the social pressure over recent years to obtain and maintain a slimmer figure. In the literature, this has been operationalized and studied in various ways but the gender differences found are similar.

Jackson et al. (1988) used the term 'body image', operationalized as physical appearance, physical fitness and physical health, and looked at its relation to gender and gender roles. In their literature review, Jackson et al. stressed the non-equivalent relation between gender and body image. They showed that women, in comparison with men, evaluate their bodies less favourably; they express more dissatisfaction with their bodies (and particularly with their weight), more often view their physical appearance as important, perceive a greater discrepancy between body image and body ideal, and are more likely to suffer from eating disorders associated with a negative or distorted body image.

Leary et al.'s (1994) review of the literature considered 'self-presentation and health', and revealed several ways in which people's self-presentation motives can be hazardous to their health. As far as gender differences are concerned, females' physical health is more at risk than that of males, with appearance and body weight seen as more important in making an impression on other people for women than for men. Perceptions of women, but not of men, are affected by how much they eat. Unusually slim female silhouettes are judged as most feminine, while normal-weight male silhouettes are judged as most masculine. The authors concluded that cultural views of femininity may contribute to eating disorders in women, by prescribing unrealistically slim body shapes and sizes. They suggested that the increase in anorexia nervosa and bulimia in the last 30 years is the result of the idealization of slimness in Western cultures.

Hayes and Ross (1987) studied the relation between appearance, health beliefs and eating habits and found that, for the average person, appearance is as large a motivating factor in eating habits as is concern with health, and that women generally are more concerned with their appearance than men. However, they found an interesting, statistically significant interaction between employment status and gender; employed men were more concerned with their appearance than non-employed men whereas employed women were less concerned with their appearance than women who were not employed. Women who were not employed were most concerned with their appearance, and men who were not employed the least. Hayes and Ross discussed these results in terms of bargaining power, arguing that employed women did not need to rely on their appearance as much as unemployed women as their paid work provided them with an alternative source of power.

In a further literature review, Silberstein et al. (1988) concluded that men and women differ in two key aspects of body-image satisfaction, namely the dimensions which underlie body-image satisfaction and the direction of body-image satisfaction. In their own research, which studied relationships between body satisfaction, self-esteem, dieting and exercise, they found that body-esteem was correlated with self-esteem for both men and women. However, measures of weight dissatisfaction were not related to self-esteem for women. The explanation for this could be that weight-dissatisfaction for women is so frequent that it has become a norm, or a 'normative discontent', and serves as a buffer to self-esteem.

More recently, Tiggemann (1994) has built a tentative causal model which proposes that actually being overweight leads to body dissatisfaction. This causes the person to diet, with inevitable failures to control weight and loss of self-esteem. The model was seen as applicable to women but not to men as she concluded that being overweight was more important and of more central concern to women than men. Being overweight was not found to have any impact on the self-esteem of men.

More recently, various eating disorders, but in particular bulimia, have been linked to particular sex-role models for women. Aspiration towards the 'superwoman' role model (that is, being all things to all people – the good homemaker, the ambitious career woman, the athlete, the mother) may lead women, and particularly young women, to be pulled in conflicting directions as regards their body image. They wish to be thin yet curvaceous, athletic yet lean, and with this in mind the relationship between aspiration towards the superwoman ideal and bulimia becomes understandable.

Feeling healthy

Macran et al.'s (1996) overview of definitions of health and illness points out that 'feeling healthy' is a subjective statement by an individual. Qualitative studies have shown that most people hold a complex, multi-dimensional conception of health. 'Feeling healthy' is generally operationalized either as the absence of physical symptoms, or in terms of subjective feelings of health or illness. In some cases, a distinction is made between a current 'health state' ('How do I feel today?') and a long-term general 'health status' ('How do I feel in general?'). In addition, an individual's use of the healthcare system has been used as an index of health state.

Results of research on gender differences and 'feeling healthy' are quite consistent across the Western world. These indicate high morbidity (sickness) rates for women and higher mortality (death) rates for men (Wingerd, 1984; Verbrugge, 1989; Anson et al., 1990; Gijsbers van Wijk et al., 1991). The highest death rates for both men and women result from cardiovascular diseases, cancers and cerebrovascular diseases (for example, strokes). While women more frequently suffer illness and disability, their problems are less often life-threatening ones. Men suffer more from chronic life-threatening diseases, causing permanent disability and earlier death. Men have higher rates of heart disease before the age of 50 years, higher injury rates at all ages, and a higher risk of all the leading causes of death. Indeed, men have an average life expectancy which is seven years less than that of women, and the risk of death is higher for males than females at all ages. As Verbrugge (1985) remarks, 'One sex is sicker in the short run, and the other in the long run' (p. 163). It has also been found, from both medical records and the monitoring of health service records, that women use the health services more than men (for example, Gijsbers van Wijk et al., 1991), even when typical female problems such as menstruation and menopausal symptoms are discounted (Popay et al., 1993). Women are also more frequently involved in other types of illness behaviour, such as having days of restricted activity and of bed-disability and of using medication (Meininger, 1986).

That women live longer than men is not a blessing *per se* (see Chapter 13). As Haug and Folmar (1986) suggest, 'The benefits of longer life may be offset by deteriorating health, cognitive deficits, death of family and friends, and financial hardship' (p. 332).

Healthy behaviour

Analytic reviews of mortality and morbidity trends have shown the importance of behavioural factors. The behaviour of individuals as a determinant of health status and functional capacity has become one of the major focuses in the health sectors of Western nations. The World Health Organisation has developed a number of programmes under the rubric of 'lifestyle' in order to influence or change the health-related behaviours of individuals, with tobacco and alcohol consumption, eating habits and exercise being the primary targets for most lifestyle projects (Dean, 1989).

It has been shown that men's higher mortality rates are due mainly to behavioural influences, such as higher rates of cigarette smoking, type A behaviour patterns and alcohol consumption (Waldron, 1976). It is accepted that smoking is one of the most significant risk factors for cardiovascular disease, the leading cause of death for men and women, and the condition responsible for approximately one half of all deaths in the US. Smoking one packet of cigarettes a day is estimated to increase one's risk of coronary heart disease by two-and-a-half times and smoking is also the major cause of lung cancer (Chesney and Nealey, 1996).

Gender differences in tobacco use have been well documented (Grunberg et al., 1991). Studies not only show that men are more likely to use tobacco products then women but also that culture, time of day and type of tobacco product play their part. In Japan, for example, almost 70 per cent of men smoke cigarettes whereas fewer than 15 per cent of women smoke. In Indonesia, 75 per cent of men smoke in comparison with 5 per cent of women. In contrast, in countries such as the US, Canada or the UK, the prevalence of smoking among men and women is similar. In Western countries, men smoke more, inhale more deeply and use stronger cigarettes than women. However, while the initiation rate for smoking has been decreasing among boys since 1960, it has increased for girls, and in addition cessation rates indicate that men are better at abstaining from cigarettes than women. Chesney and Nealey (1996) expressed their concern about increases in women's smoking, the prevalence of smoking among adolescent girls being higher than or equal to that among boys.

Gender differences in alcohol use and abuse have long been an issue of interest and debate in social science and medical research (Lex, 1991; Huselid and Cooper, 1992). The conclusions of the research are consistent. Men drink more often, more heavily, and experience more alcohol-related problems than women. Women are less likely to drink daily, to drink continuously, or to engage in binges. Furthermore, women become less frequently intoxicated and are less likely to abandon personal control while drinking (Robbins and Martin, 1993). However, women's drinking problems are more likely to develop later in life, when they can progress rapidly through the later stages of alcoholism.

Because of the high incidence of cardiovascular diseases in most West European countries, authorities have given substantial attention to the importance for health of a diet which is low in cholesterol, calories, colourings and additives, and high in fruits and vegetables. In their review article, Rolls et al. (1991) showed that women tend to have a healthier diet than men: men eat more meat, dairy products and carbohydrate-rich foods such as breads, cereals, desserts and sweets; women are more likely to consume fruit, yoghurt and low-calorie beverages. Eating rhythms also differ; men eat more often, larger amounts, and at a faster speed than women. Hayes and Ross (1987) also found that women's diet was better than men's, in the sense of avoiding cholesterol and artificial additives, and eating more fruit and vegetables. In addition, studies looking at the health habits of elementary schoolchildren have found that girls have healthier food habits than boys (Cohen, Brownell and Felix, 1990).

Gender differences in sport and exercise are also well documented (see Chapter 17). Up to the age of 12, boys and girls seem equally to enjoy exercise and sport but thereafter men are more interested and participate more often in sporting activities than do women (Wersch et al., 1991). The positive effects of exercise on physical health are well established (for example, Ransford and Palisi, 1996). As far as health maintenance behaviour is concerned, Dean (1989) found that women are more likely to show behaviour which may protect or promote their health, such as taking vitamins, sleeping regularly and practising an enjoyable hobby. The only health maintenance behaviour shown by men more than women is the use of medication or alcohol as a form of health protection.

Psychological explanations for gender differences

To begin, it would be fair to say that there are a number of shortcomings in relation to theory-building in this area. While gender differences in physical health have been explained from particular theoretical perspectives, these have often been either hypothetical or commonsense. Although researchers appear to acknowledge the likelihood of other than the obvious biological reasons for gender differences, where psychosocial explanations appear they are rarely supported within a firm theoretical framework

Shortcomings of existing research

Weinstein (1993) has presented a review of the four main theories of health-protective behaviour (health belief model; theory of reasoned action; protection motivation theory; and subjective expected utility theory). However, these models have rarely been used to good effect by the studies already reviewed in this chapter. For example, the health belief model or the theory of reasoned action is mentioned in the introduction to a number of reports, but a clear interpretation of results within this theoretical framework is rarely proffered.

Studies have tended to make more use of heuristic models than of theories, models either devised by the researchers or derived from other research. An example is Huselid and Cooper's (1992) use of a model to explain why men drink more alcohol than women. According to this model, women with traditional gender-role attitudes drink less, while men subscribing to conventional gender-roles drink more. The results of Huselid and Cooper's study support this model, though they concluded in a rather *ad hoc* fashion that the results could also be interpreted within a framework of functional coping styles (for which, however, no reference or explanation is given). Thus, the majority of research in this area has tended to provide no theoretical basis for discussion.

This deficiency in (or absence of) underlying theoretical frameworks can make it difficult to understand or interpret the gender differences which have been found in empirical studies. Lack of theory can also lead to problems in the operationalization and use of instruments, for example where measures of validity and reliability have not been documented. Indeed the variety of measurement techniques can make it almost impossible to compare or to generalize among studies. For example, most research has relied on self-report measures, which sometimes consist of only one question (Ransford and Palisi, 1996). What researchers understand by 'physical health' is not always made clear in such studies. For example, are they interested in self-reports of looking healthy and feeling healthy, or in healthy behaviour, or combinations of each, and are they looking at current health state or health state in general, or both?

Social-psychological explanations

The main gender differences in physical health and illness which have been identified are that women, on average, live seven years longer than men; men less often report being ill; men are more likely to die of the main causes of death; more men use alcohol and cigarettes; and more women make use of the healthcare system and have problems with their body image and weight-control.

Most social-psychological explanations for these gender differences can be categorized under three headings: social norms, stress and personality. The corollary behind these explanations is that in Western cultures men and women are socialized according to their gender. Male characteristics, or values associated with masculinity, are being physically strong, powerful, dominant, competitive, assertive and rational. Female characteristics, or values associated with femininity, are being friendly, warm, understanding, caring and emotional. These values are constructed and represented in society through gender-specific normative standards for both personality traits and behaviour (whether at work, in the family or at leisure) (Anson et al., 1993).

Explanations for the high morbidity rate of women have tended to focus on social norms. Because women are socialized to be affective and emotional, they can report feelings of discomfort more easily than men (perception-reporting hypothesis: Mann, 1996). It is more a part of their role to ask for help, either professional or from friends or family (social support). Another explanation is that traditionally women stay at home as housewives and mothers, and as a result can feel lonely and deprived of challenge and social support (Hibbard and Pope, 1993). Their general unhappiness with their prescribed social role leads them to develop complaints and physical symptoms. Support for this explanation is found in the research of Anson et al. (1990) in Israel. In kibbutzim, where male and female social roles are more similar than in other Western cultures, gender differences in morbidity and mortality are less marked. Haavio-Mannila (1986), on the other hand, found that in countries where more women stay at home, their physical health is poorer and their reporting of illness more frequent. This was also the case in Verbrugge's (1989) research. With less involvement in paid labour, greater feelings of stress and unhappiness, and feelings of vulnerability to illness, the morbidity rates for these women were significantly higher than those of the men. When these variables were controlled for, gender differences largely disappeared. Gender differences in morbidity and mortality also disappeared in Bird and Fremont's (1991) study when they controlled for social roles. These were operationalized as time spent on commitments to various role-related activities, such as household labour, childcare, helping others, and leisure and sleep.

The traditional housewife role is also used as an explanation for women's disturbed body image, and their vulnerability to eating disorders. For women at home, physical appearance (according to the feminine image, this is being extremely slim and lightweight) is a more important contribution to self-esteem than for women who work, or for men regardless of whether they work or not (Hayes and Ross, 1987).

The higher male mortality rate has been explained from a social norms perspective too. According to Copenhaver and Eisler's (1996) discussion of masculine gender-role stress, men are not supposed to be ill, feel pain, have physical complaints or go to the doctor. They should be strong and healthy, adhering to the masculine stereotype. This could be an explanation as to why men give a more favourable report of their health, and why their attendance at health care facilities is lower. Men are also more exposed to (acquired) risk than women, for example through their choice of hobbies or sports, or through their work (Verbrugge, 1985). To validate their masculinity, men are predisposed to engage in employment with a higher risk and in high-risk leisure activities, and indeed these high-risk activities may contribute significantly to the higher male death rates in accidents of all kinds (Copenhaver and Eisler, 1996).

Gender differences in behaviour such as alcohol and cigarette use have been explained from the social norm, as well as the stress, perspective. Smoking and drinking are behaviours which are regarded as consistent with the masculine characteristic of being strong and powerful. Gender-role stereotypes are likely to facilitate these behaviours for men (congruence models) and inhibit them for women (deviance models) (Robbins and Martin, 1993). However, this is clearly not the case for women who deliberately place themselves in opposition to traditional gender roles, hence perhaps the increase in smoking among young women. Alternatively, the recent increased smoking behaviour of girls has been explained from a social norm perspective in terms of young women's desire to look feminine, in the sense of being slim and underweight. It is noteworthy in this respect that the most frequently mentioned reason for girls' smoking behaviour is weight control (Chesney and Nealy, 1996). From the stress perspective, men's use of alcohol and cigarettes is seen as a coping mechanism in time of stress (for example, Anson, 1993; Chesney and Nealy, 1996), while women seem more likely to buffer their stress by social support (Carmel et al., 1991).

Explanations for gender differences from the personality perspective focus on gender-related personality traits (Shifren and Bauserman, 1996) or self-theory (Silberstein et al., 1988). The rationale behind the gender trait theory is that it is not gender *per se* which is important for explaining differences in health and illness, but rather the combination of masculine and feminine qualities (Bem, 1981; Spence, 1993). From this perspective, the androgynous personality seems to be the healthiest and to suffer least from illnesses, while those whose traits are neither strongly masculine nor feminine (the undifferentiated personality) suffer most (Shifren and Bauserman, 1996).

Self-theory is used to explain gender differences in body image, weight satisfaction, self-esteem and health. Because men are traditionally seen as more competent across different areas of life, their self-esteem is often higher and this has a positive effect on their health. For more women than men, there is a gap between ideal self and perceived self – in most cases because of weight dissatisfaction – which can lead to self-criticism and damaged self-esteem; and, in turn, to many kinds of physical complaint (Silberstein et al., 1988).

Conclusions

This brief review throws up two major concerns for psychologists and others working in this area. One is the female obsession with being very slim and underweight; the other is males' undervaluation of attention to bodily symptoms. Change is necessary. For women, this could be achieved by the presentation of a new feminine body ideal in magazines, films and other media, suggesting a rounder and fuller body than the contemporary ideal of the anorexic beanstalk. Another route to change, which is already fast developing, is to encourage women to see multi-tasking in a positive light and through the pursuance and recognition of competence across a wide range of social roles to enhance self-esteem and to devalue physical appearance as the only index of self-confidence.

In turn, men should be encouraged to pay more attention to pain and other bodily signals, and to ask for professional advice instead of stubbornly being 'brave' and ignoring them until it is too late. They should also be educated in trying to use healthier coping mechanisms than smoking and drinking in the event of stress. Psychologists and other social scientists could play their part in devising and evaluating educational programmes for such change. Future research in gender differences and physical health and illness would assist the programmes, but only if the theoretical and methodological problems identified above are genuinely addressed.

REFERENCES

Anson, O., Levenson, A. and Bonneh, D.Y. (1990). Gender and health on the kibbutz. *Sex Roles* **22**, 213–31.

Anson, O., Paran, E., Neumann, L. and Chernichovsky, D. (1993). Gender differences in health perceptions and their predictors. *Social Science and Medicine* **36**, 419–27.

Bem, S.L. (1981). Gender schema theory: a cognitive account of sex typing. *Psychological Review* **88**, 354–64.

Bird, C.E. and Fremont, A.M. (1991). Gender, time use, and health. *Journal of Health and Social Behavior* **32**, 114–29.

Carmel, S., Anson, O., Levenson, A., Bonneh, D.Y. and Maoz, B. (1991). Life events, sense of coherence and health: gender differences on the kibbutz. *Social Science and Medicine* **32**, 1089–96.

Chesney, M.A. and Nealey, J.B. (1996). Smoking and cardiovascular disease risk in women: issues for prevention and women's health. In Kato, P.M. and Mann, T. (eds), *Handbook of diversity in health psychology*. (pp. 199–218). London: Plenum Press.

Cohen, R.Y., Brownell, K.D. and Felix, M.R.J. (1990). Age and sex differences in health habits and beliefs of schoolchildren. *Health Psychology* **9**, 208–24.

Cohen, S. and Rodriguez, M.S. (1995). Pathways linking affective disturbances and physical disorders. *Health Psychology* **14**, 374–80.

Copenhaver, M.M. and Eisler, R.M. (1996). Masculine gender role stress. A perspective on men's health. In Kato, P.M. and Mann, T. (eds), *Handbook of diversity in health psychology*. (pp. 219–35). London: Plenum Press.

Dean, K. (1989). Self-care components of life-styles: the importance of gender, attitudes and the social situation. *Social Science and Medicine* **29**, 137–52.

Gijsbers van Wijk, C.M.T., van Vliet, K.P., Kolk, A.M. and Everaerd, W.T.A.M. (1991). Symptom sensitivity and sex differences in physical morbidity: a review of health surveys in the United States and the Netherlands. *Women and Health* **17**, 91–110.

Grunberg, N.E., Winders, S.E. and Wewers, M.E. (1991). Gender differences in tobacco use. *Health Psychology* **10**, 143–53.

Haavio-Mannila, E. (1986). Inequalities in health and gender. *Social Science and Medicine* **22**, 141–9.

Haug, M.R. and Folmar, S.J. (1986). Longevity, gender and life quality. *Journal of Health and Social Behavior* **27**, 332–45.

Hayes, D. and Ross, C.E. (1987). Concern with appearance, health beliefs, and eating habits. *Journal of Health and Social Behavior* **28**, 120–30.

Hibbard, J.H. and Pope, C.R. (1993). The quality of social roles as predictors of morbidity and mortality. *Social Science and Medicine* **36**, 217–25.

Huselid, R.F. and Cooper, M.L. (1992). Gender roles as mediators of sex differences in adolescent alcohol use and abuse. *Journal of Health and Social Behavior* **33**, 348–62.

Jackson, L.A., Sullivan, L.A. and Rostker, R. (1988). Gender, gender role and body image. *Sex Roles* **19**, 429–43.

Leary, M.R., Tchividjian, L.R. and Kraxberger, B.E. (1994). Self-presentation can be hazardous to your health: impression management and health risk. *Health Psychology* **13**, 461–70.

Lex, B.W. (1991). Some gender differences in alcohol and polysubstance users. *Health Psychology* **10**, 121–32.

Macran, S., Clarke, L. and Joshi, H. (1996). Women's health: dimensions and differentials. *Social Science and Medicine* **42**, 1203–16.

Mann, T. (1996). Why do we need a health psychology of gender and sexual orientation? In Kato, P.M. and Mann, T. (eds), *Handbook of diversity in health psychology.* (pp. 187–97). London: Plenum Press.

Mann, T. and Kato, P.M. (1996). Diversity issues in health psychology. In Kato, P.M. and Mann, T. (eds), *Handbook of diversity in health psychology.* (pp. 4–14). London: Plenum Press.

Mechanic, D. (1995). Sociological dimensions of illness behavior. *Social Science and Medicine* **9**, 1207–16.

Meininger, J.C. (1986). Sex differences in factors associated with use of medical care and alternative illness behaviors. *Social Science and Medicine* **22**, 285–92.

Popay, J., Bartley, M. and Owen, C. (1993). Gender inequalities in health: social position, affective disorder and minor physical morbidity. *Social Science and Medicine* **36**, 21–32.

Ransford, H.E. and Palisi, B.J. (1996). Aerobic exercise, subjective health and psychological well-being within age and gender subgroups. *Social Science and Medicine* **42**, 1555–9.

Robbins, C.A. and Martin, S.S. (1993). Gender, styles of deviances, and drinking problems. *Journal of Health and Social Behavior* **34**, 302–21.

Rolls, B.J., Fedoroff, I.C. and Guthrie, J.F. (1991). Gender differences in eating behavior and body weight regulation. *Health Psychology* **10**, 133–42.

Shifren, K. and Bauserman, R.L. (1996). The relationship between instrumental and expressive traits, health behaviors, and perceived physical health. *Sex Roles* **34**, 841–64.

Silberstein, L.R., Striegel-Moore, R.H., Timko, C. and Rodin, J. (1988). Behavioral and psychological implications of body dissatisfaction: do men and women differ? *Sex Roles* **19**, 219–32.

Spence, J.T. (1993). Gender-related traits and gender ideology: evidence for a multifactorial theory. *Journal of Personality and Social Psychology* **64**, 624–35.

Tiggemann, M. (1994). Gender differences in the interrelationships between weight dissatisfaction, restraint, and self-esteem. *Sex Roles* **30**, 319–30.

Verbrugge, L.M. (1985). Gender and health: an update on hypotheses and evidence. *Journal of Health and Social Behavior* **26**, 156–82.

Verbrugge, L.M. (1989). The twain meet: empirical explanations of sex differences in health and mortality. *Journal of Health and Social Behavior* **30**, 282–304.

Waldron, I. (1976). Why do women live longer than men? *Social Science and Medicine* **10**, 349–62.

Waldron, I. (1983a). Sex differences in human mortality: the role of genetic factors. *Social Science and Medicine* **17**, 321–33.

Waldron, I. (1983b). Sex differences in illness incidence, prognosis, and mortality: issues and evidence. *Social Science and Medicine* **17**, 1107–23.

Wingerd, D.L. (1984). The sex differential in morbidity, mortality, and lifestyle. *Annual Review of Public Health* **5**, 433–58.

Wech, B.A. (1983). Sex role orientation, stress, and subsequent health status demonstrated by two scoring procedures for Bem's scale. *Psychological Reports* **52**, 69–70.

Weinstein, N.D. (1993). Testing four competing theories of health-protective behavior. *Health Psychology* **12**, 324–33.

Wersch, A. van, Turner, I.F. and Trew, K. (1991). Post-primary school pupils' interest in Physical Education: age and gender differences. *British Journal of Educational Psychology* **62**, 56–72.

Further reading

Anson, O., Levenson, A. and Bonneh, D.Y. (1990). Gender and health on the kibbutz. *Sex Roles* **22**, 213–31.

Copenhaver, M.M. and Eisler, R.M. (1996). Masculine gender role stress: a perspective on men's health. In Kato, P.M. and Mann, T. (eds), *Handbook of diversity in health psychology*. London: Plenum Press.

Mechanic, D. (1995). Sociological dimensions of illness behavior. *Social Science and Medicine* **9**, 1207–16.

Verbrugge, L.M. (1985). Gender and health: an update on hypotheses and evidence. *Journal of Health and Social Behavior* **26**, 156–82.

Weinstein, N.D. (1993). Testing four competing theories of health-protective behavior. *Health Psychology* **12**, 324–33.

Discussion questions

1. Which is more important, looking healthy, feeling healthy or behaving healthily? Why?
2. To what extent does the contemporary ideal of a slender female body damage women's health?
3. Is men's health more or less affected by gender stereotypes than women's? Why?
4. Are women (or men) likely to damage their health if they behave contrary to gender stereotypes? Why (not)?
5. Why would it be useful if more empirical studies adopted a clear theoretical perspective on gender differences in health and illness?

15

PSYCHOPATHOLOGY

Bridie Pilkington and Michael Lenaghan

INTRODUCTION

From the moment of our birth, the complex interaction between gender, culture, roles and experiences begins to exert an influence on a great many aspects of our psychological development, including our mental health and psychological well-being. This chapter is an attempt to describe the role and significance of gender in predisposing individuals to particular social experiences and, more especially, psychological disorders. In a chapter of this length it would not be feasible to review all clinical areas in detail and hence we propose to focus attention on the major emotional disorders, anxiety and depression, and on two phenomena with a particular gender dimension, sexual abuse and Gender Identity Disorder (GID).

GENDER-RELATED DISORDERS

In reviews of work on gender-related disorders, anxiety and depression often feature prominently. Both are included in the International Statistical Classification of Diseases and Related Health Problems (ICD 10), with their classification as mild, moderate or severe being dependent on the number and severity of symptoms. In terms of gender differences, the available evidence suggests that women outnumber men who are treated for depression by a ratio of 2:1, and these differences first emerge as early as adolescence, if not before (Ruble et al., 1993). In addition, a range of anxiety-based disorders include more women than men. Of all anxiety-related disorders, agoraphobia is associated with the largest gender differences in referral rates. Agoraphobia, defined as the inability to stay in public situations or alone at home because of the fear of being overwhelmed by panic attacks and/or experiences of depersonalization, is approximately four times more likely to be diagnosed in women than men in either clinical or community samples (Chambless and Mason, 1986).

Research on gender differences in psychological disorders remains in its infancy and hence exactly why gender differences occur remains unclear. Weissman and Klerman (1979), on the basis of a detailed review of empirical evidence on depression, found no evidence to support the suggestion that the higher rates may be due to the fact that women admit to their symptoms more easily than men. Therefore they concluded that the gender difference was a true difference and not an artefact, a finding later confirmed by Bourdon et al. (1988) in relation to phobias.

It has been argued that gender differences may be attributable to the fact that symptoms are labelled differently for men and women. In other words, the difference reflects a diagnostic gender bias either when there is a diagnosis that the disorder is present, or a misdiagnosis that the disorder is absent. It is now generally acknowledged that the diagnosis of a mental disorder is not an objective, value-free judgement, and furthermore there is evidence that gender stereotypes do have an influence on clinicians' diagnoses of women (Ussher, 1991). Albino et al. (1990) report evidence of therapist bias against women, such that women were seen for longer periods of time in therapy and were given stronger prescriptive medications than men. Accordingly, there is evidence that men and women receive different responses within therapy and these differences appear to be most pronounced during the treatment of depression. Approximately 20–26 per cent of women will experience diagnosable depression at some time in their lives, compared with 8–12 per cent of men (Wetzel, 1984). In sharp contrast, a significantly higher proportion of men than women are diagnosed as suffering from alcohol abuse (Robins et al., 1984; Russo and Green, 1993).

Over time, researchers have attempted to conceptualize gender differences in relation to key variables. In the earlier research, gender roles were suggested as an explanation for the differences in prevalence rates between men and women. More specifically, it was suggested that being female meant taking on certain roles in society and that these roles were associated with greater psychological distress. For example, women have primary responsibility for childcare yet often must combine this with a career outside the home, thus leading to role conflict and low self-worth. In the past there has been support for this hypothesis, with research indicating that married women had a higher rate of mental illness than married men while single women had a lower rate of mental illness than single men (Gove, 1978). Jeanne Marecek (1978) suggested that the loss of status and independence experienced by many married women, as well as difficulties associated with being a mother, created severe stress and led to emotional problems. While it is reasonable to assume that the trend towards dual earner couples in society over the last twenty years means that loss of status and independence is not so great a problem, it remains likely that women, more so than men, run the risk of suffering from what Etaugh (1990) described as role conflict and role overload.

At the same time, evidence suggests that multiple roles *per se* may not be the root cause of the problem. Instead, Horowitz (1982) has concluded that power was the most significant mediating factor. He defined power in terms of having a dominant role in the family and controlling resources, and found that those who occupied powerful roles had fewer psychological disorders in comparison with those who occupied powerless roles. Married, employed women without children, for example, had few problems, but unemployed married men had many problems. More recent research has indicated that among those women who do work, greater job satisfaction is associated with lower levels of role strain and is predictive of greater family cohesion and lower levels of family conflict. However, husbands' negative attitudes towards their wives' paid employment, with resultant marital conflict, and husbands' lack of participation in childcare, may erode these potential beneficial effects (Dennerstein, 1995).

Recent studies have implicated culturally defined gender-role characteristics as significant factors predisposing women to psychological problems. For example, higher femininity scores on the BSRI are associated with greater depression, while the opposite is true for masculinity (Sanfilipo, 1994). Bekker (1996), on the basis of a review of the empirical research, concluded that the high (emotional) dependence and low (psychological) autonomy which are characteristic of femininity play a significant role in precipitating and maintaining agoraphobia.

There is some evidence that gender differences in terms of coping strategies may also contribute to the differential prevalence of psychological disorders among men and women. For example, data have indicated that gender roles are involved in the ways in which men and women cope with depression, with men tending to engage in active behaviours that distract them while women tend to ruminate (Nolen-Hoeksema, 1987). One active strategy for coping with anxiety is taking alcohol, but unfortunately excessive use of alcohol by men may lead them to be labelled as alcoholics, distracting both clinicians and patients themselves from their emotional symptoms.

Bekker (1996) has suggested that the social roles played by men, particularly in relation to economic factors, may mean that they are less likely to employ the avoidant coping strategies which are characteristic of patients suffering from agoraphobia. More men than women are under pressure to go outside the home to work and most agoraphobics seem to be 'housewives'. It has been suggested that it is easier for full-time homemakers than for employed men and women to avoid going out into public or other situations where agoraphobic patients experience extreme distress. However, the relationship between unemployment and agoraphobia is unclear. While the onset of agoraphobia often precedes unemployment, actually having a job outside the home may represent a protecting factor.

Evidence does suggest that sex-role stereotyping plays a role in agoraphobia and depression, in that the absence of masculine traits such as assertiveness and active-approach behaviour are related to both agoraphobia and depression. However, the relationship between sex roles and these disorders deserves more attention, especially with regard to questions relating to specificity. As Bekker (1996) has commented, 'the fact that only a small proportion of Western women (and an even smaller proportion of Western men) develop these symptoms needs to be researched' (p. 144).

Theoretical explanations

A number of psychological theories have been employed to help understand why these factors may adversely affect rates of depression and/or anxiety in women. Hyde (1996) has provided a useful summary of dominant theoretical perspectives, at the same time acknowledging that the hypotheses associated with these theories often remain to be tested systematically through clinical research.

Rotter's (1966) concept of locus of control suggests that people who have an internal locus of control have a greater sense of perceived control over their lives and lower levels of depression. Research is not consistent in demonstrating whether men have a more internal locus of control than women, although Ryff (1989) reported that men had significantly higher scores on internal control than women.

Learned helplessness theory (Seligman, 1975) has also been proposed to explain the prevalence of depression among women. The theory suggests that depression is caused by a person having learned that s/he is helpless or unable to control important outcomes in life. It is hypothesized that a lack of power leads to learned helplessness for women and predisposes them to more psychological problems. From a feminist perspective, a number of authors have argued that the lack and abuse of power experienced by women at the hands of men contribute significantly to the higher rate of psychological disorders among women, including depression and anxiety. Prominent among these writers in the UK has been Jane Ussher, with this sentiment encapsulated in the title of her 1991 book *Women's Madness: Misogyny or Mental Illness?* According to feminist writers, so long as men continue to exercise control over the determination of what is 'normal', and hence by inference abnormal or clinical, then gender differences in referral and treatment rates become inevitable.

The ultimate abuse of male power manifests itself in experiences of sexual abuse, domestic violence, rape and harassment, and there is overwhelming evidence that women suffer these experiences more frequently than men (see Chapter 18). A reformulated learned helplessness model (Peterson and Seligman, 1983) has also been proposed to explain the emotional numbing and maladaptive passivity that sometimes follows victimization. There can be little doubt that victimization in interpersonal relationships is a significant risk factor in the development of psychological disorders, as will be discussed later.

In a complementary fashion, the cognitive model of emotional disorders, which has evolved from social learning theory, takes cognizance of the individual's perception or interpretation of life events. The model suggests, for example, that depression is maintained by a dynamic interaction between thoughts, feelings and behaviours, and can be precipitated by a critical incident which activates core negative assumptions. It is believed that core assumptions, or schemata, are laid down in childhood as a result of early childhood experiences. So, for example, an early history of victimization or sexual abuse would lead to core negative self schemata characterized by assumptions of worthlessness; later these assumptions could be triggered in response to significant life events, such as during the establishment of close relationships.

The cognitive model suggests that the cycle of depression, or indeed anxiety-related disorders, may be maintained by negative thoughts, poor mood state and avoidant behaviour. The major theme underlying depression is that of loss, while for anxiety it is one of poor self-esteem. The higher prevalence of depression in women may be due to the fact that women suffer more victimization or adverse social experiences than men, a sentiment which would find sympathy with feminist writers.

There is empirical evidence that the socializing experiences of men and women differ from early childhood, and Ruble et al. (1993), for example, would argue that the onset of gender differences in depression during adolescence is likely to be due to differences in gender socialization processes. There is a vast literature describing the importance of childrearing factors in the development of anxiety and depression and despite certain methodological limitations, there is surprising consistency indicating that rejection and control by parents may be positively related to later onset of anxiety-related disorders and depression.

The cognitive model suggests that these early negative childhood experiences contribute to core negative self schemata, which may be triggered by later life experiences and lead to the experience of emotional disorders. These findings are consistent with the model proposed by Nolen-Hoeksema and Girgus (1994) which suggests that girls are more likely than boys to carry risk factors for depression even before adolescence. These risk factors lead to depression only in the face of challenges that increase in prevalence in early adolescence.

Recent research goes further, suggesting that a schema-focused cognitive model could provide a useful way of conceptualizing psychological disorders. The model takes cognizance of early childhood and socialization processes and hypothesizes that, in the case of victimization, core schemata of powerlessness and self-denigration lead to emotional difficulties. There is some recent empirical evidence to support a schema-focused mediational model for understanding the long-term effects of sexual abuse for women. However, there is clearly a need for further research to investigate the relationship between gender, socialization processes, cognitive schemata and predisposition to psychological disorders. Furthermore, there is a need for research to focus on gender differences in relation to coping with social experiences and psychological disorders.

Childhood sexual abuse

The existence of child sexual abuse (CSA) has long been recognized, although before the mid- to late 1970s it was a phenomenon which, acording to Sgroi (1978), society abhorred in the abstract but tolerated in reality. It is only within the last 25 years that CSA has become more visible. It is now regarded as a problem of increasing concern, with major implications for the psychological health and well-being of both children and adults.

The growing awareness of, and concern about, CSA has given rise to a proliferation of clinical and research studies which have attempted to clarify, among other issues, the incidence and prevalence of abuse, its origins, impact and how best to manage its aftermath. The literature is extensive but qualitatively deficient, with findings often equivocal and at times contradictory. In defence, researching CSA raises numerous problems, but existing methodologies have often failed to address the full interactive complexity of the many variables which contribute to its occurrence and impact. This area is, as Dempster et al. (1991) have stated, 'a methodological quagmire'.

With improved methodologies and more powerful and robust statistical techniques, significant gains have been made in terms of understanding the contribution of specific variables and their interactions with other variables in the determination of abuse impact and outcome. In addition, newly emerging information processing models of trauma (Hartman and Burgess, 1993; Putnam and Trickett, 1993; Gil, 1996), coupled with the above, have undoubtedly enhanced our understanding. Interestingly, however, the one variable about whose influence surprisingly little is known is gender. The role of gender is difficult to determine given that most studies investigating abuse-specific gender differences have been retrospective and *ad hoc* in nature, and have included relatively small numbers of male victims (most likely caused by the cultural biases and negative connotations associated with homosexuality, alongside other factors leading to lower levels of male disclosure). That so little is known about the influence of gender is surprising, given the close links between sexuality and gender. As Fracher and Kimmel (1987) state, 'that we are sexual is determined by a biological imperative towards reproduction, but how we are sexual, where, when, how often, with whom and why, has to do with cultural learning, with meaning transmitted in cultural setting . . . the foundation on which we construct our sexuality is gender' (p. 86). For some considerable time after CSA emerged more fully into general social and professional awareness, it was widely assumed and believed that only girls suffered sexual abuse, and that the perpetrators of such abuse were inevitably men. These assumptions clearly no longer hold. Such beliefs have changed as, over time, it has become more apparent that boys too experience sexual abuse and that women also sexually offend. That said, however, there can be little doubt that most CSA involves the victimization of girls, usually by older adolescent and adult males.

Pilkington and Kremer (1995a; 1995b) reviewed a large number of major epidemiological studies of CSA. Although their review articles dealt specifically with prevalence rates for females, information regarding rates for males was also included. While within-gender prevalence rates among both community and clinical samples indicated considerable variation (most likely a function of study methods and geography), between-gender comparisons showed consistently higher rates for females across both samples, irrespective of method and/or geography. The figures reported in these reviews are broadly in keeping with those reported elsewhere and in particular by Watkins and Bentovim (1992). In a review of research into the sexual abuse of male children and adolescents, these authors reported a ratio of between 2:1 and 4:1 of females to males in community samples and from 2:1 to 9:1 in clinical samples (but with a narrowing of these ratios over time). How does one account for these male/female differences and change in prevalence rates for males in particular?

CSA, in all the varying forms it may take, is above all a power-based phenomenon, involving the inappropriate use and expression of power in a sexualized form and manner. It is widely accepted that attitudes towards power and its expression, and to the expression of emotion and sexuality, are significantly shaped by contemporary culture, gender expectations and roles.

As individuals we are, albeit to varying degrees, socialized and conditioned to believe that certain, specific emotions are inappropriate to our respective genders. This conditioning can be seen as a process beginning early in life and one which leads boys and girls, men and women, to suppress and possibly even to repress specific emotions (see Chapter 7). In extreme cases, this process of conditioning can lead to the repression of certain emotions and not infrequently to the complete denial of emotions, a response which is potentially debilitating when, as a result either of general developmental experience or sexual abuse, someone may have been deeply emotionally and psychologically wounded. Such scripting and conditioning contributes significantly not only to differential rates of abuse but also to the inhibition of sexual abuse disclosures by males, to the development of deviant sexual arousal and to the cycle of victimization.

Watkins and Bentovim (1992) maintain that there has been an under-reporting of the sexual abuse of boys for three primary reasons:

- that few males in fact suffer child sexual abuse
- that the impact of such abuse is minimal, an assumption which has been shown to be erroneous
- that males may find disclosure more psychologically and socially stigmatizing given cultural and societal attitudes, although as such attitudes have changed so disclosures by males have increased.

There may very well also be a physiological substrate contributing to gender differences in the prevalence of sexual abuse. Although studies exploring the physiological and hormonal changes of adolescence and their links to behaviour are only in their infancy, these studies point tentatively to the possibility that hormones may have a direct activational influence on the increase in male aggressiveness and sexual behaviour during early adolescence, and on the intra-individual variation of such behaviour in males (Montemayor et al. (eds), 1990). In fact, adolescence is increasingly recognized as a time when many adult male offenders begin their abusive behaviours.

Impact of CSA

There are a number of ways in which one can consider the impact of CSA, in terms of its immediate, short-term and longer-term effects. While a full review of this extensive impact literature is beyond the scope of this chapter, a number of independent and major reviews, including those by Beitchman et al. (1991; 1992), Kendall-Tackett (1993), Green (1993) and Becker et al. (1995) seem drawn to similar conclusions concerning impact. Specifically,

- Sexually abused children of both genders show considerably higher levels of general emotional distress than non-abused children, similar to those seen in clinical child samples. Depression, anxiety, low self-esteem and, in the case of younger children, problems with self-regulation are among the most commonly occurring symptoms.
- Male victims suffer from psychological trauma at least commensurate in severity with that suffered by females (Hunter, 1991).
- There are clear links between CSA and adult psychosocial maladjustment for both females and males.
- At present there is insufficient evidence to make clear statements regarding differential short- and/or long-term severity and outcome.
- While many of the general effects and difficulties that follow CSA in females are similar to those seen in males, because of gender differences and societal expectations, there may be some differences in the ways in which abusive experiences are processed, and some responses which are more or less unique to males and females.

There may be a tendency for girls to internalize distress associated with CSA and therefore to react by showing more internalizing symptoms of emotional distress, such as anxiety and depression. Conversely, boys may have a greater tendency to react in an under-controlled, externalizing manner with angry, aggressive and acting-out behaviours.

Clinical experience of work with sexually abused adolescents and adult males has highlighted three specific effects of sexual abuse which have increasingly come to be regarded by clinicians (Watkins and Bentovim, 1992; Friedrich, 1995) as more or less unique to male victims of CSA. These factors are:

- recapitulation of the victim experience
- inappropriate attempts to reassert masculinity
- gender-identity confusion.

GENDER-IDENTITY DISORDERS

Gender-identity confusion and disorders of gender identity (GID) can manifest themselves in children and adolescents for reasons other than the experience of CSA. The past two decades have seen a growing awareness of, and interest in, developmental disorders associated with confused gender identities and roles. Early clinical formulations of such disorders found their way into psychiatric classification in the 1980s, with more full and complete diagnostic criteria present by the mid-1990s.

Available data suggest that disorders of this kind are rare relative to other child psychiatric phenomena, but they have attracted the attention of clinicians because of a range of associated short- and longer-term behavioural, emotional and cognitive difficulties. For example, Coates and Person (1985) have provided evidence to indicate that problems with anxiety, depression, learning difficulties and in the case of some adolescents, suicidal behaviours, may be among the more commonly associated clinical problems. In addition, Zucker and Green (1992) have suggested a clear link between GID in boys (the condition being diagnosed more often in boys than in girls) and the presence of general psychological difficulties, and have also noted higher rates of longer-term bisexual or homosexual orientation.

The most well-developed and substantive explanatory theories for GID can be subsumed under the two broad headings of hormonal and contextual/relational. Hormonal theories appear to be of two broad kinds. Direct-acting theories suggest that hormonal level or milieu gives rise directly to disorder; direct-organizational theories propose that the level of pre-natal hormone affects brain organization and development, setting in place a pathway for behavioural and emotional development in childhood which either gives rise to, or contributes to, GID.

In contrast, social-contextual models posit two main routes by which GID may emerge and be shaped. Direct contextual models suggest that GID has its origins in specific parental influences and attitudes and in social conditioning and reinforcement; mediated contextual models suggest that early contextual, relationship and environmental influences give rise to general social relationship difficulties, and it is from within this context that GID emerges.

Ultimately it seems likely that no one single factor or theory will be sufficient to explain the origin, dynamics and maintenance factors in GID. Instead we must look to multifactorial models which are able to bring together influences including the genetic, hormonal and contextual. As Green et al. (1985) have stated, 'the development of sexual identity is a complex phenomenon and indeed it should be, for it permeates so much of human behaviour. It would be a paradox within human development if there was a simple answer to how such complexity unfolds' (p. 1160).

Conclusions

It is only within the last twenty years that the relationship between gender and psychological disorders has been recognized and the role which gender plays in the occurrence of specific psychological disorders is not yet fully understood. It seems unlikely that gender alone is sufficient to explain the occurrence of psychological ill health, rather its interaction with a range of other factors needs to be fully explored. The recent development of theoretical models which take cognizance of information processing, cognitive appraisal and the transaction between variables, coupled with more powerful statistical techniques such as structural equation modelling, may allow us to assess and delineate the role of gender in a range of psychological phenomena and disorders in a more systematic way. As our understanding of the contribution of gender improves, so too may our approaches to treatment need to be modified. There can be little doubt that gender issues are firmly on the agenda, and it is likely that they will continue to have considerable implications for education, training and clinical practice in the years ahead.

References

Albino, J., Tedesco, L. and Shenkele, C. (1990). Images of women: reflections from the medical care system. In Paludi, M.A. and Steuernagel, G.A. (eds), *Foundations for a feminist restructuring of the academic disciplines*. (pp. 225–53). New York: Haworth.

Becker, J.V., Bigfoot, D.S., Bonner, L., Geddie, L.F., Henggeler, S.W., Kaufman, K.L. and Walker, C.E. (1995). Empirical research on child abuse treatment: report by the child abuse and neglect treatment group. *American Psychological Association Journal of Clinical Child Psychology* **24** (Supp.), 23–46.

Beitchman, J.H., Zucker, K.J., Hood, J.E., DaCosta, G.A. and Akman, D. (1991). A review of the short term effects of child sexual abuse. *Child Abuse and Neglect* **15**, 537–56.

Beitchman, J.H., Zucker, K.J., Hood, J.E., DaCosta, G.A., Akman, D. and Cassavia, E. (1992). A review of the long term effects of child sexual abuse. *Child Abuse and Neglect* **16**, 101–18.

Bekker, M.H.J. (1996). Agoraphobia and gender: a review. *Clinical Psychology Review* **16(2)**, 129–46.

Bourdon, K.H., Boyd, J.H., Rae, M.D.S., Burns, B.J., Thompson, J.W. and Locke, B.Z. (1988). Gender differences in phobias: results of the ECA Community Survey. *Journal of Anxiety Disorders* **2**, 227–41.

Chambless, D.L. and Mason, J. (1986). Sex, sex-role stereotyping and agoraphobia. *Behaviour Research and Therapy* **24**, 231–5.

Coates, S. and Person, E.S. (1985). Extreme boyhood femininity: isolated behaviour or pervasive disorder? *Journal of the American Academy of Child Psychiatry* **24**, 702–9.

Coates, S. and Person, E.S. (1991). Child sexual abuse research: a methodological quagmire. *Child Abuse and Neglect* **15**, 593–5.

Dempster, H.L. and Robert, J. (1991). Child sexual abuse: a methodological quagmire. *Child Abuse and Neglect* **15**, 593–5.

Dennerstein, L. (1995). Mental health, work and gender. *International Journal of Health Services* **25(3)**, 503–9.

Etaugh, C. (1990). Women's lives: images and realities. In Paludi, M.A. and Steuernagel, G.A. (eds), *Foundations for a feminist restructuring of the academic disciplines*. (pp. 39–68). New York: Haworth.

Friedrich, W.N. (1995). *Psychotherapy with sexually abused boys: an integrated approach.* London: Sage.

Fracher, J.C. and Kimmel, M. (1987). Hard issues and soft spots: counselling men about sexuality. In Scher, M., Stevens, M., Good, G. and Eichenfield, G.A., *Handbook of counselling and psychotherapy with men*. (pp. 83–96). London: Sage.

Gil, E. (1996). *Treating abused adolescents.* London: Gilford Press.

Gove, W.R. (1978). Sex differences in mental illness among adult men and women: an evaluation of four questions raised regarding the evidence of higher rates in women. *Social Science and Medicine* **12**, 187–98.

Green, A.H. (1993). Child sexual abuse: immediate and long term effects and interventions. *Journal of the American Academy of Child and Adolescent Psychiatry* **32(5)**, 890–902.

Green, R., Williams, K. and Goodman, M. (1985). Masculine or feminine gender identity in boys: development differences between two diverse family groups. *Sex Roles* **12**, 1155–62.

Hartman, C.R. and Burgess, A.W. (1993). Information processing of trauma. *Child Abuse and Neglect* **17**, 45–8.

Horowitz, A.V. (1982). Sex-role expectations, power and psychological distress. *Sex Roles* **8**, 607–24.

Hunter, J.A. (1991). A comparison of the psychosocial adjustment of adult males and females sexually molested as children. *Journal of Interpersonal Violence* **16(2)**, 205–17.

Hyde, J.S. (1996). *Half the human experience: the psychology of women.* (5th edn). Lexington, MA: D.C. Heath.

Kendall-Tackett, K.A., Williams, L.M. and Finklehor, D. (1993). Impact of sexual abuse on children: a review and synthesis of recent empirical studies. *Psychological Bulletin* **113(1)**, 164–80.

Maracek, J. (1978). Psychological disorders in women: indices of role strain. In Frieze, I., Parsons, J., Johnson, P., Ruble, D. and Zellman, G. (eds), *Women and sex roles: a social psychological perspective*. (pp. 256–76). New York: Norton.

Montemayor, R., Adams, G.R. and Gullota, T.P. (eds) (1990). *From childhood to adolescence: a transitional period?* London: Sage.

Nolen-Hoeksema, S. (1987). Sex differences in unipolar depression: evidence and theory. *Psychological Bulletin* **101**, 259–82.

Nolen-Hoeksema, S. and Girgus, J.S. (1994). The emergence of gender differences in depression during adolescence. *Psychological Bulletin* **115(3)**, 424–43.

Peterson, C. and Seligman, M.E.P. (1983). Learned helplessness and victimisation. *Journal of Social Issues* **39**, 103–16.

Pilkington, B.T. and Kremer, J. (1995a). A review of the epidemiological research on child sexual abuse: community and college samples. *Child Abuse Review* **4**, 84–98.

Pilkington, B.T. and Kremer, J. (1995b). A review of the epidemiological research on child sexual abuse: clinical samples. *Child Abuse Review* **4**, 191–205.

Putman, F.W. and Trickett, P.K. (1993). Child sexual abuse: a model of chronic trauma. *Psychiatry Interpersonal and Biological Processes* **56(1)**, 82–95. Special issue: Children and violence.

Robins, L.N., Hezler, J.E., Weissman, M.M., Orvaschel, H., Gruenberg, E., Burke, J.D. and Regier, D.A. (1984). Lifetime prevalence of specific psychiatric disorders in three sites. *Archives of General Psychiatry* **41**, 949–58.

Rotter, J.B. (1966). Generalized expectancies for internal and external control of reinforcement. *Psychological Monographs* 80(609).

Ruble, D.N., Greulich, F., Pomerantz, E.M. and Gochberg, B. (1993). The role of gender-related process in the development of gender differences in self-evaluation and depression. *Journal of Affective Disorders* **29**, 97–128.

Russo, N.F. and Green, B.L. (1993). Work and family roles: selected issues. In Denmark, F.I. and Paludi, M.A. (eds), *Psychology of women: handbook of issues and theories*. (pp. 379–436). Westport, CT: Greenwood.

Russo, N.F., Horn, J.D. and Schwartz, R. (1992). US abortion in context: selected characteristics and motivations of women seeking abortions. *Journal of Social Issues* **48(3)**, 183–202.

Ryff, C. (1989). Happiness is everything, or is it? Explorations on the meaning of psychological well-being. *American Psychologist* **57**, 1069–81.

Sanfilipo, M.P. (1994). Masculinity, femininity and subjective experiences of depression. *Journal of Clinical Psychology* **50(1)**, 144–57.

Seligman, M.E.P. (1975). *Helplessness: on depression, development and death.* San Francisco, CA: Freeman.

Sgroi, S.A. (1978). A national needs assessment for protecting child victims of sexual assault. In Burgess, A.W., Groth, A.N., Holmstrom, L.L. and Sgroi, S.A. (eds), *Sexual assault of children and adolescents.* (pp. xv–xxii). Lexington Books.

Ussher, J.M. (1991). *Women's madness: misogyny or mental illness?* London: Harvester Wheatsheaf.

Watkins, B. and Bentovim, A. (1992). The sexual abuse of male children and adolescents: a review of current research. *Journal of Child Psychology and Psychiatry* **33**, 197–248.

Weissman, M.M. and Klerman, G.L. (1979). Sex differences and the epidemiology of depression. In Gomberg, E.S. and Franks, V. (eds), *Gender and disordered behavior.* New York: Brunner/Mazel.

Wetzel, J.W. (1984). *Clinical handbook of depression.* New York: Gardener Press.

Zucker, K.J. and Green, R. (1992). Psychosexual disorders in childhood and adolescents. *Journal of Child Psychology and Psychiatry* **33(1)**, 107–51.

FURTHER READING

Beitchman, J.H., Zucker, K.I, Hood, J.E., Da Costa, G.A., Akman, D. and Cassavia, E. (1992). A review of the long term effects of child sexual abuse. *Child Abuse and Neglect* **16**, 101–18.

Bekker, M.H.J. (1996). Agoraphobia and gender: a review. *Clinical Psychology Review* **16(2)**, 129–46.

Nolen-Hoeksema, S. and Girgus, J.S. (1994). The emergence of gender differences in depression during adolescence. *Psychological Bulletin* **115(3)**, 424–43.

Zerbe, K.J. (1995). Anxiety disorders in women. *Bulletin of the Menninger Clinic* **59(2)**, Supp. A, 38–52.

Zucker, K.J. and Green, R. (1992). Psychosexual disorders in children and adolescents. *Journal of Child Psychology and Psychiatry* **33(1)**, 107–51.

Discussion questions

1. How may gender stereotypes influence clinicians' diagnoses of men? Of women?
2. If depression is related to women's social roles and status, why aren't all women depressed?
3. To what extent do you believe that parents can be held responsible for the development of depression or anxiety in their adult offspring?
4. Discuss the issues of power and victimization and their contributions to gender differences in psychopathology.
5. Why is the impact of sexual abuse on male victims different from its impact on female victims?

16

CRIME

Juliet Lyon

INTRODUCTION

> In scale and constancy, the sex difference far outweighs any other factor which we have yet been able to associate with delinquent behaviour. No one seems to have any idea why; but hardly anyone seems to have thought it worthwhile to try to find out.
>
> (Wootton, 1959, p. 318)

> Sex differences in criminality are so sustained and so marked as to be, perhaps, the most significant feature of recorded crime.
>
> (Heidensohn, 1996, p. 11)

As these quotes clearly illustrate, crime is gendered. By way of example, 84 per cent of recorded crime in the UK is committed by men, men comprise 96 per cent of the prison population in England and Wales, and one in three men born in 1953 had been convicted of an offence by the age of 30. Despite these statistics, until comparatively recently, the 'maleness' of crime has been taken as an accepted fact. It is almost as though the sheer size of the statistical difference has rendered it invisible. In contrast to the 'ordinariness' of male crime, the few early studies of female offenders have focused on their extraordinariness, as odd or ill creatures out of the norm. In the 1970s, feminist perspectives began to develop within criminology and at this time the neglect of gender, and women in particular, was highlighted. To redress the balance, research studies began to focus on women as offenders, as victims, and as gatekeepers, that is the professionals who work within the criminal justice system. In the 1990s the focus has shifted yet again, with the relationship between gender roles, and particularly masculinity, and crime falling increasingly under the spotlight.

This chapter will document some of the key issues raised by feminist criminologists and others in relation to gender and crime. It will draw on current research studies (Morris et al., 1994; Caddle and Crisp, 1997) to examine the particular characteristics, problems and needs of women in prison. The ways in which concepts of masculinity and crime are being deconstructed will be examined. Lastly, the chapter will focus on youth crime. How do children and young people grow into crime? How, and when, do the majority grow out of it? In what ways can the development of gender identity be said to intertwine with the development of a criminal identity? A recent large-scale self-reported delinquency study (Graham and Bowling, 1995) presents a more complex picture of gender differences, and similarities, than a review of recorded crime figures alone. This section will also draw on the action research studies conducted by the Trust for the Study of Adolescence (TSA), in the course of constructing specialist training materials for staff who work with young men and young women in prison. Gender is the focus of this chapter. Arguably it is, or should be, a central variable in any study of crime. However, gender and crime can only be fully explored within the context of culture and society taking account of key variables such as race, class, family, economic circumstances and individual difference.

WOMEN AND CRIME

Stereotyping

Women who break the law may also be seen to have offended against societal expectations. Lloyd (1995) in *Doubly Deviant, Doubly Damned* comments, 'when women commit violent crimes they are seen to have breached two laws: the law of the land which forbids violence and natural law which says women are passive carers not active aggressors' (p. 36). Feminist criminologists have highlighted the way in which, by committing a crime, women move from one particular set of stereotypes to another (Smart, 1977; Cain (ed.), 1989; Carrington, 1993; Gelsthorpe, 1989). Simplistically, law-abiding women are labelled good girls, virgins, madonnas, good mothers. They are submissive and agreeable. Law breakers, on the other hand, are labelled bad girls or mad women, witches. They are wanton and unruly, devious and manipulative. The image of witch remains at the top of a 'pyramid of related images of deviant women as especially evil, depraved and monstrous' (Heidensohn, 1996, p. 92). Analyses of media representations of female criminality show the salacious nature of this coverage (Naylor, 1995), with its 'restricted range of media typifications revolving round the sexually-based dichotomies of chaste/unchaste, virgin/whore' (Muncie and McLaughlin, 1996, p. 46). A preoccupation with her sexuality, and femininity, or lack of it, can be found not only in media representations, but also in a wide range of documentation on the female offender including academic studies and court reports.

Just over a hundred years ago, female offenders were described as non-women, pale imitators of men (Lombroso and Ferraro, 1885). In what ways, if any, do stereotyping and the social construction of masculinity and femininity pervade the criminal justice system today? There is considerable evidence to suggest that men and women are treated differently within the criminal justice system. Three examples have been selected from many to show explicitly how ideas and attitudes about what constitutes normal behaviour for men and women affect the way in which female offenders are treated. The examples demonstrate that gender bias is a complex, rather than a straightforward issue.

A recent large-scale study of women (Hedderman and Gelsthorpe, 1997) showed that for virtually every type of offence, women are treated more leniently than men. Part I of this two-part study consisted of a multivariate analysis of sentencing patterns for 13,000 cases, using samples of men and women convicted of shoplifting, violence and drug offences during 1991. In Part II, 200 magistrates were interviewed about what they thought were the main influences on their decision-making. Women were consistently more likely than men to be discharged even when their circumstances appeared, on the basis of the available data, entirely comparable. Magistrates were reluctant to fine women, especially those with dependent children. They were more likely to define women offenders as troubled rather than troublesome and to see their crimes as motivated by need rather than greed. The authors comment, 'the difficulty to be addressed is one of finding ways to challenge stereotypical pictures of men and women, without ignoring the fact they often (but not always) do have different needs and responsibilities (and these are precisely the needs and responsibilities which fuel the stereotypes)'. (p. 58)

A recent review of women in prison (HM Chief Inspector of Prisons, 1997) emphasizes the importance of paying attention to the real needs of female offenders:

> This review does not seek favoured treatment for women prisoners. All prisoners, male or female, should be held in safe custody, treated with respect, with no greater restrictions on them than their real security risks demand. They should be given the opportunity to tackle their offending behaviour and to prepare for resettlement in the community. However, women have different physical, psychological, dietary, social, vocational and health needs and they should be managed accordingly. As one correspondent put it to us, "It is not merely a question of women receiving equal treatment to men; in the prison system equality is everywhere conflated with uniformity; women are treated as if they are men." We heard the description "Cons in skirts" at one establishment.
>
> (Para 3.46, p. 28)

However, where stereotypical rather than real difference is recognized, this can have negative consequences for women. While in prison, women are charged proportionately far more frequently than men with offences against discipline, breaking prison rules and disobedience and disrespect (NACRO,

1993a, b). A female governor of a women's prison hazarded the possibility that this could be because

> women are expected to obey rules, treat staff with respect, remain passive – and generally meet these expectations. This would set an institutional context and an expectation against which minor infractions would be viewed severely. Men may be expected to disobey rules, treat staff with disrespect and be aggressive, creating a context and expectation in which minor infractions are tolerated.
>
> (Egan, 1996, p. 167)

Lastly, women, and especially black women, would appear to face greater discrimination than men on release from prison as regards housing and employment opportunities (Carlen, 1990; NACRO, 1993b). A detailed qualitative study of 34 women after prison shows clearly how hard women have to struggle against stigmatization, institutionalization and structural discrimination (for example blocking access to housing, education, health and social services) in order to regain some control over their lives (Eaton, 1993). As we have already seen, women represent a tiny minority (4 per cent) of the prison population. It may be that discriminatory treatment after prison is linked to women's statistical deviance in the crime figures. Female offenders are viewed, by some at least, as unnatural or pathologically deviant.

Victims of crime

A high proportion of female offenders have themselves been the victims of crime. Profiles of female offenders and surveys of their needs show a continuum from victimization to offending (American Correctional Association, 1993; Carrington, 1993; Morris et al., 1994; Chesney-Lind, 1997). In *The Invisible Woman: Gender, Crime and Justice*, Belknap comments: 'Many of these accounts confirm that prior victimization, offending (especially prostitution, running away and drug offences) and subsequent incarceration are interrelated' (Belknap, 1996, p. 7). In a large-scale survey of the needs of women in prison in England and Wales, nearly half reported experience of either physical abuse as children or domestic violence as adults, and one third reported sexual abuse (Morris et al., 1994). The inspectorate, in its interviews with 234 women in prison, found similar proportions of women disclosing abuse. In addition, 'in the majority of cases the abuser was male and well known to the woman (for example father or partner)' (HM Chief Inspector of Prisons, 1997, p. 14).

Arguably, young women involved in prostitution can be seen as both victims and perpetrators of crime. Some very young women become involved in prostitution through relationships with adults who offer accommodation and an introduction to a drug habit. The Children's Society estimated that at least 5,000 children under the age of 16 are used for prostitution in Britain. Indeed, the number of girls aged 16 years and under who were convicted between 1989 and 1994 was up by 79 per cent (Lyon and Coleman, 1996).

Professionals who work with women who are on probation or in prison have a delicate balance to strike. To work effectively with female offenders, and to empower them to take more control over their lives, full account has to be taken of their history, culture, social circumstances and current needs (Lyon and Coleman, 1996; HM Chief Inspector of Prisons, 1997). On the other hand, an overemphasis on, or labelling of, women as victims deprives them of their moral agency. This can feed into the concept of learned helplessness and increase dependency on institutional care. Again, according to Egan (1996), 'There is some evidence of the infantilisation of women in the criminal justice system, and a lingering idea that women are not responsible for their own criminality' (p. 167).

Women in prison

There are significant differences between men and women in custody. They have different criminal profiles and differing social histories. Women's most common crimes are theft and property-related crimes, with a rising incidence of drug-related offences and crimes of violence against the person. Women are more likely than men to be in prison for the first time, with about 70 per cent being 'first-timers' (NACRO, 1993a; HM Chief Inspector of Prisons, 1997). They are less likely to re-offend on release; over 80 per cent of male young offenders re-offend within two years as compared to less than 50 per cent of young women.

Gender differences in mental health needs among prisoners reflect in an extreme way those found in the general population (Barnes and Maple, 1992). Women in prison are more likely than men to suffer from depression, to harm themselves, to abuse drugs or alcohol, to seek medical help and to be prescribed, and often to depend on, medication. Women are more likely to be accommodated far from home and to be affected adversely by custody. The negative impact of incarceration was described by two young women in prison interviewed by TSA (Lyon and Coleman, 1996): 'They don't take any notice of you unless you cut up or start a fight, or smash up your cell. You just have to kick off' (p. 189); 'Some young women they come in and they're OK and then they get really loud. They go a bit mental. They go mad in here really' (p. 190).

The majority of women in prison have dependent children for whom many retain considerable responsibility. Mothers and fathers in prison differ markedly in their preparedness to maintain any responsibility for their families. A comprehensive study of mothers in prison (Caddle and Crisp, 1997) showed that, of 1,766 women prisoners surveyed, 1,082 (61 per cent) were mothers of dependent children. One third were single parents and 55 per cent had had their first child in their teens. They had a total of 2,168 children between them and a third were under 5 years old. The study documents their reliance on temporary carers, financial hardship at home, efforts to stay in touch by letters, telephone calls and visits, the particular difficulties faced by foreign nationals and finally the behavioural problems of the children separated from their mothers. The negative impact of their mother's custody on her children has been well documented (The Howard League, 1993; 1994; Lloyd, 1995). Three quarters of the mothers planned to rejoin their children after release. However, accommodation and employment opportunities had been lost by many and financial difficulties were often anticipated.

MEN AND CRIME

Masculinity and crime

> Gender is no longer simply a 'code word' for women and femininity, but also refers to men and masculinity.
>
> (Dobash et al. (eds), 1995, p. 9)

Men so dominate the criminal justice system as perpetrators of crime, as victims and as policy makers and managers, that their existence within it has been taken as given. Only recently have their gender, and the construction of their masculinity, been seen as valid areas for study in their own right (Brittan, 1989; Miedzian, 1992; Jenkins, 1994; Dobash et al. (eds), 1995; Ruxton, 1996). A discourse has opened between biological determinism and social construction theory. Are men born to take risks, challenge authority, become violent and commit crimes? Do they learn these behaviours? Is crime the context in which their masculine identity develops and is affirmed? Dominelli, in her work on male sex offenders, stated that, 'men who are unable to acquire power successfully in the public domain and negotiate their male role effectively in that sphere will exercise male power in the private domain inhabited by socially less powerful women and children without regard to their needs or persons' (Dominelli, 1991, p. 92).

Violence

The victims and the perpetrators of violent crime are mostly men, apart from sexual offences and domestic violence (both thought to be be under-reported and usually involving men as perpetrators with women as victims). Over three quarters of the victims of violent crime are male, of which 43 per cent are victims of either pub or street brawls, according to the British Crime Survey of 1993. What compels some men to use physical or symbolic violence? 'Showing hard' or 'fronting up' are certainly characteristics of young male offenders (Little, 1990; Lyon and Coleman, 1994). A qualitative, ethnographic study of 30 male offenders, focusing on life-history interviews, sought to make sense of the connections between violence and masculinities (Thurston and Beynon, 1995). The men's own stories were collected and 'read' as accounts of cultural codings of male identities. These methods were designed as an intervention to encourage men to reassess their histories, attitudes and cultural and subjective positions of power but at the same time demonstrated the powerful links between masculinity and violence.

Gatekeepers in the criminal justice system

A gendered perspective on the criminal justice system shows clearly that most gatekeeping roles which carry power and authority are held by men. Women make up only 15 per cent of legal partners, 6 per cent of police sergeants and 10 per cent of judges (Office for National Statistics, 1997). In the prison and probation services, almost all the clerical staff are women. Approximately a third of disciplinary staff in the prison service and over half the officer-grade staff in the probation service are women, but women only occupy a tiny minority of senior management posts in these services. 'Criminal justice professions are seen quite simply as male professions; it is man's work requiring the characteristics of men' (Morris, 1987, p. 135).

Over the last few years, work has begun on the implications of this gender imbalance (Senior and Woodhill (eds), 1992; Martin and Jurik, 1996). Male practitioners are being challenged to view their own masculine identity as relevant in their professional work with male offenders.

> We believe that the occupational sub-culture of male probation officers is not that different from male police officers or male prison officers. We share the same history. We are under the same pressure to conform to the masculine stereotype, to the cultural norms of patriarchy. We are just as frightened of emasculation, of being called a 'wimp', with all the slur on sexual orientation implied in that epithet. We experience the same pressures to be firm, strong and decisive; in all situations and at all costs. All this is reflected in the organisations for which we work
>
> (Cordery and Whitehead, 1992, p. 33)

Growing into crime

Gender identity development

Gender identity development is inextricably linked with the development of social, cultural and racial identity – what it means to be a boy or girl growing up in a particular context and at a particular time. For most children, parents are the primary influence on identity development and the development of self-concept and self-esteem. During the transition from childhood to adulthood, adolescents are open to influence from parents and other significant adults and, increasingly, from their peer group. Teenagers think about 'Who am I? What am I going to become? Who do I want to be like?' (Lyon and Coleman, 1996) and role models are sought within and outside the family (see Chapter 10).

In what ways, if any, can the development of gender identity be said to intertwine with the development of a criminal identity? The importance of peer-group influence is relevant here: 'As a result of anxiety and uncertainty, and because of the importance of being accepted by the group, young people may go through a strong conformist stage, when it becomes very important to look like others of your own age group, and indeed behave like them as well' (Lyon and Coleman, 1994, p. 5, Module 4). Risk-taking, challenging authority and defending honour, characteristics of adolescence in general, seem to have greater significance for young men than young women (Dobash et al. (eds), 1995), with involvement with delinquent peers, for example, having an important influence on the incidence of offending behaviour (Graham and Bowling, 1995; Farrington, 1996). For young men in particular the development of a criminal identity may well stem from a watershed event such as a first conviction. From this the young man gains a public reputation for offending (Emler and Reicher, 1995), and hence being labelled as deviant becomes a predictor of future offending behaviour.

In *Adolescence and Delinquency*, Emler and Reicher (1995) document four significant differences in terms of risk, opportunity, social control and upbringing, which link gender identity development with criminality.

> In the first place, girls are less often on the streets, in public places and shops, which is to say in the common settings for delinquent activities. In a direct sense their opportunities to offend are limited. Second, their more limited public lives also reduce the incentive for the kind of self-protection that a delinquent identity in a delinquent group might seem to afford. Third, there will also be fewer abrasive encounters with authority. Finally, because they are more likely to congregate in homes, operating in what McRobbie and Garber (1976) call 'the culture of the bedroom', their friends are more likely to come into contact with their parents. Under these conditions it is difficult to be one thing to parents – dutiful, obedient daughter – and quite another – tough, reckless, rebellious – to peers. Consequently a dissonance between filial and delinquent identities is harder for girls to sustain.
>
> (Emler and Reicher, 1995, p. 24)

Young people usually appear as perpetrators of crime rather than victims in criminological studies, despite the fact that young people under 25 years are more likely to be victims of crime than any other age group. Goodey's quantitative study, 'Fear of crime: children and gendered socialization', offers a gendered analysis of child and adolescent development emphasizing the way puberty affects identity and attitudes. She comments, 'What has been established is that fear amongst eleven to sixteen year olds is gendered, with girls expressing greater fear when outside, greater fear of "people", and more specifically greater fear of men, and with more girls than boys having been worried by "someone" when outside' (Goodey, 1995, p. 310).

Of course, one question this research raises is how possible it is for adolescent males to express fear. An analysis of the qualitative section of this study may provide some answers. Certainly the new research focus on masculinity and crime seeks to challenge popular images of young men as yobs or thugs and to call into question the 'natural' involvement of young men in offending. A central message to parents and professionals in *Boys Won't Be Boys: Tackling the Roots of Male Delinquency* (Ruxton, 1996) is simply 'don't give up on boys'.

Crime and the family

Increasingly research has pointed to the key role of the family in relation to youth crime and offending behaviour (Utting et al., 1993; Lyon and Coleman, 1994; 1996; Farrington, 1996; Graham and Bowling, 1995). On the one hand, the family can be the most important protective factor, acting as a buffer against negative peer pressure and forming strong affectionate bonds with children. On the other hand, key risk factors for involvement in crime are harsh or erratic discipline and poor supervision or neglect by parents. Other family risk factors include low-income households, parent(s) with a criminal record, and having parents whose attitudes condone law breaking and other kinds of anti-social behaviour. The importance of good family relationships cannot be overstated. Young women who are most at risk of involvement in crime are those who have not been protected by their parents and have run away from home prior to the age of 16 following abuse or neglect in the family (Graham and Bowling, 1995). In addition, those young people taken into the care of the local authority following damage or disruption in families are more likely to become involved in crime and subsequently receive a custodial sentence. Although only 2 per cent of 16–18-year-olds in Great Britain have been in care, they make up over 40 per cent of the young prison population.

In a political culture which has encouraged blame of (rather than support for) parents of teenagers, it is working mothers and lone parents (over 90 per cent of whom are mothers) who have been singled out for particular attention. However, in their overview, *Crime and the Family*, Utting et al. (1993) show that the quality of the parent–child relationship rather than the quantity, that is one parent or two, is the underlying influence. Indeed they point to the importance of the role of fathers, and the significance of their absence following divorce or due to imprisonment, in determining delinquency. Conversely, close supportive relationships with their fathers are seen as significant protective factors for children. In their self-report delinquency study Graham and Bowling (1995) state clearly that poor relationships with fathers were found to be more prevalent than poor relationships with mothers. With such results in mind, an important initiative within the prison service in Great Britain has been the development of education for fatherhood programmes in the majority of young offender institutions, with the aim of trying to break the cycle of crime (Caddle, 1991; Lyon and Coleman, 1994).

It seems clear that gender differences in parenting roles and responsibilities and differential treatment of boys and girls within the family provide important clues to understanding the differences between male and female offending.

Young people and crime

The criminal statistics given in Figure 16.1 show clearly the stark difference between men and women in relation to recorded crime. Age, as well as gender, is a very important factor. The peak age of offending is 15 for women and 18 for men. While self-report delinquency studies (Utting et al., 1993; Graham and Bowling, 1995) reveal a more subtle picture, powerful differences, particularly of prevalence and persistence, still remain. In their study of 1,720 young people aged between 14 and 25, with a booster sample of 800, Graham and Bowling (1995) found that in short, while young women grow out of crime, increasingly young men do not. Graham and Bowling summarized their views as to why: 'The key to answering this question seems to be embedded within the different conditions, opportunities and constraints experienced by males and females during the transition from childhood to adulthood' (p. 94). Much of the literature on gender and crime focuses on adults. Only a few of the recent studies of young people and crime (Emler and Reicher, 1995; Graham and Bowling, 1995) have chosen to explore gender difference as a key variable. Far too little attention has been paid to gendered socialization of children and young people within the family, within schools and within society, yet adolescence is the peak life-stage for involvement in crime and offending behaviour. If only because youth crime is a very expensive business (Audit Commission, 1996), policy makers, practitioners

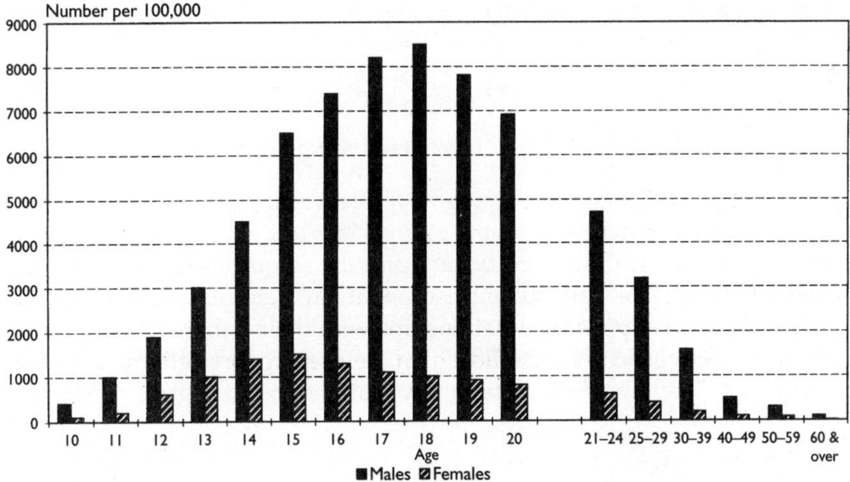

FIGURE 16.1 Persons found guilty of, or cautioned for, indictable offences per 100,000 population by age, 1995

SOURCE: *Criminal statistics, England and Wales, 1995*. London: HMSO. (Reproduced in Coleman, J., *Key data on adolescence*. Brighton: TSA Publishing, 1996.)

and researchers must turn their attention to the way in which children and young people grow into crime. They should consider and evaluate strategies for prevention and early intervention. To understand more about gender and crime we need to go back to child and adolescent development and explore how masculine and feminine identities are constructed.

Conclusions

Gender has to be a crucial variable in any study of crime. New developments in research, policy and practice all indicate a growing awareness of the significance of gender within the criminal justice system, but at the same time, stereotypes about gender and crime do still have to be challenged. The recent thematic review of the prison service (HM Chief Inspector of Prisons, 1997) has usefully documented the social circumstances of women in prison, and has made clear recommendations for their care and custody without in any way excusing their crimes. Equally, a growing body of research places the spotlight on masculinity and crime, and usefully counters the traditional 'blindspot' in relation to the maleness of crime. This work opens the possibility for exploring how gender identity development in childhood and adolescence links with the development of a criminal identity. Lastly, a new policy and practice emphasis on parenting and parent education as a primary strategy for crime prevention will take account of gender and family relationships, and in the process will further enhance our understanding of the complex interplay between gender and crime.

References

American Correctional Association (1993). *Female offenders: meeting needs of a neglected population.* Laurel, MD: ACA.

Audit Commission (1996). *Misspent youth... Young people and crime.* London: HMSO.

Barnes, M. and Maple, N. (1992). *Women and mental health: challenging the stereotypes.* Birmingham: Venture Press.

Belknap, J. (1996). *The invisible woman: gender, crime and justice.* Belmont, CA: Wadsworth.

Brittan, A. (1989). *Masculinity and power.* Oxford: Blackwell.

Caddle, D. (1991). *Parenthood training for young offenders: an evaluation of courses in young offender institutions.* Home Office Research and Planning Unit, Paper 63. London: Home Office.

Caddle, D. and Crisp, D. (1997). *Imprisoned women and mothers.* Home Office Research Study 162. London: Home Office.

Cain, M. (ed.) (1989). *Growing up good: policing the behaviour of girls in Europe.* London: Sage.

Carlen, P. (1990). *Alternatives to women's imprisonment.* Buckingham: Open University Press.

Carrington, K. (1993). *Offending girls: sex, youth and justice.* Australia: Allen & Unwin.

Chesney-Lind, M. (1997). *The female offender.* London: Sage.

Cordery, J. and Whitehead, A. (1992). 'Boys don't cry': empathy, warmth, collusion and crime. In Senior, P. and Woodhill, D. (eds), *Gender, crime and probation practice.* (pp. 28–34). Sheffield Hallam University: Pavic Publications.

Dobash, R.E., Dobash, R.P. and Noakes, L. (eds) (1995). *Gender and crime.* Cardiff: University of Wales Press.

Dominelli, L. (1991). *Gender, sex offenders and probation practice.* Norwich: Novata Press.

Eaton, M. (1993). *Women after prison.* Buckingham: Open University Press.

Egan, M. (1996). Differences: some differences between men and women in custody. In Lyon, J. and Coleman, J. (eds), *Understanding and working with young women in custody.* (pp. 167–168). Brighton: TSA (Crown Copyright).

Emler, N. and Reicher, S. (1995). *Adolescence and delinquency.* Oxford: Blackwell.

Farrington, F. (1996). *Understanding and preventing youth crime.* York: Joseph Rowntree Foundation.

Gelsthorpe, L. (1989). *Sexism and the female offender.* Aldershot, Hants: Gower Press.

Goodey, J. (1995). Fear of crime: children and gendered socialization. In Dobash, R.E., Dobash, R.P. and Noakes, L. (eds), *Gender and crime.* (pp. 295–312). Cardiff: University of Wales Press.

Graham, J. and Bowling, B. (1995). *Young people and crime.* Home Office Research Study 145. London: Home Office.

Hedderman, C. and Gelsthorpe, L. (1997). *Understanding the sentencing of women.* Home Office Research Study 170. London: Home Office.

Heidensohn, F. (1996). *Women and crime.* 2nd edn. Basingstoke: Macmillan.

HM Chief Inspector of Prisons (1997). *Women in prison: a thematic review.* London: Home Office.

Jenkins, J. (1994). *Men, masculinity and offending.* London: Inner London Probation Service Benevolent and Educational Trust.

Little, M. (1990). *Young men in prison.* Aldershot, Hants: Dartmouth.

Lloyd, E. (1995). *Prisoners' children: research, policy and practice.* London: Save the Children Publication Sales.

Lloyd, A. (1995). *Doubly deviant, doubly damned: society's treatment of violent women.* London: Penguin.

Lombroso, C. and Ferraro, O.W. (1885). *The female offender.* London: Fisher & Unwin.

Lyon, J. and Coleman, C. (1994). *The nature of adolescence: working with young people in custody.* Brighton: TSA (Crown Copyright).

Lyon, J. and Coleman, C. (1996). *Understanding and working with young women in custody.* Brighton: TSA (Crown Copyright).

Martin, S.E. and Jurik, N. (1996). *Doing justice. Doing gender. Women in law and criminal justice occupations.* London: Sage.

McRobbie, A. and Garber, J. (1976). Girls and subcultures: an exploration. In Hall, S. and Jefferson, T. (eds), *Resistance through rituals.* (pp. 209–22). London: Hutchinson.

Miedzian, M. (1992). *Boys will be boys: breaking the link between masculinity and violence.* London: Virago.

Morris, A. (1987). *Women, crime and criminal justice.* Oxford: Blackwell.

Morris, A., Wilkinson, C., Tisi, A., Woodrow, J. and Rockley, A. (1994). *Managing the needs of female prisoners.* London: Home Office.

Muncie, J. and McLaughlin, E. (1996). *The problem of crime.* London: Sage.

NACRO (1993a). *Young women in the criminal justice system.* NACRO Briefing Paper. London: NACRO Publications.

NACRO (1993b). *Opening the doors: women leaving prison.* London: NACRO Publications.

Naylor, B. (1995). Women's crime and media coverage. In Dobash, R.E., Dobash, R.P. and Noakes, L. (eds), *Gender and crime.* (pp. 77–95). Cardiff: University of Wales Press.

Ruxton, S. (1996). Boys won't be boys: tackling the roots of male delinquency. In Lloyd, T. and Wood, T. (eds), *What next for men?* London: Working With Men.

Office for National Statistics (1997). *Labour force survey. Spring 1996.* London: HMSO.

Senior, P. and Woodhill, D. (eds) (1992). *Gender, crime and probation practice.* Sheffield Hallam University: Pavic Publications.

Smart, C. (1977). *Women, crime and criminology: a feminist critique.* London: Routledge.

The Howard League (1993). *The voice of a child: the impact on children of their mother's imprisonment.* London: Howard League for Penal Reform.

The Howard League and Girls' Friendly Society (1994). *Families matter.* London: Howard League for Penal Reform.

Thurston, R. and Beynon, J. (1995). Men's own stories, lives and violence: research as practice. In Dobash, R.E., Dobash, R.P. and Noakes, L. (eds), *Gender and crime.* (pp. 181–201). Cardiff: University of Wales Press.

Utting, D., Bright, J. and Henricson, C. (1993). *Crime and the family.* London: Family Policy Studies Institute.

Wooton, B.F. (1959). *Social science and social pathology.* London: Allen & Unwin.

Further reading

Dobash, R.E., Dobash, R.P. and Noakes, L. (eds) (1995). *Gender and crime.* Cardiff: University of Wales Press.

Lloyd, A. (1995). *Doubly deviant, doubly damned: society's treatment of violent women.* London: Penguin.

Lyon, J. and Coleman, C. (1994). *Understanding and working with young women in custody.* Brighton: Trust for the Study of Adolescence (TSA; Crown Copyright).

Newburn, T. and Stanko, E. (1994). *Just boys doing business? Men, masculinities and crime.* London: Routledge.

Walklate, S. (1995). *Gender and crime.* London: Harvester Wheatsheaf.

Discussion questions

1. Why should gender be a central variable in any study of crime?
2. Describe ways in which you think research into gender and crime can be applied to practice.
3. Should studies of gender and crime be about women and crime, or men and crime, or both? Why?
4. In what ways could the differences between male and female involvement in crime be described as socially constructed?
5. In what ways does a consideration of young people and crime help to shed light on gender and crime?

Group exercise: anti-social or offending behaviour

When you were a teenager did you ever:

- Break rules?
- Tell lies?
- Disobey your parents or carers?
- Stay out late?
- Get into trouble at home?
- Run away from home?
- Get into trouble at school?
- Truant from school?
- Get suspended from school?
- Steal from your family?
- Steal from a friend?
- Accept something you thought was stolen?
- Steal from a shop?
- Trespass on someone else's property?
- Damage something deliberately?
- Travel on a bus or train without a ticket?
- Drink in a pub when under age?
- Get into a fight?
- Get banned from a youth club or team?
- Copy tapes or videos without copyright permission?
- Commit a motoring offence?
- Get in trouble with the police?
- Set out to scare or harm someone?
- Get blamed for something you had not done?
- Blame someone for something you had done?

Choose one or two of these to discuss with your partner.
What led up to the incident and what happened as a result of it?

Notes to tutors: This exercise is designed to prompt memories of offending behaviour in early and mid-teens. It can be used to lead to a group discussion of the prevalence of offending behaviour; gender differences and similarities; family and peer influences and reasons for desistance from crime. Some questions are drawn from the International Self-Report Delinquency Study (ISRD). It is important to tell participants only to disclose behaviour that they are prepared to discuss with others. The exercise has been piloted extensively prior to publication (Lyon and Coleman 1994, 1996). It is reproduced here by kind permission of HM Prison Service and TSA.

17

SPORT AND EXERCISE

Deirdre Scully

INTRODUCTION

Gender issues have enjoyed considerable prominence within sport and exercise psychology over recent years (see Costa and Guthrie, 1994) although it is still difficult to identify a coherent research strategy which spans across this literature. At the same time, historical trends in the area have tended to mirror those found in other branches of mainstream psychology (Gill, 1994a), with an emphasis on biological differences giving way to consideration of gender roles as aspects of personality. More recently, prominence has been afforded to social psychological perspectives which emphasize social constructionist and feminist analyses of gender and sport.

Over the years, the majority of work has tended to be North American. Interestingly, although significant contributions have been made by Europeans, most of the research identifiable as gender related has been carried out not within sport and exercise psychology but within the allied disciplines of sport sociology, leisure studies, cultural studies, physical education and health psychology. To overview this literature, the chapter will first place the study of gender issues in sport and exercise psychology in its historical context. The second section will outline the major theoretical perspectives and contemporary research trends since the 1970s, while the third section will focus on the recent proliferation of work relating to gender across the emerging subdiscipline of exercise psychology.

GENDER AND SPORT HISTORY

As you may expect, the sport and exercise sciences have not been immune from androcentrism. Parratt (1994) and others have argued that traditional analyses of the history of sport have omitted or downplayed the rich variety of women's sporting experience and indeed Kennard and Carter (1994) go on to suggest that the reality of sport's past may well have been very different from many retrospective descriptions. Through recourse to diverse primary sources these authors propose that both men and women were involved in sport's origins, and that sport certainly was not always a male domain, as is so commonly portrayed in most historical accounts.

This aside, historical accounts of Western sport invariably acknowledge the clear divergence during the mid-nineteenth century between 'sport' (the implicit meaning being 'men's sport') and 'women's sport'. At this time physical education for girls developed, in response both to educational reforms and a more general call from health reformers, who lamented what they saw as women's poor physical development. However, and despite these concerns, overriding any campaign for increasing women's physical fitness and well-being was the misplaced and continuing belief in women's inherent fragility. The theory of 'constitutional overstrain' developed at this time and subsequently held sway well into the twentieth century. This theory was based on pseudo-scientific biological explanations which argued that women were physically incapable of vigorous, aggressive and long-endurance activities. It was also thought that women were more vulnerable to injury in contact sports and that vigorous physical activity could impair women's capacity for reproduction.

The net result was the development of gender-specific activities and a gendered world of sport which has persisted to the present day. For example, men's sports were originally 'adapted' or made safe for women by limiting space, speed and contact (men's basketball v. women's netball) or limiting contact through use of an implement (women's hockey and lacrosse). Even initiatives such as the Women's League of Health and Beauty, which sought to promote a positive view of womankind, did so only insofar as this view conformed with the accepted sociocultural image of femininity (Hargreaves, 1994).

In the more recent past, from the 1960s to the 1980s, several factors have influenced gender relations in the world of sport. For example, in the USA the introduction of various civil rights acts, and in particular Title IX of the Higher Education Act (1972), brought about sweeping changes in sport and physical education by encouraging movement towards equality of opportunity between the genders. From the 1960s onwards, some of the myths surrounding what is masculine (that is, competitive sport) and what is feminine (that is, slim, graceful and aesthetic recreation) were challenged and it became increasingly acceptable for women to seek out sport and competition, leading to a steady influx of women into the sport arena which has continued to the late 1990s.

At the same time, while women may appear to have infiltrated successfully this male domain, palpably they have not succeeded in becoming as involved or as active in all areas of sport and exercise as men. For example, the largest increases in women's participation rates have occurred in sports such as keep-fit and aerobics which continue to emphasize traditional notions of femininity. Also there remain restrictions on opportunities for women in sport, even at the Olympic level where there are substantially fewer events for women. In addition, women are massively under-represented in sports' infrastructure, including positions such as coaches, administrators, journalists and leisure managers, and women's sport continues to receive less sponsorship and less media coverage (Plaisted, 1995). So, in retracing the history of women in sport we can see that historical traditions, while not entirely immutable, often show surprising resistance to change.

Gender in sport psychology

The study of gender issues in sport and exercise psychology has a history principally dating from the women's movement during the 1970s, leading to the current challenge for 'researchers and practitioners to treat gender as a complex, socially dynamic and multifaceted phenomenon which has a profound influence on both male and female sport and exercise behaviour' (Plaisted, 1995, p. 538). This call appears to reflect upon a number of historical and contemporary forces, including the shift in social attitudes towards sport and healthy criticism of traditional scientific approaches to knowledge development within psychology as a whole.

Most early academic reviews of gender differences in sport and exercise have adopted an essentialist approach, arguing that any observed behavioural differences must be attributable to basic biological sex differences. Underlying this assumption is the belief that apparent biological sex differences are dichotomous, with males and females represented at opposite poles. This distinction, based on genetically predetermined physiological characteristics, is often invoked as the definition of 'sex', whereas the term 'gender' is reserved to highlight the psychosocial dimensions of sex, such as cultural customs, roles and expectations associated with being male or female.

Recent research from across several disciplines is in agreement that this definitional process, while attractive, is far too simplistic. It does not allow for the considerable overlap that occurs not only in psychological characteristics and behaviours associated with being male or female but also in the biological variables themselves. The sporting domain offers us an excellent example of this confusion in action, through the use of the 'sex test' (recently renamed the 'gender verification test') which is obligatory for all international female competitors. The gender verification test is supposedly sensitive to the presence of the male Y chromosome, that is an XX reading signifies female and an XY reading signifies a male chromosomal make-up. However, Oglesby and Hill (1993) report on female athletes who have been disqualified from competition because they show cell chromosome structures of XOY or XXY, which hardly seems fair when medical examples of such confusions in sex assignment are known to exist. For this reason it seems wise to accept a more tolerant notion of sex categorization, where each individual is seen as comprising a mosaic of male and female biological components.

Generally speaking, by focusing on gender differences, the danger is that gender similarities are disregarded. As Diane Gill (1994a) notes, males and females not only share the same sex hormones (albeit in different distributions) but the genders overlap across a wide range of biological, psychological and behavioural elements. For example, although a male basketball player is on average taller than a female basketball player, a female basketball player is likely to be taller than the average man. Similarly, although we usually think of women as being less aggressive or confident than men it is certainly possible to find many sportswomen who possess a greater abundance of these characteristics than most men. At the same time, much of the research in this area has been so confounded by the influence of cultural and sex-role expectations and stereotypes that it is very difficult, if not impossible, to establish just how much of our gendered behaviour reflects biology and how much culture. In sport and exercise psychology as elsewhere, the early search for exclusively biological bases of behaviour proved futile, leading eventually to an alternative focus on the individual's sex-role orientation, or psychological sex.

CONTEMPORARY THEORY AND RESEARCH

Social roles and processes

Clearly, discussion of sex-role stereotypes (see Chapter 2) is particularly salient to sport because the qualities traditionally associated with being masculine are seen as so closely linked to involvement in competitive sport. In contrast, femininity can easily be portrayed as 'unsportsmanlike'. Surveys of sport involvement consistently show that overall participation rates vary considerably by gender, with males demonstrating higher participation rates than females (Kane and Snyder, 1989). One possible explanation is related to the gender-appropriate behaviours which society encourages; it is that sport in general provides an arena in which men can prove their masculinity while women are restricted to selected sports which are labelled 'feminine', including gymnastics, ice skating and dance.

Gender stereotypes in sport were first discussed over 30 years ago (Methany, 1965) when it was identified that competitive team sports were perceived as masculine whereas individual sports (often of a non-competitive nature and emphasizing aesthetic qualities) were seen as feminine. Recent surveys suggest that very little has changed in the intervening years (Scully and Clarke, 1997). For example, boys continue to enjoy games which are highly complex, competitive, rule-infused, large in size and goal-directed, whereas girls enjoy small intimate groups engaging in similar independent activities which focus on enjoyment rather than winning (Adler, Kless and Adler, 1992).

The origins of such gendered sport stereotypes are thought to be located early in life. A small number of studies have considered the development of play and motor skills in infancy and have found that fathers tend to encourage vigorous play and 'roughhousing' with boys, and while they are actively involved in teaching gross motor skills to their sons, their daughters receive less attention (Greendorfer, 1992). Indeed, girls in general appear to be given very little systematic instruction in motor skills by either parent. Furthermore, girls are often punished for engaging in vigorous physical activity whereas boys are not. Other research has shown that from a very early age boys are encouraged to actively explore their environment, whereas young girls are more likely to be picked up or restricted in their interaction with a play environment (Lewko and Greendorfer, 1988). Hence it is little wonder that by early adolescence girls have learned that they may risk jeopardizing their popularity or self-image as a female if they take part in contact sports which require strength and power or that sport often comes to assume a low priority in women's lives.

Role conflict and gender schema

As regards the 'why' of sport participation, the notion of role conflict was first put forward as an attempt to explain the reason for more men becoming involved in sport than women. As most sports emphasize masculinity it was argued that women who were involved in sport would experience role conflict because they were running against their sex-role stereotype. However, empirical research designed to examine the extent of rôle conflict experienced by women athletes has yielded little support for this hypothesis.

A more fruitful line of enquiry next developed from Bem's (1974; 1978) work on gender-role orientation and the construct of androgyny as a gender-role category associated with masculine and feminine personality traits. Sport psychologists were quick to follow the lead taken by Bem and others, with numerous studies showing that athletes and exercise participants exhibited more masculine or androgynous traits than non-participants (Henderson et al., 1988). Nevertheless, despite initial support for these ideas, the limits of the gender-role orientation perspective are now generally acknowledged and instead they have been supplanted by more complex and encompassing perspectives which emphasize the relationship between gender and social cognitive processes.

In this vein, Gill (1994b) has suggested that the gender-schematic processing of the behaviour of significant others may be vitally important in influencing the involvement of young people in sport and exercise, a position supported by many physical educationists. For example, powerful and traditional attitudes are still revealed in the outlook of PE teachers, who reinforce stereotypes of boys as being more dominant and as possessing greater physical prowess in comparison with girls, who tend to be described in terms of their appearance and presentation and not their ability (Scraton, 1992).

Alongside these perspectives based on social cognition, sport sociologists now argue for the incorporation of feminist frameworks and alternative approaches, such as critical theory and social constructionism. They argue that women's experiences differ from men's and that researchers must place gender, and more particularly women, at the centre of their analyses (Hall, 1988). To this end, feminist scholars focus on the social context of sport and exercise experiences in an effort to understand why and how gender differences occur (Krane, 1994). A recent addition to this perspective is the growing number of male theorists, both European and American, who utilize a feminist perspective to examine the complex relationships between masculinity and sport (Messner and Sabo, 1990).

Gender and achievement in sport

Martina Horner's psychological construct of 'fear of success' (FOS; Horner, 1972), so prominent in much gender research in the 1980s, was also proposed as a factor which could explain women's relative scarcity in sport. It was suggested that women may fear that their success in male-dominated environments, such as in sport, might lead to a perceived loss of femininity and possible social rejection by their peers, hence FOS. Despite the intuitive appeal of such a proposition, the subsequent empirical research efforts failed to find convincing support to link FOS to women's achievement behaviour in sporting contexts. More recently, the approach has been criticized because the FOS construct does not appear to be significantly related to gender and is not necessarily stable as a personality disposition. Furthermore, use of the construct has been criticized because it may serve to perpetuate societal stereotypes, implying that, in some way, women's lower participation rates in sport are their own fault (Birrell, 1988).

This aside, two general findings remain. First, men consistently score higher than women on measures of competitiveness, and second, gender influence is strongest and most consistent for competitive sport behaviour rather than general achievement or sport goal orientation (Gill, 1994b). Recent research suggests that a different dispositional variable, named *hyper-competitiveness*, can predict level of sporting involvement for both men and women. Other studies have shown a marked gender difference in preference for competitive activity. For example, boys thrive on competition while girls dislike being put in competitive situations and fail to be motivated when required to display competitive behaviour.

A second psychological variable which reveals consistent gender differences is self-confidence. In general terms, women tend to have lower expectations of success and to make fewer achievement-oriented attributions than men (Deaux, 1984). Similarly, in relation to physical activities numerous studies show women to be less confident than men (Gill, 1994b). Recent British research on elite athletes has also demonstrated gender influences on levels and patterning of pre-competitive anxiety and self-confidence, with the suggestion that effects may be mediated by differences in perceived gender roles and competitiveness (Swain and Jones, 1991). A meta-analysis of the motor performance literature has suggested that gender differences in self-confidence may be not as large as originally thought, with a key mediating variable being the sex-linked nature of the task. For example, when the task is female-oriented then gender effects disappear (Lirgg, 1991). These disparate findings further underline the necessity to understand the importance of social context in any discussion of self-confidence. If men and women only display equal levels of self-confidence in carefully contrived situations then we need to seriously reconsider current policies and practices for coeductional PE and mixed sport and exercise settings.

With this in mind, a major concern of academics and practitioners dealing with PE in schools throughout the 1980s was the role to be played by coeducational PE in secondary schools. Ensuring 'equality', by providing boys and girls with access to coeducational PE, does not necessarily provide equality of opportunity or equality of outcome. In fact, equal access to coeducational PE can often mean equal access for all students to male PE. Applied research has consistently supported this hypothesis, with boys' performances regarded as the norm or benchmark against which girls' performances should be measured (Talbot, 1993).

A number of models of achievement orientation have been proposed to explain participation and continuance motivation in sport (see Weiss and Chaumeton, 1992). In terms of gender influences on achievement, Eccles's model (1985) is currently the most popular, partly because Eccles and Harold (1991) recently expanded the model to consider specifically gender differences and influences in sport achievement. The model adopts a standard expectancy/value framework, taking into account both individual interpretations and perceptions and also accommodating sociocultural factors. The work is important for many reasons, not least because it points to the necessity for considering gender within a much wider sociocultural context of sport and exercise. While potentially valuable, further research is required not only to aid understanding of the mechanisms mediating gender differences but also to discover whether current socioculturally developed stereotypes and attitudes are modifiable for the benefit of future generations' participation in sport and exercise.

Gender, exercise and health

Up until this point, discussion has centred on gender issues within sport but with few specific references to exercise behaviour *per se*. However, it is in the area of exercise and health that many fascinating new contributions to research with a particular gender dimension are found (see Berger and McInman, 1993). While the primary focus of this research has been women, a greater number of these contemporary contributions emphasize the importance of treating gender as a relational process and therefore including an analysis of men's involvement alongside women's.

A great deal of recent research has considered the effects of exercise on mental health, both in clinical (see Martinsen, 1995) and non-clinical settings (see Mutrie and Biddle, 1995). In examining the psychological benefits of exercise, researchers typically use measures of anxiety, tension, depression, anger or more general mood profiles. These data support a general consensus that, within limits, a strong and positive relationship exists between physical activity and mental well-being. Additionally, more recent analyses suggest that the mental health benefits of exercise hold equally for men and for women (McDonald and Hodgdon, 1991). Health benefits associated with cardiovascular fitness include reduced incidence of coronary heart disease, hypertension and diabetes. However, as with work on exercise and mental health, earlier research often failed either to include women as subjects or to look specifically at the cardiovascular health benefits of exercise to women. One exception was a large-scale epidemiological study conducted in the USA on 3,000 women (Blair et al., 1989). Not only did the study show that death rates from cardiovascular disease, cancer and other causes were four and a half times higher in the lowest fitness group compared to the highest fitness group but the authors also speculated that if all unfit women were to become fit the death rate among women could drop by 15 per cent. While demonstrating the health benefits for women of increased fitness, when set against current levels of inactivity these results only tend to underscore the need to develop practical policies to encourage women's participation in and adherence to fitness programmes.

Looking to women's issues in particular, it is interesting that the current concerns within biomedical sciences are strikingly similar to those noted by nineteenth-century physicians, namely menstrual irregularities and the implications of exercise for pregnancy and childbirth. However, in place of the dire warnings issued to women regarding the dangers associated with physical exercise, we are now witnessing biomedical research which may enable us to identify the importance of early physical training and exercise in optimizing women's health and motor development. Over recent years, research efforts have been directed towards examining the relationship between exercise and menstrual cycle irregularities, including amenorrhoea (fewer than one period in the previous six months) and oligomenorrhoea (a menstrual cycle lasting longer than 35 days). In particular, these conditions have been associated with women participants in certain sports including long-distance running, gymnastics and dance. Factors influencing these menstrual irregularities are thought to include nutrition, body fat, stress and the impact of intensive training, with major health implications for athletes, coaches and parents relating to the long-term relationship with infertility and osteoporosis (De Souza et al., 1994).

One aspect of this work examines the relationship between exercise and pre-menstrual syndrome (PMS). Given the long-established claims for the health benefits of exercise, it may be worthwhile considering the possibility of using physical exercise as a treatment for menstrual cycle disorders, especially as it is estimated that at least half of all menstruating women experience some form of dysmenorrhea (painful periods) (see Cockerill et al., 1992) and that even regular exercisers suffer menstrual disturbances (Broocks et al., 1990). Empirical studies have shown that moderate physical exercise can be effective in the reduction of various physical and psychological symptoms associated with PMS, although it is possible to 'overdo it'. For example, studies by Cockerill et al. (1992) and Choi and Salmon (1995) have both found that women engaging in strenuous exercise (that is, more than four times a week) actually experience PMS symptoms which are more similar to sedentary groups than low- or moderate-exercise groups.

Body image and eating disorders

The dangers of women using exercise to pursue an elusive 'ideal' gender-role stereotype have already been discussed here and elsewhere. Linked with this work there is an emerging literature associating body image with eating disorders and exercise addiction (see Annett et al. (eds), 1995). Despite the fact that exercise may enhance self-esteem and body image, even physically active women can be damaged by the pressures of sociocultural stereotypes of unattainable ideal female physiques, for example the superwoman ideal, being slim yet curvaceous. It is difficult to determine the prevalence of eating disorders among women, although it has been estimated that 90 per cent of all eating-disordered individuals are women and that a very high proportion of women have at least some experience of eating disorders, from unhealthy dieting through to clinical anorexia and bulimia nervosa. Furthermore, it is maintained that the cultural pressure to be lean is a major contributory factor, acting alongside various cultural, familial and individual factors.

Recent research (see Thompson and Sherman, 1993) supports the idea that athletes may be more likely to develop eating disorders than non-athletes due to sports' emphasis on low body fat and the drive for perfection. It has also been acknowledged that certain sports, known as 'thinness-demand sports', such as gymnastics, ice-skating, running, dancing and diving, may account for the greatest proportion of such disorders. However, owing to the relative paucity of research it is difficult to determine whether participation in sport increases the occurrence of disorders, or whether individuals with a tendency toward disorders are more likely to choose certain activities as a means of 'covering' their predisposition. A number of recent studies have emerged which purport to examine the nature of eating disorders in selected sports (for example, Reel and Gill, 1996), or focus on the psychological attitudes of athletes predisposed to eating disorders (for example, Parker et al., 1994), or examine coaches' attitudes to weight control (for example, Griffin and Harris, 1996). Taken together, the evidence suggests that women in specific sports present with pathological weight control behaviours, display attitudes towards food and dieting which are similar to clinically diagnosed eating disorders, and have coaches who indirectly may encourage pathogenic weight loss due to their own relatively negative attitudes towards, and limited knowledge about, weight and weight control.

Finally, it has also been suggested that there are strong links between exercise addiction and eating disorders. For example, Davis et al. (1995) found a significant relationship not only between exercise dependence, weight preoccupation and obsessive-compulsive personality traits among eating disordered women but also between physical activity and obsessive-compulsiveness among high-exercising women without eating disorders. The authors proposed that a self-perpetuating loop may develop between physical activity, starvation and obsessive-compulsiveness and what is more, this pattern of behaviour appears to be highly resistant to change. Given the relatively high incidence of eating disorders among women athletes, these results are disconcerting although clearly further research needs to be conducted, particularly in relation to identified high-risk sports.

As to the future, while traditionally men have suffered from eating disorders less frequently than women, there is growing evidence that more young men are feeling pressured to attain culturally valued body images associated with leanness and high muscle definition. While the literature relating body image to eating disorders and exercise among men is in its infancy, given current social trends it may well assume greater significance over the coming years.

CONCLUSIONS

As Gill (1994b) suggests, much of sport and exercise behaviour is interpretable only when social context is taken into account. For this reason, a number of sport and exercise psychologists agree that future research should be devoted to establishing more encompassing conceptual frameworks based around theories of social cognition. In addition, it has been pointed out that the social context of sport changes continually over time and place (Kremer and Scully, 1994) and such changes are often matched by fundamental shifts in gender-role stereotyping. Such shifts in gender belief systems may have their positive side, in allowing women greater freedom, but there is also a downside. In particular, the recent research looking at the relationship between physical exercise, body image and eating disorders highlights the dangers of women using exercise to chase after unattainable gender-role ideals. The only sensible way forward would appear to be through an approach which acknowledges the biological and physical aspects of sport but as part of a dynamic social process, or to move further towards the development of sophisticated biopsychosocial models (Gill, 1994b) which offer scope for acknowledging the complexities of cognition, emotions and behaviours associated with gender, sport and exercise.

REFERENCES

Adler, P.A., Kless, S.J. and Adler, P. (1992). Socialization to gender roles: popularity among elementary school boys and girls. *Sociology of Education* **65**, 169–87.

Annett, J., Cripps, B. and Steinberg, H. (eds) (1995). *Exercise addiction: motivation for participation in sport and exercise.* Leeds: British Psychological Society.

Bem, S.L. (1974). The measurement of psychological androgyny. *Journal of Consulting and Clinical Psychology* **42**, 155–62.

Bem, S.L. (1978). Beyond androgyny: some presumptuous prescriptions for a liberated sexual identity. In Sharman, J. and Denmark, F. (eds), *Psychology of women: future directions for research.* (pp. 1–23). New York: Psychological Dimensions.

Berger, B.G. and McInman, A. (1993). Exercise and the quality of life. In Singer, R.N., Murphey, M. and Tennant, L.K. (eds), *Handbook of research on sport psychology.* (pp. 729–60). New York: Macmillan.

Birrell, S. (1988). Discourses on the gender/sport relationship: from women in sport to gender relations. In Pandolph, K. (ed.), *Exercise and sport science reviews*, vol. 16. (pp. 459–502). New York: Macmillan.

Blair, S.N., Kohl, H.W., Paffenbarger, R.S., Clark, D.G., Cooper, K.H. and Gibbons, L.W. (1989). Physical fitness and all-cause mortality: a prospective study of healthy men and women. *Journal of the American Medical Association* **262**, 2395–401.

Broocks, A., Pirke, K.M., Schweiger, U., Tuschl, R.J., Laessle, R.G., Strowitzki, T., Horl, E., Horl, T., Haas, W. and Jeschke, D. (1990). Cyclic ovarian function in recreational athletes. *Journal of Applied Physiology* **68**, 2083–6.

Choi, P.Y.L and Salmon, P. (1995). Symptom changes across the menstrual cycle in competitive sportswomen, exercisers and sedentary women. *British Journal of Clinical Psychology* **34**, 447–60.

Cockerill, I.M, Nevill, A.M, and Byrne, N.J. (1992). Mood, mileage and the menstrual cycle. *British Journal of Sports Medicine* **26**, 145–50.

Costa, D.M. and Guthrie, S.R. (1994). *Women and sport.* Champaign, IL: Human Kinetics.

Davis, C., Kennedy, S.H., Ralevske, E., Dionne, M., Brewer, H., Neitzert, C. and Ratusny, D. (1995). Obsessive compulsiveness and physical activity in anorexia nervosa and high-level exercising. *Journal of Psychosomatic Research* **39**, 967–76.

Deaux, K. (1984). From individual differences to social categories: analysis of a decade's research on gender. *American Psychologist* **39**, 105–16.

De Souza, M.J., Arce, J.C. and Metzger, D.A. (1994). Endocrine basis of exercise-induced amenorrhea. In Costa, D.M. and Guthrie, S.R. (eds), *Women and sport.* (pp. 185–209). Champaign, IL: Human Kinetics.

Eccles, J.S. (1985). Sex differences in achievement patterns. In Sonderegger, T. (ed.), *Nebraska Symposium of Motivation, 1984: Psychology and gender.* (pp. 97–132). Lincoln, NB: University of Nebraska Press.

Eccles, J.S. and Harold, R.D. (1991). Gender differences in sport involvement: applying the Eccles expectancy-value model. *Journal of Applied Sport Psychology* **3**, 7–35.

Gill, D. (1994a). A feminist perspective on sport psychology practice. *The Sport Psychologist* **8**, 411–26.

Gill, D. (1994b). Psychological perspectives on women in sport and exercise. In Costa, D.M. and Guthrie, S.R. (eds), *Women and sport* (pp. 253–84). Champaign, IL: Human Kinetics.

Greendorfer, S. (1992). Sport socialization. In Horn, T.S. (ed.), *Advances in sport psychology* (pp. 201–18). Champaign, IL: Human Kinetics.

Griffin, J. and Harris, M.B. (1996). Coaches' attitudes, knowledge, experiences, and recommendations regarding weight control. *The Sport Psychologist* **10**, 180–94.

Hall, M.A. (1988). The discourse on gender and sport: from femininity to feminism. *Sociology of Sport Journal* **5**, 330–40.

Hargreaves, J. (1994). *Sporting females: critical issues in the history and sociology of women's sports.* London: Routledge.

Henderson, K.A., Stalnaker, D. and Taylor, G. (1988). The relationship between barriers to recreation and gender-role personality traits for women. *Journal of Leisure Research* **20**, 69–80.

Horner, M.S. (1972). Toward an understanding of achievement related conflicts in women. *Journal of Social Issues* **28**, 157–68.

Kane, M.J. and Snyder, E. (1989). Sport typing: the social 'containment' of women. *Arena Review* **13**, 77–96.

Kennard, J. and Carter, J.M. (1994). In the beginning: the ancient and medieval worlds. In Costa, D.M. and Guthrie, S.R. (eds), *Women and sport.* (pp. 15–26). Champaign, IL: Human Kinetics.

Krane, V. (1994). A feminist perspective on contemporary sport psychology research. *The Sport Psychologist* **8**, 393–410.

Kremer, J. and Scully, D. (1994). *Psychology in sport.* London: Taylor & Francis.

Lewko, J.H. and Greendorfer, S.L. (1988). Family influences in sport socialization of children and adolescents. In Smoll, F.L., Magill, R.A. and Ash, M.J. (eds), *Children in sport,* 3rd edn. (pp. 287–300). Champaign, IL: Human Kinetics.

Lirgg, C.D. (1991). Gender differences in self-confidence in physical activity: a meta-analysis of recent studies. *Journal of Sport and Exercise Psychology* **13**, 294–310.

McDonald, D.G. and Hodgdon, J.A. (1991). *Psychological effects of aerobic fitness training: research and theory.* New York: Springer-Verlag.

Martinsen, E.W. (1995). The effects of exercise on mental health in clinical populations. In Biddle, S. (ed.), *European perspectives on exercise and sport psychology* (pp. 71–84). Champaign, IL: Human Kinetics.

Messner, M. and Sabo, D. (1990). *Sport, men and the social order.* Champaign, IL: Human Kinetics.

Methany, E. (1965). Symbolic forms of movement: the feminine image in sports. In Methany, E. (ed.), *Connotations of movement in sport and dance* (pp. 43–56). Dubuque, IA: Brown.

Mutrie, N. and Biddle, S. (1995). The effects of exercise on mental health in nonclinical populations. In Biddle, S. (ed.), *European perspectives on exercise and sport psychology* (pp. 50–70). Champaign, IL: Human Kinetics.

Oglesby, C.A. and Hill, K.L. (1993). Gender and sport. In Singer, R.N., Murphey, M. and Tennant, L.K. (eds), *Handbook of research on sport psychology.* (pp. 718–28). New York: Macmillan.

Parker, R.M., Lambert, M.J. and Burlingame, G.M. (1994). Psychological features of female runners presenting with pathological weight control behaviors. *Journal of Sport and Exercise Psychology* **16**, 119–34.

Parratt, C.M. (1994). From the history of women in sport to women's sport history: a research agenda. In Costa, D.M. and Guthrie, S.R. (eds), *Women and sport.* (pp. 253–84). Champaign, IL: Human Kinetics.

Plaisted, V. (1995). Gender and sport. In Morris, T. and Summers, J. (eds), *Sport psychology.* (pp. 538–74). Brisbane: Wiley.

Reel, J. and Gill, D. (1996). Psychosocial factors related to eating disorders among high school and college female cheerleaders. *The Sport Psychologist* **10**, 195–206.

Scraton, S.J. (1992). *Shaping up to womanhood: gender and girls' physical education.* Milton Keynes: Open University Press.

Scully, D. and Clarke, J. (1997). Gender issues in sport participation. In Kremer, K., Trew, J. and Ogle, S. (eds), *Young people's involvement in sport.* (pp. 25–56). London: Routledge.

Swain, A.B.J. and Jones, G. (1991). Gender role endorsement and competitive anxiety. *International Journal of Sport Psychology* **22**, 50–65.

Talbot, M. (1993). A gendered physical education: equality and sexism. In Evans, J. (ed.), *Equality, education and physical education.* (pp. 74–89). London: Falmer Press.

Thompson, R.A. and Sherman, R.T. (1993). *Helping athletes with eating disorders.* Champaign, IL: Human Kinetics.

Weiss, M and Chaumeton, N. (1992). Motivational orientation in sport. In Horn, T.S. (ed.), *Advances in sport psychology.* (pp. 61–99). Champaign, IL: Human Kinetics.

Further reading

Gill, D. (1994). A feminist perspective on sport psychology practice. *The Sport Psychologist* **8**, 411–426.

Kennard, J. and Carter, J.M. (1994). In the beginning: the ancient and medieval worlds. In Costa, D.M. and Guthrie, S.R. (eds), *Women and sport.* (pp. 15–26). Champaign, IL: Human Kinetics.

Oglesby, C.A. and Hill, K.L. (1993). Gender and sport. In Singer, R.N., Murphey, M. and Tennant, L.K. (eds), *Handbook of research on sport psychology.* (pp. 718–28). New York: Macmillan.

Plaisted, V. (1995) Gender and sport. In Morris, T. and Summers, J. (eds), *Sport psychology.* (pp. 538–74). Brisbane: Wiley.

Scully, D. and Clarke, J. (1997). Gender issues in sport participation. In Kremer, J., Trew, K. and Ogle, S. (eds), *Young people's involvement in sport.* (pp. 25–56). London: Routledge.

Discussion questions

1. Which sports would you identify as being perceived as masculine, feminine or androgynous? Which of these sports would you choose to watch and to play?
2. Which sports did you play at school? Can you remember why you chose those sports and would you regard them as sex-typed?
3. Did you choose to continue or discontinue those sports when you left school? Why? Would you return to those sports now? Would your friends?
4. In an ideal world, which sports would you choose to take part in?
5. Thinking of the sport stars that come to mind, both men and women, discuss whether or not you feel that they provide good gender role models.

18

VIOLENCE

Geraldine Moane

Introduction

Violence is clearly an extremely wide-ranging term which can encompass an enormous variety of behaviours. This chapter will focus on specific forms of violence, namely that between men and women, or more specifically, sexual violence. It will begin by describing the forms and patterns of such violence and consider the ways in which this violence is embedded within a broader social context involving attitudes and social structures. It is necessary to adopt this contextual approach in order to understand the psychological aspects of violence from the perspective both of women, who are largely at the receiving end of sexual violence, and of men, who are largely the perpetrators.

Patterns of violence

Before the advent of the women's movement in the late 1960s, sexual violence against women was largely unrecognized and rarely publicly discussed or acknowledged in most Western societies (Kelly and Radford, 1991). Up until then, sexual violence such as rape, sexual assault and battery certainly occurred, but a combination of attitudes made it very difficult for women to speak out or take action against men who committed acts of violence against them. By way of example, it was accepted practice for a husband to strike his wife, and women who were raped were normally seen to have 'asked for it'. In turn, these behaviours were supported by laws which, for example, failed to make rape in marriage illegal, or which made certain acts of violence legal within marriage (most notoriously the 'rule of thumb' which allowed a husband to beat his wife with a stick so long as it was no thicker in diameter than his thumb).

As women began to speak out against sexual violence, and as research uncovered the extent of such violence and its many different forms, it became increasingly recognized as a serious problem. Today, most countries in North America and Western Europe have changed many of their laws, and have also provided resources to help women who have been victims of violence. There has also been a greater level of understanding of why men commit violence against women, and programmes are being developed to help men better understand why they behave in violent ways towards women (Dobash and Dobash, 1992; McWilliams and McKiernan, 1993; Ferguson and Sinnott, 1995; O'Connor and Wilson, 1995; Buzawa and Buzawa, 1996; Task Force, 1997; Working Party, 1996).

By way of example, in Ireland there has been considerable research, much new legislation and several innovatory social programmes dealing with sexual violence. In 1996, a government Task Force on Violence against Women was established. Its report stated that 'The existence and extent of violence against women was, until recent times, largely hidden within Irish society' (Task Force, 1997, p. 11). The establishment of such a task force was itself a response to the growing level of concern about violence against women, expressed by Irish women themselves in a variety of contexts. For example, surveys consistently indicated that violence, and particularly sexual violence, was a major source of anxiety and stress for women. Formal consultative processes carried out, for example, by the Irish Department of Health and by the Department of the Tanaiste, highlighted violence as a major concern. Community women's groups, rape crisis centres, and battered women's shelters constantly reiterated the problem of violence against women (Task Force, 1997; Working Party, 1996). On the other hand, in a trend that was typical of studies elsewhere across Western Europe and North America, men were much less likely to be concerned about violence or to be aware of sexual violence as a problem (Leonard, 1993; Dobash and Dobash, 1994). Research shows that men are very unlikely to be victims of violence by female partners. Fewer than 10 per cent of domestic violence cases involve female violence, and where women are violent it is most often in response to their partner's violence (Dobash and Dobash, 1992).

Violence against women takes a number of forms. It obviously includes rape (including marital rape) and also battery and sexual assault. Physical violence includes beating up, pushing, bruising, kicking, strangling or choking, and even manslaughter and murder. It is often perpetrated in a sustained way over a long period of time, resulting in serious bodily injuries, and physical and mental health problems. Mental abuse includes verbal attacks, emotional outbursts and blackmail, threats of violence, withholding of money, and interrogation. It is generally reported that over half of such violence, including rape, takes place in the context of an intimate relationship, and such violence is found across socio-economic class, urban–rural or other social contexts (Hyde, 1994; Hester et al., 1996; Rollins, 1996; Task Force, 1997; Working Party, 1996).

Prevalence

It is extremely difficult to establish the prevalence of such violence across any population because of a lack of systematic research, and because of the very strong pressures exerted on women to remain silent about such crimes. For example, in the case of rape, international research estimates that overall only about 10–15 per cent of rapes are reported to police. In Ireland, the Dublin Rape Crisis Centre has reported that only 28 per cent of women seeking counselling (which itself is an unknown percentage of women who have been raped) had reported the crime to the police, and of those cases reported to the police, only between 20 per cent and 40 per cent, depending on the year of study, led to criminal proceedings. Again in Ireland, a five-year study of conviction rates from 1986 to 1991 found that only 7 per cent of rapes reported to the Garda (police) led to conviction (Connolly, 1993; Working Party, 1996).

Figures on reported violence or on conviction rates are therefore less than adequate in assessing the extent of violence against women. The use of survey research is also problematic, primarily because it encounters the problem of low rates of disclosure, as mentioned above. That aside, a study based on a national representative sample commissioned by Women's Aid in Ireland found that 7 per cent of respondents said that they had been abused in the past year by a partner or ex-partner, and 18 per cent had been subjected to violence at some time by a current partner. A majority of those surveyed knew a woman who had been subjected to violence by a partner. The scale of the problem is indicated by the number of phone calls to Women's Aid helplines (8,000 in 1996), to Dublin Rape Crisis Centre (6,100 in 1995), and to the Garda Domestic Violence and Sexual Assault Unit in Dublin (6,000 in 1996; Task Force, 1997). Studies in Britain also suggest that up to 20 per cent of women have experienced rape or attempted rape, while many more have been subject to some form of violence by a male friend or partner (Walby, 1990; Dobash and Dobash, 1992; Hester et al., 1996).

In the USA, considerable research based on college samples has shown that over one third of female students had already experienced some form of harassment by the time they left college, and between 5 per cent and 10 per cent of women stated that they had been raped (Rollins, 1996). Studies of male students also found that up to one quarter reported that they had used aggression, ranging from being disagreeable and offensive to using outright physical intimidation, in order to get what they wanted sexually (Koss et al., 1987; Hyde, 1994). This research also shows that sexual aggression occurs in all forms of heterosexual relationships, ranging from casual dates to steady relationships. It is also clear that men and women differ in their attitudes to sexual aggression. Men are far more likely to think that sexual aggression is acceptable, and in addition to underestimate its hurtful effects on women.

Such attitudes to women are also reflected in a more pervasive form of violence or coercion, namely sexual harassment, where women are subject to bullying, harassment and humiliation of a sexual nature. Sexual harassment is defined by the European Commission in their Recommendation and Code of Practice on the Protection of the Dignity of Women and Men at Work (1991) as 'unwanted conduct of a sexual nature or other conduct based on sex affecting the dignity of women and men at work' (p. 9). Examples provided by the EC include the display of sexually suggestive or pornographic pictures or calendars, and physical sexual harassment. That sexual harassment in the workplace is widespread is not questioned. Surveys show that a very high proportion of women, perhaps as high as 80 per cent, have experienced such harassment, either in the workplace, in public places or in the home (Schneider, 1993), and that a common response is to leave work or seek a transfer.

So far the discussion has emphasized the many ways in which sexual violence can occur, showing that there is a variety of forms of sexual aggression, that sexual aggression occurs quite frequently both in casual relationships and in intimate relationships, including marriage, and that there are differences between men and women in their attitudes to sexual violence. It must also be said that although all women may not be direct victims of violence or sexual harassment, almost all women experience problems because of the pervasiveness of violence and harassment. Studies in Europe and North America reveal that up to 80 per cent of women worry about sexual assault, and restrict their behaviours out of fear of sexual assault (Gordon and Riger, 1989; Stanko, 1993). In an Irish replication of an American study aptly entitled *The Female Fear*, based on a sample of mature students who ranged in age from 18 to 55, O'Neill (1991) found that 64 per cent of women worried about sexual assault sometimes, frequently, or very frequently, compared with 11 per cent of males. One third of males worried about physical assault, but this was not indicated separately for females, who worried about both physical and sexual assault. Around 50 per cent of females took precautions such as not walking alone (compared with 15 per cent of males), or not dressing in a sexy manner (compared with 14 per cent of men). This fear is thought to be reinforced through depictions of high levels of violence against women, and of women as victims, in mass media, popular culture and pornography (Gordon and Riger, 1989; Stanko, 1993).

Social structures and sexual violence

The above discussion has touched on some of the ways in which the structures of society are implicated in sexual violence. Sexual violence is not just something that occurs between a man and a woman in isolation from social and cultural forces. Indeed, it occurs with sufficient frequency to make it clear that its occurrence is linked to economic, political-judicial and sociocultural factors. Sexual violence may be said to be institutionalized, to the extent that the major institutions of society which are charged with preventing such violence not only fail to do so but actually create barriers to women attempting to enlist their help. For example, women who have written of the trauma of rape and battery, which will be discussed more fully below, have also described the difficulties which they encountered in disclosing the crime and in pursuing legal proceedings (Buzawa and Buzawa, 1996). This is because violence against women occurs in a cultural context in which both ideology and socio-legal services tend to support the view that women deserve to be violated ('asking for it'), that women will make false claims, and that men are not responsible. Fear, the threat of further violence, the shame and stigma attached to violence, and economic dependency are among the factors which prevent women from disclosing experiences of violence. Many women report that those to whom they have disclosed, including social workers, have not believed their stories, and have subjected them to intrusive and humiliating interrogation. Through its summing up and sentencing policy, the judicial system continues to reflect considerable ambivalence about the responsibility for sexual violence (Fennell, 1993).

In theorizing about violence against women, feminist writers have concluded that the pervasiveness and patterning of violence against women, and the way in which it is handled – or mishandled – by social institutions, requires a social structural analysis (Walby, 1990; Dobash and Dobash, 1992; O'Connor and Wilson, 1995; Hester et al., 1996). Male violence cannot be explained simply as the isolated actions of exceptional individuals. As Walby states, 'Male violence against women is sufficiently common and repetitive, with routinized consequences for women and routinized modes of processing by judicial agencies to constitute a social structure ... Male violence is thus a form of power over women in its own right' (Walby, 1990, p. 143). The significant role which power motives play in sexual violence has been indicated by international research, including an Irish study in which 40 men convicted of rape and/or indecent assault were extensively interviewed (Cullen, 1989). Three quarters of the men believed that the woman was in his company against her will. Cullen reports that, 'Feelings of power or domination were reported by half of the group. One third of the men reported feelings of anger towards the woman, and over a third experienced feelings of hatred' (Cullen, 1989, p. 16).

Hence a variety of factors converge to make violence a serious problem for women, and one which permeates their everyday life, which imposes restrictions on their movements and which prevents them from participating fully in society. These factors include cultural attitudes which are highly ambivalent about violence against women and which maintain a considerable degree of silence about the problem. Social and legal systems, from which women often have been excluded, historically reflect these attitudes and fail to recognize or respond appropriately to the problem. Women's economic dependency on men, and their isolation within the home, often make it extremely difficult for women to resist violence. The end result is that the vast majority of women have directly experienced sexual violence and/or harassment, and the vast majority of women restrict their behaviours out of fear of sexual violence. Furthermore, women live in a climate in which sexual violence against women is constantly depicted through pornography, mass media and advertising.

Psychological effects on women of sexual violence

As the above research shows, the pervasiveness of sexual violence has an impact on most women by creating fear and restriction. Obviously, women who have actually been victims of sexual violence, particularly rape, battery or sexual assault, suffer even more serious consequences. Rape, which usually involves forced sexual intercourse, is extremely painful and humiliating, and has a number of harmful psychological consequences. Battery, in which women are terrorized, physically assaulted and raped over a long period of time, also has long-term psychological consequences. In both cases, the immediate or acute responses to assault include terror, pain, shame, humiliation, and helplessness (Herman, 1992; Hyde, 1994; Rollins, 1996).

The long-term effects of sexual violence appear to depend on a variety of factors. These include how severe and prolonged the incidence of violence was, the relationship between the women and the assailant, the amount of support the woman receives following the assault, and the degree to which the woman blames herself for the assault. The first three factors operate in relation to other crimes as well. Effects are more severe when serious violence has occurred, where the assailant is known to the woman, and where the woman receives very little support afterwards. Unlike other crimes, however, self blame is particularly prevalent among women who have been raped, perhaps reflecting society's attitudes to the victim's role in rape. The degree to which the woman blames herself also increases the severity of the effects (Foa et al., 1991; Herman, 1992).

The phrase 'rape trauma syndrome' has been developed to refer to the psychological effects of being raped, and in many ways the syndrome is seen as similar to post-traumatic stress disorder (PTSD). Research shows that it can take a woman from two to six months to recover from the immediate after-effects of rape. These immediate after-effects include intense fear of being raped or assaulted again which prevents the woman from relaxing even in her own home, and which produces a state of hypervigilance, where she is constantly watchful and suspicious. Flashbacks of the rape or assault can occur which are extremely distressing. Feelings of shame and guilt almost always occur even if the woman does not blame herself, often accompanied by obsessive thoughts about how and why the rape occurred. Anger and a desire for revenge can also play a strong role in the woman's emotional reactions. Physical effects include stomach aches, headaches, sleep problems and loss of appetite, as well as bruising, bleeding and pain brought about directly by the assault. Sexual activity is very difficult, even more so if a woman's partner has a negative attitude or blames her for the assault (Herman, 1992; Hyde, 1994; Rollins, 1996).

Rape is almost always a very severe trauma, and even when these immediate after-effects subside, there are longer-term effects. Fear of assault continues, although not as intensely as in the acute phase. Other reactions which continue in varying degrees are nightmares, flashbacks, insomnia, sense of detachment, inhibited emotions, lack of trust, loss of interest in sexual activity, and reduced interest in socializing. Women may make changes in their lives, usually out of fear, such as moving to a different area or changing jobs. Research suggests that many women will have recovered from these symptoms after about two years, but the severity and duration of these symptoms depends on the factors mentioned above (Herman, 1992; Rollins, 1996). If a woman reports the rape it is often more difficult for her to recover, but this may be counterbalanced by the self-esteem to be gained by speaking out against her attacker (Kelly, 1988).

Construction of masculinity and sexual violence

It is clear from the research reviewed above that a substantial proportion of men will behave in sexually aggressive ways towards women, and that there is a considerable gap between men and women in their attitudes towards this behaviour. These observations suggest that male sexual violence is more likely to be related to sex-role socialization and power differences in society than it is to individual personality factors, and this is supported by research. Research on rapists and on batterers has failed to find any consistent set of characteristics which differentiate them from other men (Leonard, 1993; Dobash and Dobash, 1994; Hyde, 1994). Survey research on men who admit to sexual aggression, or on men's attitudes, also fails to identify particular psychological characteristics (Leonard, 1993). Not surprisingly, men who are sexually aggressive are more likely to express negative attitudes towards women. Research on pornography also suggests that viewing pornography is associated with more negative attitudes towards women, greater willingness to be aggressive towards women, and a greater tendency to believe myths about rape such as that women enjoy being raped (Weaver, 1992).

These findings suggest that sexual violence is more heavily influenced by society's attitudes towards women and particularly violence against women, and by power issues, than by individual characteristics such as pathological aggression or sexual deviance. Research referred to above which found that men themselves said that the need for power and control was part of their motivation to rape supports the emphasis on power and control as the key factors in explaining sexual violence (Cullen, 1989; Scully and Marolla, 1993; Dobash and Dobash, 1994). This is particularly evident in research on men who batter their partners, where battery is almost always accompanied by controlling behaviours such as isolation and interrogation (Ferguson and Synott, 1995). Patterns of sexual harassment also highlight the role played by power differences, because such harassment more often occurs in relationships such as that between a boss and a subordinate or a lecturer/professor and student, which are marked by power differences (Schneider, 1993).

These different areas of research on sexual violence suggest that features of society, particularly the facts that men occupy more positions of power than women and that the mass media and pornography reinforce these power differences by showing men in positions of power and behaving more aggressively than women, are contributing to sexual violence. This is supported by a cross-cultural study by Sanday, who studied 156 tribal societies and found that those societies which were more male-dominated had higher levels of rape and sexual violence. These factors also influence behaviour through their impact on sex-role socialization, where men are socialized to be more aggressive, to express anger more readily, and to have difficulty expressing feelings of vulnerability and love compared with women (Sanday, 1981).

Conclusions

Research on the pattern and extent of sexual violence indicates that it is a serious social problem, with important implications for men and women and for relationships between men and women. Sexual violence is in part a product of power differences between men and women in society, and in turn it also reinforces these power differences. Sexual violence is reflected in popular culture, mass media and pornography, and it has psychological effects for both women and men. Women in general experience fear and suspicion about being assaulted, and also towards men whom they do not know. Women who have been assaulted suffer traumatic effects for a considerable period of time afterwards, and often have their lives seriously disrupted. Men in general have difficulty with anger and with vulnerability, and may not realize the extent to which sexual violence disrupts their relationships with women. Sexual violence enters into almost all sexual relationships between men and women because it permeates mass media and popular culture, and is part of the construction of heterosexuality.

Up to the present day, primarily it has been women who have spoken out about sexual violence, and indeed who have done most of the research which has aided in understanding the nature of sexual violence and its effects on women and men. A consistent finding from research on rape, battery and even sexual harassment is that many more women than men consider these behaviours to be a problem, and that men underestimate how prevalent and how damaging these behaviours can be. The provision of rape crisis centres and shelters for battered women, although completely inadequate in numbers, has helped to alleviate the damage to women from experiencing sexual violence. However, if sexual violence is to be prevented, it is important for all to acknowledge that it is a serious problem. The research reviewed in this chapter suggests that ultimately, sexual violence will only be prevented if there are changes in the power structures of society and in the social construction of gender.

REFERENCES

Buzawa, E.S. and Buzawa, C.G. (1996). *Domestic violence: the criminal justice response.* London: Sage.

Connolly, J. (1993). *The question of a separate legal representative for complainants in cases of rape: an Irish reform?* Unpublished LLM thesis, University of Edinburgh.

Cullen, R. (1989). *Forty men convicted for sexual offences in the Irish prison system: a descriptive and comparative study.* Dublin: Department of Justice.

Dobash, R.E. and Dobash, R.P. (1992). *Women, violence and social change.* London: Routledge.

Dobash, R.P. and Dobash, R.E. (1994). Men, masculinity and violence against women. In Stanko, E. (ed.), *Perspectives on violence* (pp. 82–93). London: The Women's Press.

Fennell, C. (1993). Criminal law and the criminal justice system: women as victim. In Connelly, A. (ed.), *Gender and the law in Ireland.* (pp. 151–70). Dublin: Oak Tree Press.

Ferguson, H. and Synott, P. (1995). Intervention into domestic violence in Ireland: developing policy and practice with men who batter. *Administration* **43(3)**, 57–81.

Foa, E.B., Rothbaum, B.O., Riggs, D.S. and Murdock, T.B. (1991). Treatment of post-traumatic stress disorder in rape victims: a comparison between cognitive-behavioural procedures and counselling. *Journal of Consulting and Clinical Psychology* **59**, 715–23.

Gordon, M.T. and Riger, S. (1989). *The female fear.* Springfield, IL: Collier.

Herman, J.L. (1992). *Trauma and recovery.* New York: Basic Books.

Hester, M., Kelly, L. and Radford, J. (eds) (1996). *Women, violence and male power.* Buckingham: Open University Press.

Hyde, J.S. (1994). *Human sexuality.* 5th edn. New York: McGraw-Hill.

Kelly, L. (1988). *Surviving sexual violence.* Cambridge: Polity Press.

Kelly, L. and Radford, J. (1991). Nothing really happened. *Critical Social Policy* **30**, 39–53.

Koss, M.P., Gidyez, C.A. and Wisniewski, N. (1987). The scope of rape: incidence and prevalence of sexual aggression and victimization in a national sample of higher education students. *Journal of Consulting and Clinical Psychology* **55**, 162–70.

Leonard, M. (1993). Rape: myths and reality. In A. Smyth (ed.), *Irish women's studies reader.* (pp. 107–21). Dublin: Attic Press.

McWilliams, M. and McKiernan, J. (1993). *Bringing it out in the open: domestic violence in Northern Ireland.* Belfast: HMSO.

O'Connor, M. and Wilson, N. (1995). Violence against women: a human rights issue. *UCG Women's Studies Centre Review* **3**, 193–200.

O'Neill, M. (1991). *Fear of sexual assault in college students.* Unpublished M.Psych.Sci. thesis, University College Dublin.

Rollins, J.H. (1996). *Women's minds, women's bodies: the psychology of women in a biosocial context.* Upper Saddle River, NJ: Prentice Hall.

Sanday, P.R. (1981). The socio-cultural context of rape: A cross-cultural study. *Journal of Social Issues* **37**, 5–27.

Schneider, B. (1993). Put up or shut up: workplace sexual assaults. In Bart, P. and Moran, G. (eds). *Violence against women: the bloody footprints* (pp.). London: Sage.

Scully, D. and Marolla. J. (1993). Riding the bull at Gilley's: convicted rapists describe the rewards of rape. In Bart, P. and Moran, G. (eds). *Violence against women: the bloody footprints* (pp. 26–46). London: Sage.

Stanko, E. (1993). Ordinary fear: women, violence and personal safety. In Bart, P. and Moran, G. (eds). *Violence against women: The bloody footprints.* (pp. 155–64). London: Sage.

Task Force on Violence against Women (1997). *Report*. Dublin: Office of the Tanaiste.

Walby, S. (1990). *Theorizng patriarchy.* Oxford: Basil Blackwell.

Weaver, J. (1992). The social science and psychological research evidence: perceptual and behavioural consequences of exposure to pornography. In Itzin, C. (ed.), *Pornography: women, violence and civil liberties.* (pp. 284–309). Oxford: Oxford University Press.

Working Party on the Legal and Judicial Process for Victims of Sexual and other Crimes of Violence against Women and Children (1996). *Report.* Dublin: National Women's Council of Ireland.

Further reading

Dobash, R.P. and Dobash, R.E. (1994). Men, masculinity and violence against women. In Stanko, E. (ed.), *Perspectives on violence.* (pp. 82–93). London: The Women's Press.

Hester, M., Kelly, L. and Radford, J. (eds) (1996). *Women, violence and male power.* Buckingham: Open University Press.

Koss, M.P, Gidyez, C.A. and Wisniewski, N. (1987). The scope of rape: incidence and prevalence of sexual aggression and victimization in a national sample of higher education students. *Journal of Consulting and Clinical Psychology* **55**, 162–70.

Schneider, B. (1993). Put up or shut up: workplace sexual assaults. In Bart, P. and Moran, G. (eds). *Violence against women: The bloody footprints* (pp.). London: Sage.

Weaver, J. (1992). The social science and psychological research evidence: Perceptual and behavioural consequences of exposure to pornography. In Itzin, C. (ed.), *Pornography: women, violence and civil liberties* (pp. 284–309). Oxford: Oxford University Press.

Discussion questions

1. To what extent do you think it is useful to represent sexual violence as falling along a continuum, perhaps ranging from rape to sexual harassment?
2. Discuss the ways in which women are affected by sexual violence and the ways in which men are affected by sexual violence. Do you think that sexual violence is inevitable?
3. What could you do personally to help prevent sexual violence?
4. Why do you think that there is a gap between men and women in how they view sexual violence?
5. What do you think are the causes of sexual violence?
6. How do economic, political and cultural factors contribute to sexual violence?

AUTHOR INDEX

SUBJECT INDEX